12

The Trifone Edition

Britton Barthold

This limited edition is dedicated to the man who gave me

both my physical and creative voice, Clark Weber.

Photography done by the Darien Athletic Foundation along with Charles Barthold.

CONTENTS

12

The Men in Black

Thanksgiving Day

The Road to Redemption

The Road to 2015

A Non-Stop Affair

The Fight Goes On

his eyes and kept fighting. He smiled every second he was around us and in turn, we smiled every time we were around him. To this day, one of my more vivid memories of my high school playing career was walking up to Jim with tears in my eyes after we blew the 2014 State title to New Canaan. I knew he wanted that game so badly and I knew deep down he probably didn't have enough time on Earth to make it to the 2015 State title. I apologized to him over and over until he stopped me, telling me I had nothing to apologize for and that instead, he had something to say to me.

"Thank you."

I still to this day remember the last time I saw him alive. Sam Giorgio and I visited him at Roton Point and the disease had gotten to the point where talking had become a struggle for Jim. He still smiled though, he still laughed, he still loved us. When he died a few weeks before our season was set to begin, it was all but confirmed that ALS did not win the fight against Jim Mulhearn. Seeing him respond to what he was going through as a senior in high school, it changed everything perspective wise. Not just for me, but for my senior teammates as well.

Back to my comment about God watching us… On Jim's birthday that year, we supplanted Southington as the #1 team in the state when we beat them in the state semifinals. The next week on the 12th day of the 12th month, we won Darien's first state championship since 1996 for our 12th man. I mean, come on. You can't sit here and say, "What a coincidence." I remember when that was pointed out to us, days before the state title game and all I can remember doing is smiling and thinking to myself, *Holy shit*.

None of that though, and I firmly believe this, none of that would have happened (the perfect season, the state title) if Coach Trifone hadn't introduced us to Jim Mulhearn that day in 2014. It was bigger than sports. Coach Trifone knew that.

We didn't at the moment, but we do now. And really, it sticks with us to this day, nearly five years since the 2015 team took the field. It sticks with Coach Trifone to this day, nearly five years after one of his best friends died with a Blue Wave Football helmet by his bedside.

The interview process for 12 in 2018 was grueling, really. I remember Coach Trifone's interview for the book in his classroom at Darien High School though. I hadn't thought about Jim for quite some time leading up to the books process, but I could tell Coach Trifone had the man on his mind every single day since he died. The second I asked him to talk about Jim for the book he broke down, and as I sat there trying to remain professional in the interview setting, I fought back tears as well. That's who Jim Mulhearn was to us. That's who Jim Mulhearn will remain to us.

All in all, Rob Trifone isn't perfect. Nobody is. He's made mistakes. So have I. So have you. We live in a world where mistakes seemingly have to define us, that when we meet someone, we tend to judge them off their flaws, not their good deeds. In my opinion, Darien doesn't deserve Rob Trifone anymore, because his flaws became all too much for the town to look past, even as his good deeds towered above.

Rob Trifone loved us. He cared for us. He knew that no matter how old we got, we would still be those little goofballs running around playing the game we loved.

For this edition as well, I've included a tidbit from the incomplete sequel I was writing for 12 that I called *The Unbelievers*. The story follows a newly opened school in Virginia who struggled to build an identity and winning culture during its first few seasons. I thought it would be fun to share the first chapter or so, just to give you a look at what I was working on. I don't plan on finishing it, even though I got up to 100 pages with plenty more story to tell.

That's the one thing about writing I have learned...

Sometimes, it doesn't work. *The Unbelievers* didn't work, even though I found it to be one of the better things I have ever written. That's writing. Overall though, I am still writing. I plan to release my first fiction novel titled *Growing Up* in the coming year or so. We will see. Stay tuned, or don't.

So enjoy re-reading, reading for the first time or just skimming through the book for old time sake. Laugh, cry, do whatever your emotions tell you. But when you do close it, when you do put it down, remember to smile about the past but not to dwell in it. Remember the things you have ahead, the people who count on you, the people who love you. Take the lessons you learned from the mentors, the teammates, the coaches, and pass them on.

And one more thing, while I have you… I've always had a lot of people ask me this question: "Britton, is the book anti-Darien? Is it a criticism of Darien?"

Let me wrap up the meaning of *12* up to you in a super complicated way…

In May of 2018, I set out to tell a story… A story about a group of kids who in the mid-2000s, led by Rob Trifone, did one simple thing…

They dreamed.

- Britton Barthold
    #44

Barthold currently attends Indiana University. He is entering his fourth year with the football program at the school, working primarily with the Quarterback position. He intends to graduate in December of 2021 with degrees in both English and History.

Britton Barthold in 2008 while being coached on Rob Trifone's fifth-grade team.

A Note from Allison Mulhearn

Born and raised in Brooklyn, NY, Jim was passionate about his family, friends, faith and football. Dad grew up playing stickball with neighborhood kids in the street. He never officially played football, but was always a dedicated fan. As a teenager he would go to NY Giants games with his Sister Dorothy and Brother in Law, Danny. Jim attended the infamous November 20, 1960 NY Giants vs. Philadelphia Eagles game at Yankee Stadium. He witnessed the legendary hit by Chuck Bednarik (Eagles) on Frank Gifford (Giants), which caused injuries that paused Frank's football career for 2 years. Jim grew up as both a NY Giants fan and a Gifford fan. It made an impression on Jim and set a tone about resilience. Over fifty years later, fate brought dad and Gifford together through a mutual friend in Greenwich, CT. Jim got to share with Frank what that infamous game was like from the sidelines and how he admired Frank's talent and perseverance. In 2015, Jim and Frank passed away one day apart and both donated their brains for medical research.

Growing up, I remember walking to Greenwich high school football games with my dad decked out in our cardinal gear. We'd cheer the team on and I'd try to catch one of the small plastic cardinal footballs they would toss to fans. I vividly recall the sensational 1998 season; we were big fans of Jim Henry the junior star halfback at the time and loved attending games together. I was in awe at how my dad cared about the players, precisely called the plays and never lost faith in his team.

Jims' positivity, sense of humor, and gift of story telling never failed him. His true purpose in life was to connect, support, and laugh with other people. He brought out the best qualities in others, and people just wanted to be around him. Jim met Darien high school football coach Rob Trifone at Roton Point Beach Club in the summer of 2010. Dad loved hats and his Greenwich Cardinals football hat was a staple in his rotation. They exchanged a joke about Jim wearing the wrong teams' hat and started talking from there. The two started a friendship over their mutual love of football. Dad was inspired by Trifones' ability to motivate youth, to become their best selves on and off the field. Dad respected Trifones' talent, tenacity and endurance. Jim loved Trifone, viewed him as the greatest football coach, and was honored to call him his dear friend.

In the summer of 2014, the ALS Ice Bucket Challenge gained momentum. Trifone wanted to take part to raise awareness for ALS and invited Jim (who had been diagnosed with the disease in March of 2010). On a hot August day of training, the team honored Jim with an Ice Bucket Challenge. Trifone gave Jim an opportunity to be part of something bigger than himself and the unbreakable bond was formed. Jim started wearing a new Darien Blue Wave football hat and jersey!

Seeing the team became Jims' motivation to seize the day in his final year on earth. He had a game to get to and a team to cheer on. It gave him a purpose to keep going and live out a dream of being on the football field with people he loved. The greatest lesson Jim taught us all, was how to love and be loved. Jims' unwavering support for the Blue Wave was about the perseverance to keep going and never give up.

For both Jim and the team it was never about how many times they got knocked down on or off the field, it was always about how they leaned on each other and got back up.

Anytime dad talked about the team (which was all the time!), he would light up and smile. He would also get emotional, having cared so deeply for all of them. Jim appreciated each team members' story and valued them as individuals. He would describe them as, "Talented young gentlemen with bright futures ahead." Jim would say, "Al, when they come together and play football it's magical. Their precision, speed, agility, and coordination makes' them a dream team. And they are the nicest caring good guys."

On August 8th of 2015, dad and I had what would become our last conversation. We were at the CT Hospice in Branford looking out at the Long Island Sound. He had his Blue Wave football blanket on him. We held hands and had some quiet time just being together. We talked about Blue Wave football's upcoming season and Dad said, "I'll be rooting for the team from the sky box in the sky. They will go undefeated in 2015 and be CT State Champions." I said I got em' covered from the sidelines dad. Jims' legacy lives on in each team member and Rob Trifone. Collectively, an unbreakable bond grounded in love for each other and love of football links them all forever.

Thank you to Britton for having the courage, grit and grace to write this incredibly honest book. Thank you Coach Trifone, the team, especially the 2015 seniors and parents for helping me cope through that first 5 months without my dad. You welcomed me with open arms and gave me a sense of connectivity. What a ride it was, from the Greewich game in September when the 12th man flag was debuted (and seeing the JM tape that Hudson Hamill wore), to the semis at Boyle on what would have Been Jims' 69th birthday, and winning

States on 12.12.15. Jim's spirit and energy was all around us. I am forever grateful to be a Blue wave football fan. Roll wave.

- Allison Mulhearn

Allison with her father at a Darien High School game

A Note from Christian Trifone

Finish.

That was Jim Mulhearn's word for our 2015 senior season. A word that none of us took lightly. Everyday we took the field for practice, we carried that with a heavy heart. We had played together since 3rd grade, watching as the varsity team lost time and time again to arch rival New Canaan. We sought a different outcome.

We were told we had the talent and we were well aware of our depth at each position. The focus was on finishing; putting everything together and finishing what we had started. As everyone in the town knows there are distractions every step of the way. We were determined to overcome any and everything that stood in our way. It was never just about the games or the stats for us. We were brothers. It didn't matter which friend groups we belonged to or what our respective hobbies were off the field, we cared about each other and we still hold that. Some things in life can never be taken away from you and what we did that season we will hold forever.

Times change and people change but the memories we made together will never fade. Some of my best memories came on that Darien High School turf. Of course winning games was a luxury as well as finishing the season as we did.

But like I said, it was never about the games. It was about walking out of that tunnel everyday with a band of brothers. Walking out and feeling invincible because we all looked out for each other, and we weren't going to let the guy to our left or right down. One of the greatest lessons I've learned in my life reads "whatever you start, you finish." We finished, Jim.

- Christian Trifone
  #24

Christian Trifone in fifth grade, 2008

A Note from Sam Giorgio

I believe I first met Coach Trifone around the third grade when I began my first year of playing tackle football in the Darien Junior Football League. After graduating college this past spring around 12 years later, I can honestly say I had no idea how much Darien Football and Coach Trifone changed my life. I was on Coach T's DJFL team every year from third grade through eighth grade when both our DJFL teams were co-champions of the division that season. I was never in love with football when I was growing up, and I was undersized for the sport even then as an elementary schooler. Coach Trifone was the first coach and one of the only I ever had to show faith in me despite my size.

During DJFL, he would give me shots at any position from linebacker to running back to even guard at some point helping me build my confidence and love for the game. I feel like most kids like me who were on the smaller size, didn't get to play a lot normally, and were maybe even a little socially awkward would eventually grow out of football and not want to play; however, Coach Trifone made sure, from third grade, that wouldn't happen to any of us. He coached us into loving football and over our eight year football journey we all began to become a family.

Coach Trifone and I got to be better friends when he hired

me to work for him at Roton Point Association as well as a lifeguard. He quickly introduced me to another person who would have a huge impact on my life in a short amount of time, Jim Mulhern. Jim was a beloved member of not only the football community but of the Roton Point family as well. I'll never forget the inspirational speeches Jim would give myself and my teammates that worked there. He believed in us and our team so much that I think he in a way helped everyone on the team believe in themselves and motivated them to be their best selves, for Jim. It's a subject that still makes me choke up every time I talk about him and I wish he were still here with us, but I have been able to find a little solace in what we accomplished for him in 2015. I could not be the man I am today again without that 2015 State and FCIAC championship season.

The experiences I had, the life long friendships I built, and the just immense enjoyment we all got out of playing that season are, and always will be, irreplaceable to me. I could go on and on for pages about every little detail of how important that season was for me, but I think the most important thing it did was give me the confidence I needed to succeed and thrive at college. However, I'd be remiss to not say that everything we accomplished that season in 2015 was not possible without Coach Trifone.

I had mixed emotions when I heard about his retirement from Blue Wave Football because on one hand I feel the team will always need him like I did for my football career. On the other hand though, I am happy to see him move into a new chapter in his life and excited to see what great things he still has to offer, and not only as a coach. I owe Coach T, Jim, and that 2015 season the world, they helped shape me into the person I am proud of today and taught me lessons I still use everyday.

I hope that Coach T looks back happily on everything he's

accomplished over his career, and I just want to say "Thank You!" to him for everything he's done!

- Sammy Giorgio
  #33

Giorgio graduated from Villanova University with a Bachelor's degree in Biology in May of 2020. While he applies to medical school, he plans to work both as an Emergency Room Technician and assist with John Carlozzi. He dreams of one day working as an orthopedic surgeon with a specialty in major sports teams, especially football.

Sam Giorgio in 2011 on the 8th grade championship team.

A Note from Hudson Hamill

It is hard to state how much of an impact Coach Trifone and Jim Mulhearn have had on my life. Coach T taught me so much about preparation and accountability. These are things that I have used throughout my college career and will continue to use in the real world. His willingness to welcome Jim to the team also reflects the type of character Coach T possesses.

As for Jim, he was the motivating factor for our whole team. He taught us about how to handle adversity and how to always have a positive mindset no matter how tough things might be. I owe so much to both Coach T and Jim and will never forget my years playing at Darien High School.

- Hudson Hamill
  #22

Hamill graduated from Washington & Lee University in May of 2020. He spent his entire college career on the Generals lacrosse team, where in 2019 he was named a Third Team All-American. He was a team captain his senior year and ranks ninth all-time on the school's assist leaders. He plans to move to Washington DC and work at United Bank.

Hudson Hamill in 2011 playing against Westport in eighth grade.

A Note from Mark Evanchick

Coach T - Congrats on your retirement! I cannot thank you enough for the time and effort you put into coaching and preparing us for life after football. Throughout my career, you taught me to always be prepared and most importantly, you're never out of the fight. Not only did you emphasize this, but having Jim around throughout my junior and senior year really made that point stick. To have a man that was fighting through a horrible disease and would show up every day as happy as could be, was an incredible experience.

Beyond the lessons you and Jim taught us, the 2015 season was one of the most fun years I ever had playing sports. Week in and week out, knowing that whoever was lining up across from us did not stand a chance was an unbelievable feeling and one that I will never forget. I still remember arriving at Boyle to play NC and even before we kicked off, everyone on the bus knew that we weren't going to lose that game. The confidence you instilled in us each and every week was unbelievable and played a huge part in our success that year. Even when we knew we were playing an inferior team, there was never a letdown because you refused to allow our team to play below our full potential.

Every week, while staying focused on the game ahead, you managed to keep practice fun and enjoyable for everyone.

Looking back today on that 2015 season, It still remains one of my favorite athletics seasons not only because of how successful we were, but because how close we all were and the drive we had to accomplish the goal of your first state championship at Darien High School.

I know I speak for all of your former players when I say that we are sad to see you retire, but grateful for everything you have done for all of us. Thank you again for everything you have done for all of us and I hope you enjoy retirement.

- Mark Evanchick
  #90

Evanchick graduated from the University of Pennsylvania in May of 2020. He spent all four years on the lacrosse team and spent the 2018 football season with the Quakers. He plans to move to Atlanta, Georgia and work as a loan syndication analyst for Truist Financial.

Mark Evanchick (#75) blocking against New Canaan in 2011.

The Trifone twins lead blocking for Hudson Hamill (2008)

Jim Mulhearn's birthday celebration (2014)

* * *

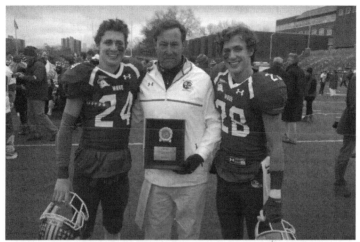

Coach Trifone with his sons after the Turkey Bowl (2014)

Sam Giorgio on Senior Day (2015)

Hudson Hamill celebrates against Southington (2015)

Timmy Graham in the 2015 State Championship vs. Shelton

Bobby and Christian Trifone after the 2015 State Championship game

Bobby and Rob Trifone after the 2015 State Championship

Preface

I think it is an understatement when I tell you that when growing up, football was my life. Really, my first vivid memories are from playing flag football all the way back in 2008 for the first time. Ever since then, I have spent every single autumn season around the game. However, there wasn't any real passion in the game of football while I played from third through seventh-grade. I honestly only played football because my two older brothers played, especially Ryan, a wide receiver on the 2010 and 2011 Darien High School football teams. As a seventh-grader in 2010, I worshipped the grounds that Ryan walked on as a high school football player, and only played simply because I wanted to be like him. There was no other reasoning behind me playing, all until the summer leading into my eighth-grade season.

That summer at 13 years old, I searched at the Darien Library for football books to read before the start of the season. I then stumbled across a book titled *Friday Night Lights* by H.G. Bissinger. I devoured the book in under a week and officially fell in love with the game of football. I related heavily to the life of soft-spoken quarterback Mike Winchell and went back to the book year after year during football seasons. Anyone close to me can tell you how addicted I am to the story of the 1988 Permian High School Panthers football team; I have read the book cover to cover six times and will probably reread it again soon.

Now, a preface is meant to tell the reader what the motivation was behind writing the book. H.G. Bissinger's tale of high school football in the heart of Texas is the main reason this book was written. Now obviously, Bissinger revolutionized sports writing with his masterpiece back in 1990, something I know I cannot replicate. However, when thinking about the book as a whole, I saw incredible differences between the two settings of Odessa (TX) and Darien (CT). Odessa was a dirt-poor oil town that Bissinger spotted in the late 80s. What stood out to Bissinger was the obsession with high school football the town had, along with the on-field and off-field lives the players had during that time.

Then, I took a look at Darien, nearly 40 years after *Friday Night Lights*. The games at Darien High School barely attract a couple of thousand fans each weekend, a decimal compared to the 20,000 that rolled into Ratliff Stadium during the 1988 Permian season. The town of Darien does not shut down on the day of the games as Odessa did; also, Darien does not qualify as a dirt-poor oil town but instead qualifies as one of the wealthiest communities in the United States of America. The two towns are utter opposites really, although they share a pretty significant similarity...

There is a slight obsession with athletics.

So for me, there was something about wanting to revisit the messages that Bissinger wrote about almost four decades ago. I wanted to put my own spin on it, and instead of focusing on one season, I wanted to focus on all three years of my high school playing career because to me, they are three fascinating years due to the circumstances surrounding them and the characters that lived through them. What I found most interesting when writing this book was the latter in that sentence; the people who played alongside me and the backstories they have. As with a lot of sports, fans in the stands see football players as people with football helmets and shoulder pads on. However, there is a lot underneath those helmets and pads. They are human beings going through a combination of things that a lot of people don't know about. The most important thing, which I like to touch on a lot, is that they are kids still, and not professional athletes.

For those who aren't familiar with Darien, there is a large notion that the town is known for putting a considerable amount of pressure on student-athletes to perform well in the classroom while being wildly successful on the athletic fields as well. That is one of the main focuses of my book, only because I, along with a lot of my teammates, struggled with that balance of academic and athletic pressure (not to mention the social pressure we felt as well).

When I decided to write 12, I felt that I needed to write it as a tribute to the years of Darien High School football that I played. But as I researched and interviewed former players and teammates, I realized there was more to just being grateful to the game of football. I saw that there were problems in Darien, may it be the underage drinking issue, the parental interference that I experienced first-hand when coaching seventh-grade football, or the sometimes extreme measures children are pushed so that they can succeed in their parent's eyes, which trickles down all the way to the youth level. There's a lot of positives in a town like Darien, yet you can't always turn a blind eye to the negatives.

When you do go on to read the book too, you will find the balance between my perspective along with my teammates' perspectives while growing up in the Darien High School system. There are some great and good things; there is some bad, and there is some ugly in the lives that we lived in 2013-2015. There is happiness, and there is sadness. In short, there are human stories that go unnoticed when the Darien Blue Wave run out onto the field at Darien High School during autumn weekends. I feel as if those stories are important to share, whether they make you laugh, smile, cry or ask more questions.

However, I don't stray away from the main roots of my book, which is to deliver a retelling of the hopes and dreams my grade and I had as little kids while we played football. Because in the end, what brings the town together is its passion for sports and the hopes and dreams of said town. And for the kids involved, which is evident through some of the stories my teammates give, it is all for one single purpose:

For the love of the game.

That is what makes high school sports and football in Darien so amazing. That is what makes the experience worth it. That is what makes running out in front of 10,000 people on Thanksgiving morning the biggest adrenaline rush ever. It is all for the love of the game.

As I conclude, I hope you enjoy the ride. In the next few hundred pages, you will experience the rise of the Darien High School football program through the eyes of those who lived it. More importantly, you will ride a rollercoaster through the three seasons with the Darien High School football senior class of 2015, which led what is considered the greatest football team in school history. You will experience the heartbreak, the joy and the beauty that makes football the greatest team sport in the world.

Once again, enjoy the ride. I absolutely loved writing this book and hope you will enjoy reading it as much as I did writing it. This book is a dream come true to me; it was a privilege to retell the stories of my teammates and to talk to the townspeople of Darien, I am forever grateful for their time and support.

Now without further ado…

Welcome to Darien.

Darien, Connecticut

When driving through, it is hard to miss. The bright green fields, the grand houses situated on acres of land, the beautifully grown gardens; it's an eye-opening affair the first time you drive down the roads of Darien, Connecticut. The real estate market booms in "D-Town," where the average median home value is an easy $1,304,227.[1] Compared to the national average of $215,600,[2] it is safe to say that Darien is well, different.

Darien has grown over the years as the stereotypical affluent town in Connecticut, only rivaled by neighboring towns like Greenwich and New Canaan. The facts support the stereotype, as Bloomberg's 2018 edition of "America's 100 Richest Places" listed Darien at #10 on its list. Alongside that, the median household income in Darien is $208,125; the national average is $55,322.[3] With all that money, the townspeople have plenty of places to spend it. Darien is home to a plethora of private member clubs and country clubs, notably Wee Burn Country Club (women could not become full members until 1999), which is one the highest taxpayers in Darien according to the Town of Darien Annual Report.

The extraordinary amount of wealth cannot hide the

checkered history within the town. Throughout the 20th century, Darien was known informally as a sundown town. Simply put, this meant the town had unwritten rules to keep African Americans out. If these families did not leave by sunset, the townspeople would take forcible, and what is now considered, horrifying action. The accusations on Darien kept on building to a high level, especially after the publication of James W. Loewen's book *Sundown Towns: A Hidden Dimension of American Racism.* Infamy only grew within Darien, notably when a high ranking officer in Connecticut's Klu Klux Klan moved to town during the Klan's peak (over 15,000 Connecticut members) during the 1920's.[4]

Racism continued in the town, as anti-semitic practices began to flow into the streets of Darien in hopes of scaring off the influx of Jewish families coming into Connecticut. The treatment of Jewish families grew to the point of national notoriety when Laura Hobson published her 1947 book, *Gentleman's Agreement*, a story set in Darien that explores the anti-semitism in and around the area. The novel received acclaim, with one contemporary critic writing that the book was "a story of the emotional disturbance that occurs within a man who elects, for the sake of getting a magazine article, to tell people that he is a Jew and who experiences first-hand, as a consequence, the shock and pain of discrimination and social snubs."[5] The book became so well known that it was eventually adapted into a film later that decade. The film, titled the same as the book, continued the setting in Darien and went on to garner eight Academy Award nominations, winning Best Picture.

Over 70 years after *Gentleman's Agreement* and after attempted improvements, the racial diversity in the town has still drawn constant criticism. In a 2016 study, Darien was found to be 89% white, while Hispanic people made up 3.28% and African Americans only made up 0.51% of the population.[6] In contrast, neighboring cities like Stamford are 49.6% white, 26.5% Hispanic and 14% African American.[7] Some people believe in the idea of Darien being a bubble, where citizens are protected and blinded from the issues in surrounding areas and towns. One coach sees the diversity effect on children as well, who says that during a summer tournament, a young child told him they were losing because the other team "has a black kid."

Through all the controversy, Darien remains a tight-knit community. Pride throughout the town is at an all-time high, as thousands gather for the Memorial Day Parade and congregate in masses for special events. The town boasts five elementary schools and Middlesex Middle School. Local private schools also cater to Darien, including St. Luke's School, Greens Farm Academy and New Canaan Country School, to name a few. Then there is the town's monument to education, Darien High School. The high school was completed in the fall of 2005 after $73 million was put forth to rebuild the demolished old aging building. Seven years later in a U.S. News article, Darien High School was ranked #1 in their "Best High Schools in Connecticut" rankings. The school holds an incredible graduation rate while sending almost all of its students off to college after leaving Darien High School.

Although there is massive educational success, Darien's passion lies in athletics. Just by looking at Darien High School from above, you can see athletics are the dominant force. The campus is home to five turfed fields (six, if you include the junior varsity baseball field which connects to the multipurpose field), two softball fields and tennis courts, all within the vicinity of the campus. Most of the turf is thanks to the Darien Athletic Foundation, which has helped fund projects across the board, most notably the funding for the stadium lights that were installed in 2017 after years of battles with the neighbors of Darien High School.

Youth programs also have a shareholder in the town's sports monopoly. The town's Little League program is one of the biggest in the nation while holding the outstanding achievement of being home to the largest Challenger Division in the country. The youth lacrosse programs and football programs carry the same amount of pride, dominating the previously mentioned fields at Darien High School almost every weekend. Where the real talent lies, however, is with the students within the halls of Darien High School. From the unstoppable juggernaut in coach Laurie LaRusso's volleyball teams to the incredible progression of the Track & Field teams, Darien High School is always in the mix for titles in the Fairfield County Interscholastic Athletic Conference (FCIAC), but more importantly, at the state level (CIAC). Yet, as of recent, two sports have been the real center of attention within the sports realm of Darien.

Darien is historically known as a lacrosse town, where head coach Jeff Brameier has delivered complete superiority. The high school boys lacrosse team in Darien have won 16 FCIAC championships, and 13 state championships, while claiming the #1 ranking in the Under Armor/Inside Lacrosse national rankings in some years. The Blue Wave win like it is nobody's business, even when national powerhouses come from New York and California to see if Darien is *that* good. The girl's lacrosse program has risen to prominence under the direction of head coach Lisa Lindley, who has helped lead the girls to 16 state championship victories. Lindley has led the girl's team since 1994 and has earned a plethora of Coach of the Year awards, although she came under fire in 2012 when during a playoff game, Lindley, who was visibly frustrated, grabbed hold of a players helmet after a costly mistake. She was suspended for the remainder of the season,[8] while the town was split down the middle on if the punishment was an overreaction.

Still, the lacrosse programs have been somewhat of a mainstay at Darien High School for decades. The football program, however, has been on and off since the 1970s. The team was dominant in the late 70s, winning the school its first CIAC State Championship in 1979 (famously beating Steve Young and Greenwich in the FCIAC Championship) with an 11-0 record while placing #2 in the state polls, which was the first true undefeated season in school history. The team struggled in the 80s, yet returned to relevance in 1987 under new head coach Mike Sangster, who led the football program to two straight state title games in the later part of the decade but lost both.

The 1990s saw a massive resurgence in the football team. In 1991 the Blue Wave rolled to a 10-2 record and a CIAC State Championship win by defeating Berlin High School 35-22. The team was not done, as the '92 squad flirted with perfection, riding an 11-0-1 record. The team was led by defensive standout Brian Merritt, who caught 56 passes for 1,027 yards while intercepting 11 passes on defense, leading the team to an incredible 10 points allowed per game. The Wave steamrolled to the title game, where they obliterated Stratford High School in the CIAC State Championship by a score of 30-0. Since taking over in '87, Coach Sangster had led the Blue Wave to four state title games with two victories, bringing new life to the football program.

Sangster and the Wave struggled to reach the title game the following years but stormed back into contention during the 1996 season. Led by running back Ryan Damon, who ran for 1,765 yards, the team reached the CIAC State Championship looking for its third title of the decade and did so in a shootout by beating Bloomfield High School, 21-16 and finishing with a 12-1 record.

Sangster had the Darien High School team in dynasty mode, and he planned on continuing the path they were on.

With his team hungry for more, the team set out on its title defense in '97 hoping to right the wrong of the one loss in 1996. The loss of Damon hurt the team though, and they struggled mightily. Three losses put them on the brink of state elimination, but they squeezed into the playoffs behind the play of quarterback Tom DiMenna. The Wave marched to the state semifinals to the surprise of most, where they upset Ansonia High School by a score of 31-20. The road led to a rematch of the 1996 CIAC State Championship, as Bloomfield returned for revenge. The Blue Wave's defense struggled in the 1997 rematch, and they lost by a score of 39-21, decimating any hope of going back to back.

The loss fueled a fire under the team. New running back Tim Stisser put on one of the most dominant shows in Darien High School history, averaging 6.4 yards per carry. The team rolled through the opposition until they got to the state semifinals against Stratford High School. The game was close, but Darien prevailed by a score of 15-12, advancing to the title game with a perfect 12-0 record while becoming the first team in school history to reach three consecutive title games. Perfection, however, was not meant for the '98 team, as in the CIAC State Championship game, the Wave's offense went missing, losing to Seymour High School 14-6.

With the loss came the end of the immensely successful tenure of head coach Mike Sangster. Sangster led the Blue Wave for 12 years, holding a 105-30-2 record, reaching seven CIAC State Championships and winning three of them. Inheriting a team that hadn't had any success since the '79 season, Sangster motivated his teams unlike any coach before him, and brought Darien High School back to relevance at the state level, creating a winning atmosphere and a culture of competition.

Following the departure of Sangster, the Blue Wave were led by now current lacrosse coach Jeff Brameier. The '99 team,

after watching two devastating losses in the title game, decided it was time to finish for their teammates what they started back in 1997. Led by Jim Muhlfeld's 18 touchdown passes, the team met hated arch-rival New Canaan in the semifinals. If Darien won, they would make history themselves, breaking their record by becoming the first Darien High School football team to reach four consecutive state title games. Darien dominated their hated rival from the opening kick, winning by a score of 23-0.

Weaver High School in Hartford awaited the Blue Wave, massacring them by 46 points and leaving the team empty-handed for the third consecutive year. The loss wasn't what made the headlines though, but instead the behavior of the Darien players towards the predominately black Weaver players. In interviews after the game, Weaver players told media members that the Darien players used racial slurs, while also saying things such as: "In five years, you'll be working for me" and "we have some bananas for you guys."

After 1999, Brameier was unable to replicate Sangster's success, as the turn of the century proved to be devastating to the Darien High School football program. The team struggled to reach the playoffs following the '99 season, making Brameier's tenure as head coach end following the 2003 season with a 27-26-1 record.

The program continued in a nosedive, resulting in back to back 4-6 seasons in 2004 and 2005. After a mediocre 5-5 record in 2006, the athletic department moved in a new direction, hiring Rob Trifone to take over the reigns of the Darien Blue Wave. Trifone was a proven winner, leading the 1994 Brien McMahon Senators to an undefeated season and a CIAC State Championship. The '94 Senators were quite possibly the most dominant team in Connecticut football history, led by future Super Bowl winner Idris Price. The defense rarely let up a touchdown, and when it happened, the first unit had been off the field for a while. Trifone, however, was given a mighty task in Darien of rebuilding a depleted football program. Ten years had passed since the Blue Wave had won a CIAC State Championship, and Darien High School football once again took a backseat to a developing Girls Volleyball powerhouse and the always dominant lacrosse teams. State competitiveness was out of the question too, since the team was struggling to stay relevant in the FCIAC alone.

In 2007, Trifone took a step back from the previous year, enduring a 4-6 record, but the team was motivated under the leadership of their new head coach. It was in 2008 though when the fortunes turned back towards Darien. Led by the offensive trio of quarterback Matty Wheelock, running back Nikki Dysenchuck and wide receiver Brian Kosnik, Trifone led the Blue Wave to a perfect record heading into the annual Thanksgiving Day clash with the New Canaan Rams. The Rams were the powerhouse of the FCIAC and state, having won four CIAC State Championships since the turn of the century and being undefeated as well. Darien had not won a Turkey Bowl against the Rams since 2001, but there was more to the game than that. The game also doubled as the FCIAC Championship game, which Darien had not won since 1998. The stakes were high, and the players and fans knew it. The game was played at Boyle Stadium in neighboring Stamford, as nearly 10,000 fans packed in to see the Blue Wave battle the Rams.

The game was a dogfight, as the Blue Wave went back and forth with the mighty Rams. It wasn't meant to be though, as New Canaan walked away with a 28-20 victory, claiming the FCIAC crown for the first time since 2000. The Blue Wave recovered quickly, entering the state playoffs for the first time since the '99 season. Trifone and his offense impressed and reached the CIAC State Championship for the first time in nine years. The joy of victory didn't last long, because waiting for them on the other side were none other than the Rams of New Canaan. In the Turkey Day rematch, Trifone was unable to create any offense as the Rams defense stifled Darien, giving New Canaan a 26-7 victory and it's fifth state title of the decade.

In hindsight, the 2008 season was a massive success for Darien High School, as it drew a record crowd on Thanksgiving and gave the fans an incredible playoff run only one year after winning four games, ending with a strong 11-2 record, good enough for #6 in the state. In the end, Trifone had earned his keep at the helm of the Wave as the future looked bright for the resurgent Darien program.

Wheelock, Dysenchuck, and Kosnik all graduated following the '08 season, causing a brutal setback in the plans of Trifone. The Wave were unable to build off the success of the previous season, finishing with a 7-3 record in '09 and no entry into the postseason. 2010 saw the return of balance at Darien High School, as Trifone and the undefeated Blue Wave stormed into the FCIAC Championship to play the Trumbull High School Eagles for the crown. Led by defensive stars Charlie Kunze and Jake Weil, the Blue Wave kept the Eagles at bay with a 17-7 win, claiming their first FCIAC Championship since 1998.

Following the FCIAC win, the Blue Wave hoped to turn it into significant momentum heading into Thanksgiving, where they planned on ending the losing streak to the Rams that dated back to 2001. The Rams, however, had different plans, destroying the Wave 42-14 on Darien's turf. The team would be eliminated in the state playoffs soon after, losing to Masuk High School in the state semifinals 41-0.

Fortunes did not get any better. The Wave went 8-2 in the 2011 season and missed out on a state playoff berth. 2012 held promise, but devastating losses at home crushed the team, as the Wave went 6-3 heading into Thanksgiving, effectively eliminating any dreams of a postseason. On Thanksgiving Day in Darien, the New Canaan Rams arrived already clinching a state playoff berth and as heavy favorites over the Blue Wave. In the face of massive adversity, the Wave prevailed, ending the long losing streak to New Canaan by defeating them 36-23. Afterward, Trifone walked off the field at Darien High School Stadium relieved with the win, but also with high expectations for the 2013 Darien Blue Wave football season.[9]

PART I
The 2013 Season
"People had doubts, and they had good reasons to have doubts because we were certainly not the most talented team, and I was not the most talented player."
- Silas Wyper on the 2013 Blue Wave

CHAPTER ONE

The Chosen Ones

Three years before the start of the 2013 season, Hudson Hamill stood alongside Bobby and Christian Trifone on a crisp Saturday afternoon at Darien High School. The varsity team was in the middle of a battle with St. Joseph's High School, struggling to get on the board going into halftime down 10-0. The score didn't matter to the 12-year-old Hamill, wearing his #11 youth jersey, who was instead enamored by the high school athletes wearing the "Blue Wave" name on their jerseys. He watched as running back Graham Maybell, donning the #22, darted through the St. Joseph defenders in the second half and eventually scored on a dump pass to put the Blue Wave up 13-10 in the fourth quarter. Hamill was quick to relate to the senior captain, who at 5'9 160 pounds was exceptionally undersized but had a ton of fight when he stepped onto the football field. At safety, Maybell took on receivers twice his size but did so with absolutely no fear, putting his body on the line every single play day in and day out.

From the day Hudson Hamill started playing football, he was counted out. The tiny frame of Hamill made him a quick and speedy target, although doubts rose very quickly from parents who would say at every youth game, "If he doesn't grow he won't make it a day at Darien High School." As a young kid, Hamill ignored those doubts but heard them constantly. "I knew I was always on the smaller side," Hamill remembers. "I also knew that I was going to run as fast as I could and knew that if I hit somebody, it would hurt them more than it hurt me." Hamill did precisely that, becoming one of the most dangerous players on both sides of the ball during his Darien Junior Football League (DJFL) career. Still, questions lingered about his long term ability in high school.

As the clock ticked down during the St. Joseph's game, Hamill and the Trifone twins stood atop the Darien High School cafeteria, looking down to Bobby and Christian's father, head coach Rob Trifone, on the field. With the sun peeking over the stadium, Hamill looked down at the superstars on the high school team while they celebrated the hard-fought win. Hamill, like everyone in our grade, wanted to be like that. However, he wanted more. He looked at Bobby and Christian atop the cafeteria and said to them:

"We're going to win a state championship one day."

It was a daunting prediction made by the 12-year-old, but it wasn't anything new to our grade either. In fact, it seemed as if the prophecy had already been bestowed upon us years earlier when we were just eight years old. With Bobby and Christian in our grade, Rob Trifone started pulling double duty after accepting the Darien High School job, while also taking the task of coaching his twin sons in third-grade youth football. It was a different experience, but Trifone refused to treat us any differently. We knew him as a God, due to his status as the varsity football coach. Trifone though knew us as a bunch of kids who were playing football for the first time. He wasn't going to change, although expectations were high.

Our lack of developed talent showed in our first few years

together, even with a football genius like Trifone at the helm. In fourth-grade, my team went winless, while the other two DJFL fourth grade teams struggled just as mightily. The fortunes didn't change in fifth or sixth-grade, as we once again failed to do anything tremendous during the regular season, consistently getting whipped by rival New Canaan and other towns in the league. Improvement, however, began to show as Trifone implemented elements of the high school offense and defense into our youth system. Entering our seventh-grade season, we had a newfound sense of swagger and confidence under the new system. The results came with that, pushing both Darien teams as far as the league semifinals, where we both fell to New Canaan.

The hope and expectations rose to massive heights leading into our eighth-grade year. With only one year until we entered the Darien High School program, Trifone and the other coaches decided to put in all the marbles for the 2011 season. With fathers like Tom Mercein, Kevin Minicus and Pete Graham (all of who played college football) helping out, our eighth-grade season was a masterpiece of skill and talent meshing perfectly with coaching excellence. The two teams combined to lose only three games, with the Mercein/Graham team beating a previously undefeated New Canaan team (not having lost since third grade), which eventually led to both of our teams being crowned co-champions.

The eighth-grade championship only created higher expectations coming into our freshman year at Darien High School. Almost immediately, some of us were hazed right off the bat as being Coach Trifone's "chosen ones" who would finally be the kids to lead Darien High School football to a state championship. Not only that, but we were also labeled as "untouchable" by seniors on the 2012 team, who made jokes left and right about how much we got pampered in the lead up to high school. Ignoring the attention, we set out as a freshman team and worked like a well-oiled machine, stringing together an undefeated season leading up to the end of year game against New Canaan. We cracked under the pressure of the game though, getting demoralized and demolished by a hungry New Canaan team.

Distraught, we returned to the drawing board for the 2013 season, where we would be sophomores on a vastly larger varsity team. The sting from the freshman year loss didn't hold long, especially for me, since I was off the walls excited about the prospect of joining the varsity squad during my sophomore year. That was my childhood dream since I first started playing football with my friends back in elementary school, to be a varsity football player on the field at Darien High School. Like Hamill and my other teammates, the high schoolers who played on Saturdays were cooler than the word cool itself to me. I worshipped the ground they walked on, thinking they were more prominent than the guys who played at the college or NFL level.

However, unlike Hamill and some of my other teammates, I wasn't a superstar in the making. I was from a middle-class family (at least in Darien terms) and grew up different than some kids in town; I did chores without allowance, I had a set bedtime, and I had to do most of the yard work/cleaning at my house. Socially, I wasn't the most popular kid but wasn't an outcast either. I was a quiet kid growing up, and even through our differences, there was still one constant that held guys like Hamill and me together; it was our unconditional love for football.

I started throughout my youth career and watched Darien High School games every Saturday, surrounding myself with the game of football at every turn. I devoured football, and the varsity team at Darien High School was better than life itself. For me, coming into 2013 with the chance to play at Darien High School at the varsity level, let alone being on the team as a sophomore, was a massive dream come true. I wasn't at Darien High to be a student. My main priority was on the football field, where I planned on working tirelessly for three years to achieve the goals I had set all the way back as a kid.

1. Become a star player.
2. Win a ring.

Spring Ball

It was early June in 2013 when Coach Trifone walked onto the turf field at Darien High School as the sun peeked over the mammoth campus. A new beginning had arrived, an opportunity to rid the wrongs of the previous year; a chance to leave no doubts and create a strong team from top to bottom. Although there was a powerful bond between Trifone and my class, we were not the priority on the field during the days of spring practice. Trifone instead was given the task of figuring out who fit where at the varsity level, trying to fill in the missing puzzle pieces after losing a good chunk of starters from the 2012 team to graduation. His biggest concern was at the quarterback position, where after losing two-year starter Henry Baldwin, he was forced to turn the reins over to unknown senior quarterback, Silas Wyper. Undersized and not acquainted to the ways of varsity football after years buried on the depth chart, it appeared Wyper would have his plate full during the spring season in order to be ready for the opener in early September.

Two sophomore players remained with the varsity squad though; one was a defensive end by the name of Mark Evanchick. Even at this time, it wasn't Evanchick's first rodeo with the varsity team. In the middle of our freshman season the previous fall, Trifone called Mark up following an injury to senior defensive end Will Lochtefeld. Evanchick, who became one of the first freshmen in school history to start on the varsity squad, eased into his role on the team, resulting in an incredible 2012 season. The 6'0 245-pound defensive end collected 4.0 sacks in the four games he played, including a crowd erupting sack against New Canaan on Thanksgiving.

The other was quarterback Timmy Graham. Senior Silas Wyper was the penciled in starter from day one, but Graham was the heir and was given the backup job over junior Cooper Drippe. Timmy was every offensive coordinator's dream, standing at 6'4 and possessing the mobility and arm strength to stretch the field. Quiet on the field, he was remarkably dedicated to his craft and wanted nothing more than success. He knew football was his life, and he wanted nothing more than to be a quarterback at Darien High School.

Following the first practice, we would be on the field for the next six days. With no conditioning or anything major, the springtime was a chance for many players to get a feel for what football at this level was like, and for me it was incredible. I loved watching the coaches discuss coverages and routes, and was in awe seeing the players screaming certain codewords at each other to adjust to what was in front of them. As an offensive lineman during my sophomore year, I took note of the other lineman and their footwork, trying to pick up everything I could during the two weeks of practice. I knew my size (standing at 6'2 165 pounds) was my weakness, so I would have to make up for it with my technique and skill.

The one thing though that I wasn't aware of until spring football were sophomore duties. I had completely forgotten that it was a thing until all of a sudden during the second day one of the seniors walked up to me and told me to get the water ready. Not even using my name, he just casually expected it to happen. I did the task but learned that getting water wasn't even half of what was to come. Putting away the pads used during practice, collecting the footballs and cleaning up any trash found on the field was all part of our sophomore duties. It wasn't something we were asked to do, but it was more or less an unwritten rule. We were expected to do it, and if we didn't, we were playing with some severe fire.

Sophomore duties, even by the namesake, wasn't something that all sophomores took part in. Guys like Mark Evanchick never had to do the water while higher-up players such as Timmy Graham and the Trifone twins were very rarely pressed to do the heavy-lifting of the duties. That was left to guys like Sam Giorgio, Mark Schmidt, Marcus Pagliarulo and I; which in hindsight, was really because of our social status within the team. Sophomore duties were just the start of the "bottom feeder" treatment that some of us received at the sophomore level; which is something Pagliarulo remembers vividly. "I was getting ready for practice one day on the field when an older player came up to me," says Pagliarulo. "He looked at me and said, 'Pags, tie my shoe.' I looked at him, and he wasn't joking, so I started to go down to his level when he walked away and started laughing."

After two weeks of practices, spring football was wrapping up as we closed in on June 16th, which was the annual Blue vs. White scrimmage. The scrimmage was like any other spring practice finale, as the team was split into separate units to compete against one another. Even though it was promoted as a scrimmage, it was a glorified practice of sorts. Still, it was a proving ground for many players who were looking to make a name for themselves in front of the coaching staff. I saw the game as a golden opportunity to showcase my skills and technique on the line to hopefully get the coaches to realize that I had the potential to be a starter down the road.

When the game started, the sophomores were promised

the entire second quarter of the game to get some playing time. When the second quarter came, I readied myself but did not hear my name called onto the field. Annoyed, I stayed on the sideline and told myself to wait until the next drive. Blue regained possession of the ball, and the same offense went in. Now pissed off, I was ready to confront my coaches on it, but decided against it, thinking that it might make me seem like a selfish person asking to go in instead of someone else. Eventually, I got in for one possession during the Blue vs. White game at left tackle, but we went three and out, ending my 2013 spring season rather quickly.

I was beaten up from the spring, my tiny frame unable to take the brutalities of a true varsity lineman. I knew I had to bulk up so that I could have a puncher's chance of getting any consideration from coaches, so that is exactly what I did. That summer, I spent nearly five days a week in the gym trying to get myself to the point where I could continue to develop into a productive player. I tried putting on weight as well so I could look more like a stereotypical lineman, but my metabolism didn't agree. I still felt myself getting stronger, and I knew that there wasn't a lot I could do about my weight. I was still growing and was only going to be a sophomore, and I had two years to fully develop into what I wanted to become in time for my senior year.

The summer flew by and in early August, the first day of practice was officially set for the 19th of the month. Time continued to go quickly, and sooner than I expected, August 18th arrived. The next morning I woke up at 6:45 am. "Hell Week" had come.

Hell Week

Hell Week is the unofficial name given to the first week of August practices, and it is indeed a test of everything your body has physically, mentally and emotionally. "You have no idea what to expect, that first practice of Hell Week," Sam Giorgio says, remembering the build-up to the first week of practices as a sophomore in 2013. "I think that is what is the scariest part of it all. You have no idea what is coming." Hell Week is the time of the year where sophomores go to die, as more players quit during this time than any other period of the season. Your legs struggle to stand, your heart beats faster than it has ever beat before, and your brain questions why you are putting yourself through this in the first place.

Hell Week is a truly legendary tale from Darien High School that goes all around the town of Darien. I first heard about Hell Week when my older brother was playing football back in 2010. He returned home after practice one day in August, and drenched in sweat; he collapsed onto the couch following a five hour day of football. It terrified me as a seventh-grader, but it intrigued me too. It didn't only spark my mind because, throughout our youth careers, my teammates and I would always talk about it while watching the varsity team practice in August. We tried calling our first week of practices Hell Week, although we came nowhere near the level of brutality of the high school practices.

Contrary to popular belief, Hell Week isn't for the coaches enjoyment to watch their players suffer. Hell Week gives the coaches an opportunity to see who has been putting in the work in the summer, and who has not. It is a medieval tactic in some people's minds. The coaches are separating the strong from the weak, the men from the boys. Students who think they can play the game of football soon realize that they are not cut out for it, and quit not even a week into practice. From the stories I had heard, I was scared to death but also excited to undertake the challenges of Hell Week.

Leading up to the 19th, the upperclassmen were extremely helpful in making sure us sophomores were somewhat prepared for what was coming. Nothing prepares you for it, but one senior shared a piece of advice that holds true for most:

"If you make it through your first Hell Week, you can make it through almost anything after that."

We arrived for practice at 8 am on the morning of the 19th, as Coach Trifone wanted to hold an introductory meeting before we kicked off the first week of practice. Trifone had entered the room quiet and stoic, and a hush fell over the crowded classroom. Walking over to his computer, he opened a powerpoint presentation, where the preseason Connecticut high school state rankings were plastered onto the white background. Darien was nowhere to be found. The laughter and joking vibe was all gone, while the seniors looked stone-faced at the screen, absorbing the disrespect the media had given the Blue Wave. Most of the disrespect fell onto Silas Wyper, who was questioned as a quarterback wherever Darien was mentioned in the press.

Following about a minute of silence, Trifone began to speak to his 2013 team. He talked about respect and disrespect, and how Darien was being counted out once again. Standing in the back, I watched in awe while Trifone delivered one of his signature speeches. It was like he had the entire team in the palm of his hand, offering a sermon that every player took to the center of their hearts. It was the senior class again who took the entirety of Trifone's speech personally. They had been behind the 2012 seniors who were supposedly the team that was going to bring glory back to Darien football but couldn't quite finish what they were supposed to do. The 2013 seniors were forgotten pieces, as the media pinned Darien down for a rebuilding year before they returned to prominence in the 2014 season.

The team meeting ended by 8:30 am, which is when we were sent down to the locker room to get ready for the first official practice of the week. Upperclassmen got out of their seats in the classroom, put on their headphones and marched down to the locker room, expressionless. The sophomores were the last to leave; the junior varsity coaches stayed back to notify us of our duties for the day.

When we left, I went down the stairs to head for the locker room but passed the training room along the way. In there sat the stars of the team, Nick Lombardo, Silas and Alex Gunn, with extreme focus as they got taped up before practice. Walking down the hallway to the locker room, you couldn't hear the music playing, but could instead *feel* it through the floors and walls. Standing in the hall, I took a deep breath and exhaled before entering the locker room. I opened the door as the music blasted into my face while I put my best game face on to match that of the seniors. It was go time.

For the next couple of hours, sweat poured off the helmets and pads of players who smashed into each other repeatedly. Footwork drills conquered the early stages of practice, as Trifone and the rest of the staff pounded the idea of the technique being the core of any success. Players began to collapse an hour in, their muscles giving up on them and cramping. Every couple of minutes, water splashed onto the faces of players exhausted by the heat, hands stayed on the heads of players who were merely trying to catch their breath. By 11 am, the first practice was over. Helmets were torn off as players gulped down water like parched buffalos. I stood there, exhausted and drenched in sweat, but with no complaints. It didn't seem that bad. The legend of Hell Week seemed to be overrated in my mind at that time.

That was my mentality right up until the head strength and conditioning coach at Darien, John Carlozzi blew his whistle, emerging from the parking lot. I turned, wondering what the big deal was, but realized it was bad news the minute the seniors started screaming some choice words at Carlozzi. Seconds later, the whistle blew, and John yelled out the infamous words that make any Darien High School football player shudder:

"ON THE LINE!"

Timmy Graham remembers the moment after all these years, terrified of the build-up to the conditioning session at the end. When Carlozzi yelled his trademark phrase, it was all fear from that point on. "Yea, I was shitting myself," says Graham.

He had every right to do that, because, for an entire hour, Carlozzi tested the will in every single player on that field. Sprints consisting of 20 yards and back (four times, mind you, for a total of 160 yards) in a set amount of time crushed our spirits. To make matters worse, if one player did not make it back in time, the whole group had to redo the sprint all over again. 30 minutes in, I felt that maybe football wasn't really for me anymore. My will was broken in half, but I refused to quit. I wanted this, I told myself, and now I have it. Deep down, I knew this was a test, a challenge, and really, a way of making me a better football player. I kept going, even against my body telling me not to. The moment stayed light though, as Marcus Pagliarulo watched in awe of Nick Lombardo sprinting back and forth like it was nothing. Between deep breaths, Pagliarulo made an unforgettable remark, turning to me and saying, "God, he's as majestic as a gazelle."

At the end of conditioning, Trifone addressed his exhausted but resilient team, speaking to us in a large huddle around midfield. "This sport isn't for everyone," Trifone said. "If it were, there would be a lot more players on this field with you today." He continued to speak about team rules and unity, reminding us of the importance of the team as a whole. After pausing, he looked at us with a stern face and stated quickly but fiercely, "...And don't do ANYTHING stupid." Trifone then walked away, and the captains gathered us in a huddle to reinforce everything Trifone had said. We broke the huddle and made our way to the locker room, beaten and battered at the end of the first official day of football practice.

Trifone's message stuck with some. For others, it went right through their ears. A few days after Trifone spoke about the importance of not doing anything dumb, a senior linebacker and captain was stopped on the roads of Darien late at night and charged with a DUI, along with possession of alcohol. The player's captainship was revoked immediately by Darien High School and the respect I had for him crashed and burned. Now all eyes, good and evil, were on us. My fellow sophomores and I looked to the other captains, as our young varsity careers had begun with controversy without even starting. The uphill climb of a season was steep initially, but this bump in the road proved to be a real test to the legacy of the senior class. Off the field issues aside, a more pressing issue on the field was rapidly approaching. Week one was days away, and all eyes were on Silas Wyper to see if the quarterback could get the job done.

The Subtlety of Silas

Silas Wyper had a chip on his shoulder, and he knew it. A shadow lingered over him after the departure of two-year starting quarterback Henry Baldwin, who had been one of the most highly touted quarterbacks in Darien High School history. Baldwin was groomed for the position ever since he entered high school, while Wyper's story was a little bit different.

Wyper in his own words describes himself as a "late bloomer." He was already behind most of his classmates when he started playing football in fifth-grade because most kids in Darien begin when they enter third-grade. When he did finally take the field for the first time, he was lost in the shuffle of his teammates, forcing him to bounce around from position to position, trying to get a feel for what was right for him. By the time he reached eighth-grade, he had begun to take a liking to the quarterback position, realizing in his mind that he could "probably be 'okay' at the position."

However, Silas wasn't your prototypical quarterback, standing at a mere 6'0 while Baldwin stood at 6'4, which gave Baldwin advantages only those blessed with that kind of height could have. But Wyper knew he could make up for it in other ways, due to his strong work ethic that almost anyone on that team can tell you about.

Fellow senior captain and center on the team, Alex Gunn, remembers something about Wyper that he had rarely seen in others during the team's winter workouts, saying, "Silas was always in the gym after us, even after Tommy Gasparino and I went home, he was always looking to get extra reps." It didn't stop there. By February, six months before August practices, Wyper was found in the gyms at Darien High School with Gunn working through his progression and footwork late into the afternoon.

Rock Stewart, a sophomore at the time working on the scout team defense against Wyper saw the same incredible work ethic. "He was so smart; I remember that it was really hard to do something like that. He was the best of the QB's at Darien to do that; he never stared somebody down, he went through his progressions, he was always calm, cool and collected. He was very impressive, and he wasn't able to do it just in games, but also in practice."

Wyper's work ethic was mostly due to his lifelong fight of being counted out. He was undersized through youth football and never felt comfortable at any position. Even after playing at Darien at the junior varsity level, his size and unconventional style of play raised concerns from media outlets. The media being doubtful of his abilities never bothered Wyper though, since there was already enough motivation around him already. "We locked (the media) out pretty good," Wyper recalls. "We didn't really need external motivation. Playing the game that we all loved together with people that we love was certainly enough motivation for us."

In short, Wyper was never about individual accolades. He couldn't care less about being an All-State quarterback or making highlight reels out of his plays. His priority was his team and his teammates, which was evident from the first day of practice. He catered to the young guys, unlike a lot of other upperclassmen varsity players. If you had a question, whether it be a football related or not, Silas was the guy in the locker room you could talk to because he was relatable to every single player. On or off the field, Wyper was unique, and Coach Trifone will be the first person to tell you that. "Silas Wyper is a special person, forget about being a player," says Trifone. "Obviously, special people as they continue to go through life, eventually succeed in whatever they put their mind to. That's Silas Wyper."

Then there was Timmy Graham, who says learning under Wyper was a dream come true. "Everything I accomplished in high school was because of what Silas taught me. The fact that he was overlooked, undersized, he wasn't a big name yet he was still competitive and had a great work ethic. His leadership too and the way he handled himself on and off the field, I took so much from him." Passionate, was the best way to describe Wyper when around Graham. Wyper knew that Graham was being groomed as the next big thing at Darien High School, and instead of ignoring the superstar in the making, Wyper embraced the young quarterback and taught him everything he could. When Wyper made a mistake, he wouldn't throw a fit on the sideline but instead would discuss what he did wrong with Timmy. If Silas saw Timmy struggling, he didn't look the other way. He would help the developing quarterback, giving him tips spanning from throwing mechanics to how to behave on the field during game situations. The lessons were priceless, and Timmy studied them whenever he got the chance to learn from his mentor.

Even before the biggest game of his life, Wyper kept true to himself. He didn't make any bold predictions, didn't go out or say anything on social media, nothing like that at all. In fact, Wyper did the exact opposite. The night before the game, Wyper did the same thing that he would continue to do for the rest of his senior year. Following the team's pasta dinner, Wyper drove down to the Goodwives Shopping Center in Darien and parked in the same spot he always parked. Going into Stop & Shop, Silas would purchase a Pedialyte to drink and stay hydrated.

Afterward, he would return home, or sometimes head over to senior captain and running back Jay Harrison's house. After sitting and watching Northern Illinois and Toledo duke it out in the Mid-American Conference Friday night slate, Wyper would get ready to call it a night. Before going to bed, he reviewed the game plan and watched some film to keep himself focused, although in this particular case, nerves were on his mind. His first varsity start was on the horizon, and it couldn't have been against a bigger and more intimidating opponent.

Silas Wyper takes the field during an early morning practice
(August 21ˢᵗ, 2013)

From left to right; Sam Giorgio, Mark Schmidt, and Marcus Pagliarulo take part in sophomore duties before a preseason scrimmage (September 5th, 2013)

CHAPTER TWO

Unfamiliar Waters

Hillhouse

The first game of the season could not have been bigger. The defending Class M CIAC State Champions were coming to town: Hillhouse High School from New Haven. Hillhouse was a Connecticut football monster, a powerhouse that ran through opposition year in and year out. The team had won four state titles since 2000 and were feared from every corner of the state. Their combination of speed, athleticism, and strength was unstoppable, creating a legendary dynasty that dominated the 21st century. Trifone refused to buy into the fear but knew the challenge ahead would be daunting. He was ready for it, knowing that a win against the defending state champions would go a long way in solidifying Darien as a threat to the rest of Connecticut.

After a week of long nights and preparations for the varsity guys, game day was upon us. In what many considered a wave of bad luck, Friday, September 13th arrived and had me up and running at 6 am with kick off scheduled for 4 pm that day at Darien High School. After what seemed like a long dragging school day, we were dismissed at 1:30 pm, allowing for the team to move down to the locker room to prepare for opening day.

After leaving my English class, I came down the stairs that led to the locker room, and I felt the music bumping against the walls. As I entered the locker room, "Simon Says" by Pharoahe Monch, bounced off the lockers straight back into my face. Never having heard the absurd song before, I stood next to Mark Schmidt who looked at me and said, "What the fuck is this?" Unfortunately, we didn't get to ponder the wonders of "Simon Says" for long because sophomore duties called; I was quickly shuffled out of the locker room with my fellow teammates to set up the field for the game. Everything from the yard markers, the water bottles on the sidelines to the sky hawk film camera was on the to-do list, so we were plenty busy. Even then, I snuck back into the locker room whenever I could to get a glimpse at the pregame preparations of guys like first-string players Gasparino and Lombardo, as their professionalism and focus astonished my 15-year-old self.

As I gazed and took in the locker room atmosphere, Coach Trifone entered. With a wave of his hand, the music was silenced, and everyone turned their attention to him. He called the seniors forward followed by the juniors, and finally us sophomores. Sam Giorgio remembers sitting in the back, looking at our head coach with wide eyes. "It was our first varsity speech," Giorgio remembers. "I was low key kind of excited to hear what Coach T had planned." We knelt around him as he spoke to us, reminding us of how we got here together. He spoke quietly at first but began to raise his voice, coming closer to the end of his speech. After he finished, a hush fell over the team. He then took a deep breath in, looked up and uttered one of the most effective two-word pep talks I have ever heard...

"FUCK HILLHOUSE!"

The team erupted, as goosebumps ran over my entire body.

The seniors led the way out of the locker room, and my heart raced for probably the 50th time that day. Walking down the hall, I could hear the faint noise of a crowd cheering while also listening to the band playing loud and proud. We turned the corner to the tunnel, where the famous "Punch In" sign stood above. The sign was a simple reminder that once you step on that field, you better punch into all things football. The seniors slapped the sign, as I got more and more excited at the back. Finally, I came up to the sign and smashed my hand against it, feeling like an absolute God.

The seniors then blasted through the tunnel to the approval of the home crowd. The people in front of me charged out like warriors going out to battle, ready to destroy anything in their paths. I stood there, realizing that I wasn't supposed to be running on my knee just yet (I had sprained my left knee during the last sprint of Hell Week), but my obsession took over, and I sprinted through the tunnel while the home crowd roared. In Darien, the hype around the game was massive. We were the underdog trying to take down the defending state champs while Hillhouse was attempting to defend its title. The game, unfortunately, did not live up to the hype, because we ran away with it from the opening kickoff.

Any doubts surrounding the abilities of Silas Wyper were put to rest right there, as he dominated the game in every single aspect. Wyper feasted on the Hillhouse defense, throwing for 239 yards with 4 TDs. He wasn't just useful in the air but on the ground as well, adding 71 yards on the ground which led the entire team that game. Nick Lombardo's speed also proved too much for Hillhouse as he racked up 106 receiving yards on four catches, three of those catches being touchdowns.

Nothing appeared to be going right for the Academics of Hillhouse, although late in the game, players on our side began to drop like flies due to cramping in their muscles. The game was stopped multiple times during the second half because of cramped up athletes on our side, causing Trifone to lose patience with his players. Right when things seemed to be picking up late in the third quarter though, storm clouds rolled over Darien High School, darkening the field and causing a delay. Lighting then struck, forcing the referees to make a decision. Hillhouse insisted on finishing the game, so it was decided that the game would be completed the following day.

We shuffled back into the locker room, holding a 40-26 lead heading into the 4th quarter. Trifone was livid, not at the referees but at his cramping players who had not stretched enough before the game started, which in turn, caused the long delay before the storm. Visibly upset, Trifone and the coaches immediately retreated up to his classroom to discuss game strategy to ensure that Hillhouse wouldn't be able to come back and defeat our persistent varsity team.

The next day the game picked up right where it started on a bright and hot Saturday afternoon. Hillhouse, however, came back with a controversial move. The previous day the team's star running back had been taken out due to a possible concussion; he was put back into the game Saturday, with the team saying he was cleared to play. Trifone was irate at this while I watched on the sideline along with Mark Schmidt. We looked at each other as Trifone stormed back to the sideline, baffled by the decision to let an injured player back into the game after the weather delay.

The return of the Academic's star running back didn't help their cause though, as our defense stopped him dead in his tracks. We would win the game by a score of 46-26, laying claim to a considerable upset and proving any doubters wrong. The team stormed into the locker room to celebrate while my sophomore teammates and I cleaned up the field. I celebrated while picking up the field with my friends. We began to discuss the possibility of playoffs and even started to think about the chance of winning a championship ring. Before Hillhouse, a state championship for Darien seemed way out of the question, yet following the upset, anything seemed possible for us. The unfortunate part was this, however. In a matter of 48 hours, the expectations surrounding our team went from a possible 6-5 season to state playoff aspirations, which is quite the change in a two-day period. The pressure, which was nonexistent until after the win, was now on the senior class to perform at an extremely high level. Nothing else would be acceptable going forward from the Blue Wave fans.

After the major upset, Trifone set his attention to the following week's opponent almost immediately. The Greenwich Cardinals were coming to town following a 22-21 come from behind victory against West Haven High School, and Trifone knew the threat of the Cardinals was substantial. Greenwich and Darien are notorious rivals, both wealthy communities in Connecticut who have an absolute disdain for each other on the sports fields. Both programs are members of the FCIAC, but the teams had not met in the regular season since the 2008 season when Darien beat the Cardinals 31-25 behind an eight catch, 127-yard receiving game from Brian Kosnik.

Five years later, Greenwich head coach Rich Albonizio knew the implications of the game well and conveyed that to the media following their win over West Haven. "It's always been a great rivalry type game," Albonizio said. "They always gave us a tough game, they're well coached, and they have great athletes."[1] Trifone stayed rather silent on his opponent within the media, opting to motivate his team inside rather than out.

As Trifone began to prepare Wyper and the rest of the

newly rejuvenated varsity team for Greenwich, I sat patiently waiting to be cleared by doctors to return to game action. A couple of days after the Hillhouse victory I got my wish, getting clearance to practice during the week leading up to Greenwich. It could not have come at a better time too. While Trifone and the varsity squad broke down and planned for the Cardinals, my sophomore teammates and I would be getting ready to play in our first games as members of the varsity team. It wouldn't be on Saturday's but would be on Monday and Wednesday afternoons, in front of a much smaller crowd. Although it seemed rather bland, the excitement rose within ourselves as we began to prepare for our junior varsity debut.

Jesus Varsity

The junior varsity team at Darien High School was a prideful part of the football program. The talent was grown and developed at the junior varsity level, where the team had not lost a game since the 2011 season. The homegrown formula had been a success over the years, and Silas Wyper was a prime example of that. Wyper was raised on the junior varsity team, along with countless other star players on the football team throughout the years. In fact, Wyper credits most of his success due to the reps he got on the junior varsity field, saying, "I think if anything, it was confidence builder... Not to be the guy for the varsity team but for *a* team. Alongside that, getting the reps under my belt so that I had some confidence going into my senior year, knowing that even if other people didn't think I could, I knew that I could play."

The players understood the importance of junior varsity games, knowing that the plays they got in these games would hopefully one day shape them into the players who played in front of the Darien High School faithful on Saturday afternoons. Things were always kept light-hearted on the junior varsity field, however, which I learned pretty quickly. During our first junior varsity game against Greenwich, I stayed extremely focused leading up to it, going through my offensive wristband and testing my knowledge of the blocking schemes on the offensive side of the ball. The non-varsity juniors seemed a little calmer on the outside, which in turn made me feel a little less stressed out about the game itself. Then, in what is probably one of my greatest memories of high school, junior Ryan Murray huddled us up to deliver a pregame speech. In it, Murray produced the fantastic line, "I know all the attention goes to the guys who play on Saturday, but we are just as important - in fact, more important. This isn't junior varsity; this is JESUS Varsity!"

"Jesus Varsity," almost like the good Lord himself had said it. Laughs ran through the huddle as we made our way onto the field. Murray knew how to excite a team because we dominated the Greenwich J.V. squad. As a grade, we got our first taste of high school football that day, but all eyes were on the man under center, Timmy Graham. The heir to the varsity throne worked the Greenwich defense, moving around the pocket and delivering on-point throws to a variety of receivers including fellow sophomores Colin Minicus and the Trifone twins. Even though the crowd was small, bigger eyes were watching from afar. From up next to the press box, Coach Trifone stood and watched Graham gun the ball all over the field. That is the beauty of junior varsity football, and Trifone knew it. He was able to mold, craft and create future assets at the lower level. The junior varsity team wasn't the only place Graham was getting reps either, because Trifone introduced the sophomore team years earlier.

Sophomore squads from different towns would play each other, mostly on Wednesdays/Thursdays in a very laid back contest. Referees took a back seat and ran the clock the entire game, but it was still valuable to guys like me who continued to get better and better on a weekly basis. In fact, playing two games a week (junior varsity and sophomore) was brutal on the body, but the practice and reps we got were precious. It was something Trifone had planned and wanted, understanding that our class was the future of Darien football, and getting Timmy Graham along with the rest of us as many reps as possible was not a bad thing whatsoever. The vast majority of us would be playing as juniors on the varsity team due to the sheer number of seniors that would be graduating, so, for Trifone, he needed us to be ready as soon as possible.

Even though the reps were valuable, there was a lighter aspect surrounding the junior varsity and sophomore games, besides Murray's declaration. The locker room pregame was laid back, the pregame speeches were sarcastic messages mocking varsity speeches (the infamous "sick and tired" speech that was made almost every varsity game became very easily mocked), and the bus rides home were parties. Guys like Spencer Stovall after a sophomore victory would lead the team in the singing of "Ain't No Mountain High Enough" which became a tradition throughout the year. After junior varsity games, we would jam to "Goofy Goober Rock" from the *Spongebob Squarepants Movie*, because why the hell not? That was the junior varsity/sophomore mentality. As long as we were winning games and playing well on the field, why not have a little fun and do stuff that would be shut down immediately on the varsity squad?

After our victories at both the junior varsity and sophomore levels, the varsity team had no troubles against the Cardinals after a week of preparation, defeating them by a blowout score of 42-21. Wyper continued to impress despite preseason doubts, throwing for 227 passing yards and two touchdowns against the Cardinals. The fortunes continued the following week against Bassick High School with a stomping of the Lions, 51-16. The game, even though it was a dull affair due to the blowout fashion, was one of the first moments I truly experienced total mistreatment from a varsity player like Marcus Pagliarulo had felt earlier on in the season.

Early in the game, a senior began cramping up and stormed towards me, ordering me to run into the training room to grab a banana for him to eat. I came back with the peeled banana when all of a sudden, the senior looked at me and said, "What the fuck is this? You peeled it wrong." Looking at him confused, I asked what he meant. Surely he was joking, how could someone peel a banana wrong? Unfortunately, he wasn't kidding, and he yelled at me to run back in and get another one, and this time to peel it right. Baffled by the stupidity of the situation, I walked back inside and got another banana, peeling it to the senior's liking. Just like that, without saying a word to me, he scarfed it down and continued playing.

Following the win, the mood in and around the team was at an all-time high. Our varsity team was 3-0 for the first time in two years, creating a sense of passion and a winning attitude in the locker room for the senior class that had been counted out only a couple weeks before.

Not only were the seniors ecstatic about the start, but I along with my sophomore classmates were as well. The 3-0 start had us dreaming big already, thinking about state playoff hopes along with the once crazy idea that maybe we could go undefeated. The media had begun to take notice too, retracting on previous statements, with one member of the press calling Wyper a "revelation."[2] Alex Gunn took notice of the change of media opinion, stating, "After we started to win, especially after the Greenwich game, that's when people started to take notice of us, and that got us excited." The seniors along with the rest of the team had every right to be excited, too. In 2012, those guys were supposed to be the ones to lead us back to state prominence. They failed, and 2013 was supposed to be a rebuilding year for the team. Now all of a sudden we were 3-0 and riding a wave of momentum. It was good for the program, even in the midst of the newfound pressure on the team to perform at a high level.

In the middle of all the culture change in the locker room, my uselessness on the varsity roster finally came to an end when during practice one week, offensive coordinator Mitch Ross called junior quarterback Cooper Drippe, junior wide receiver Dylan Cunningham, along with Timmy and me over to the sideline during a practice break. When we asked what was going on, Ross pulled out a bin full of cardboard signs with numbers and colors on them and told the four of us that we were the new play-callers on game day. The reasoning was pretty obvious: the four of us were the tallest players on the team, allowing the players to see us more easily among the other players on the sideline.

There was more to the card strategy then I realized at the time. Ross was implementing a faster pace in the offense, and the cards would allow for Wyper to run a no-huddle offense without having to run to the sideline after every play to get the call from Ross. It felt like a major promotion for me getting to stand so close to the field, all while wearing a hat to indicate what my job was. Along with that, I was relieved from the majority of my sophomore duties which made me feel a little more unique on the team during the time. "The Card Crew" is what we called ourselves, and it became somewhat of a team within the team. Right off the bat too, the chemistry within the crew was evident, especially when Cunningham sarcastically remarked that we should wear sombreros instead of white hats the day of the games to distract the other team.

The spirit of the team was high following the 3-0 start, but Trifone knew of the difficulties that lay ahead in the fourth week of the season. We were presented with the Saint Joseph High School Cadets, a private school in nearby Trumbull that held a total of ten state football titles. The Cadets were undefeated coming into the game and were averaging over 41 points a game. Leading St. Joe's was running back Mufasa Abdul-Basir, who was averaging 8.1 yards per carry over the first three games. This seemed problematic for Darien defensive coordinator Mike Forget (pronounced for-shay), as the defense was letting up 157 yards per game to opposing running backs. With that came a dynamic game plan and an aggressive week of preparation, anchored by my sophomore teammates and I on the scout offense and defense.

Yellow Headed Hogs

Every single week, the scout team took an absolute beating from the varsity starters on the opposite side of the ball. We took the field with yellow caps over our helmets, almost signaling to the varsity guys that it was feeding time. I was no stranger to this, having to line up against the defensive linemen who were almost twice my size on a regular basis. Junior defensive tackle Jack Tyrrell would pancake me to the ground like I was nothing, and I would usually wave to Marcus Pagliarulo to sub in and take my place on the line. Tyrrell would then send Pagliarulo to the cleaners, and the rotation would continue.

The beatings didn't just take on the defensive line. Life seemed a little worse for guys like Rock Stewart, who had become a favorite target of Timmy Graham's on the scout offense. Stewart has plenty of memories of the seniors picking on him while he mimicked the opposing offense, remembering the story of the time he got his clocked cleaned while running a route. "Timmy throws me a floater across the middle, and it's nowhere near me. Out of nowhere, Myles Ridder blew me up," Stewart recalls. "It's not like that happened just once. He came after me sometimes, and it's not like coach stood up and said, 'You can't do that.'"

Sam Giorgio had a similar experience on the scout team sophomore year, playing all around the field, getting beaten to a pulp by guys who were twice his size. "It was rough," Giorgio says, "I'm not going to lie, it was hard work." Giorgio also revealed one of the unwritten rules of scout team: Don't one up the varsity guys. "You don't want to make those guys work too hard because they have to start in a game in like two days, but you also don't want to make yourself look bad in front of the coaches. That's the hardest part, trying to find the balance in that."

The brutalities of scout team were like that, where we stepped off the field more bruised and battered than the guys who were playing on Saturday. The upside though was the valuable reps we got on the scout team, since playing against varsity starters every day of the week built us up. We as sophomores also decided to make some fun out of it, knowing that we didn't have any other option but to play. While playing on scout, guys like Giorgio, Schmidt, Pagliarulo and I would call out fake play names to distract and anger the varsity guys. When playing defensive end and nose tackle, Pagliarulo and I would utilize a play call known as "Zebra" in our books, which meant we would jump over one another before Wyper took the snap. "That was a blast," Pagliarulo remembers. "We'd get yelled at almost every time by the varsity players and the coaches; it was hilarious."

As always, with a string of positives come a few negatives. Not everybody was enjoying the time on the field, as sophomore players began to quit the team at an alarming rate, which unfortunately was expected. The commitment had become too much for some, with two hours of practice a day and weekends virtually unavailable. Then, there is the prospect of being a full-time student as well, which created a mounting amount of pressure and exhaustion on the body and mind of a 15-year-old. For me though, the idea of quitting seemed barbaric. I knew full well that this was what I wanted my whole life, and even if the first year of varsity football meant being a scout team bottom feeder, I knew that things would be a whole lot better down the road. The glory and fame were only a couple of years away, at least in my mind.

On a crisp early October afternoon in Trumbull, it was 14-7 Darien at halftime during the St. Joe's game. In the Darien locker room, the focus remained incredible, knowing how well the St. Joe's coaches worked adjustments.

The adjustments St. Joe's made appeared to have worked, as the Cadets outscored us 21-0 in the second half behind two rushing touchdowns from quarterback Jordan Vazzano. Wyper struggled on the offensive side of the ball in the second half, especially after senior receiver Kyle Gifford sustained a concussion after a deep pass attempt. I stood watching as the team trainer talked to Gifford, and vividly remember him looking into the trainer's eyes and saying, "Everything is yellow." I stood terrified listening to him talk through the moment.

Mark Schmidt stood there as well, stunned by the responses Gifford was giving. "I remember them asking him, 'Are your parents here? Do you know anyone here?'" Schmidt says. "And Kyle just kept saying, 'I don't know, I just don't know.' It freaked me out as a sophomore."

St. Joe's won the game by a score of 28-14, destroying any hope of an undefeated season for us. The bus ride home on the sophomore bus was silent, and a similar experience was felt on the varsity bus. Alex Gunn sat next to fellow senior lineman Nick Kunze in silence when Coach Trifone made his way towards the seniors at the back of the bus. "You know that Mufasa kid is legit, right?"

"Yep," Gunn said. State playoffs were no longer a sure thing, which was the topic of discussion on the sophomore bus. Another lose and the season would be out the window, everything to waste. The seniors had a different outlook, knowing how much potential they had. Gunn stepped off the bus with Kunze, and the conversations began to spark up. "We were upset, but a lot of the talk was 'don't get discouraged, you can't change what's happened,'" Gunn recalls. "We knew how good St. Joe's was, they were just a talented team and we got outplayed."

The varsity team bounced back with a Friday night 31-6 win over the Mustangs of Fairfield Warde High School and followed that with a home victory over Trinity Catholic High School, 56-29. Seven days later, the team avoided a scare against the 5-1 Ridgefield Tigers. Wyper struggled in that game, completing 13 passes with two interceptions. Wyper had thrown five interceptions in his last four games, raising concerns about his ability after a strong start. Also, negative attention was again on the eyes of Darien High School when five days after the Ridgefield game an assistant coach on the team was fired after being arrested for assaulting a police officer at a traffic stop. The arrest was the second of the season for the team, both related to drunk driving.

The captains kept the focus on the field for the rest of the team, and Wyper knew he needed to have a big game against Wilton on Senior Day. Wyper put on a clinic, throwing for 318 yards on 29 completions with two touchdowns and no turnovers in a 40-14 win against Wilton during his last start at his home stadium. His celebrations were minimal during the game, keeping up the notion of him being laid back, humbled and more importantly, a team-first player.

It was a mesmerizing rise for the quiet quarterback. In two

months, Wyper had become a household name in Darien following all the skepticism he was met with to start the season. Alongside him, Nick Lombardo became a favorite among the younger fans due to his impressive playmaking ability. "He was otherworldly, he was the guy you wanted to be," says Sean O'Malley, an eighth-grade football player at the time. "As a kid, I thought (he) was the best football player I had ever seen." Lombardo was putting up video game stats through the Wilton game, averaging nearly 20 yards per catch and hauling in nine touchdowns in that time span.

The "Silas/Lombo Connection" was the face of the offense. They were the guys who wowed the crowd with their speed and mobility, with flashy catches and big-time runs. On the other side of the ball, a young sophomore wasn't wowing the crowd, but overwhelming them with his speed, strength and raw power as a defensive end. He was a God among men, a legend of Darien at just 15 years of age, a hero to kids. He had 9.0 sacks in the first eight games while becoming the face of the Darien defense, although the star on the outside was a little bit different on the inside.

"My parents always told me to act like I had been there before," says Mark Evanchick. "If you do something great, whatever. I wasn't a showboater; I didn't feel like any of that was necessary because it isn't all about me, it's about us winning games." Humble is an understatement when describing Evanchick because it doesn't do him justice. He was a superstar in the making, and one wouldn't know it by the way he carried himself on and off the field. Having been one of the few people in school history to play varsity as a freshman and then become the most dominant player on defense as a sophomore, Evanchick knew all eyes were on him, which had its effects. He knew he couldn't do stupid things, or make the tiniest of mistakes. In his mind, he was being watched at every turn by players, coaches, and fans, every single day.

Evanchick himself had quite the football story coming into Darien High School. He didn't start playing the game until fifth-grade due to safety concerns, but his presence was automatically felt. He continued to grow at an incredible rate to the point where he wasn't allowed to play in his grade when he was in seventh-grade. He moved up to the eighth-grade youth team and dominated there for two straight years while dwarfing his competition. Then, he again was taken from the comforts of his friends on the freshman team, moving up to the varsity squad, a move in which he calls "a little nerve-racking."

The spotlight only shined brighter on Mark early in his sophomore year, when he gave a verbal commitment to play lacrosse at the University of Pennsylvania. Even with such a monumental decision, he stayed within himself, not bragging about the Ivy League education he was going to receive, or about the fact that he was the fastest rising star in Darien sports history. He kept it inside, creating the incredible image of "perfection" on the outside. He ate the same thing before every game (a sausage, egg, and cheese from Vavala's Deli for breakfast, hot sauce included, followed by an Italian combo for lunch from the same place), wore the same socks for four straight years, along with the same type of cleats. The fascinating tale of Evanchick didn't stop there. He also followed the same athletic taping routine, and walking off the bus before every game, Mark would listen to the same song: "Fast Lane" by Bad Meets Evil. Marching towards the field, the words would fuel the beast inside Evanchick:

Livin' life in the fast lane
Movin' at the speed of life and I can' slow down
Only got a gallon in the gas tank
But I'm almost at the finish line, so I can't stop now.

* * *

The offensive tackle lining up against him was in for a rude awakening, week in and week out.

Vanacore Field

On November 9th, 2013, the team collected another win over Harding High School by a score of 47-23. The team was 8-1 with a state playoff berth in reach for the first time since 2010, something that was unheard of back in August. With at least one win over our next two games, we would virtually be guaranteed a spot in the state playoffs. The first of those games was the final Friday night game of the year against North Haven, a high school an hour away straight in the heart of Connecticut. The teams had never met in the history of each program, creating a sense of complete mystery around the Indians of North Haven.

The team was as old school as they come, barely throwing the football and averaging 332.2 rushing yards per game. Four players on the team had rushed for more than 500 yards on the season, creating a problem for the defensive coaching staff of Darien. Traditional game plans against FCIAC foes were thrown out the window because we were about to get a taste of smash-mouth football, something that didn't exist in Fairfield County.

Trifone decided to throw all the cards into this game, knowing that a win clinched a state playoff berth. New Canaan on Thanksgiving was an uncertain game, to say the least, so the plan was to secure and go home that Friday night. We were set to debut new jersey's for the game with our names on the back too, the first time Darien had done that since the 2008 state playoffs. For the first time all season as well, Trifone put together a travel list, meaning only a select group of sophomores who would have the chance of playing would be on the coach bus Friday afternoon. The day before the game in between classes, I went down to the football locker room to grab one of my books for my English class when I realized the travel list was posted on the door. I saw my name on it and in parenthesis, "Card Crew" was written. Trifone had decided to bring the original Card Crew, even though earlier in the week he considered having non-playing juniors take over. I was through the roof excited, being one of not even ten non-varsity sophomores going to the game.

The next day, the team arrived at school wearing button downs and ties for the occasion. I sat next to Mark Evanchick in chemistry, and I could tell his focus was nowhere near what our teacher was putting on the whiteboard. In his mind, it was game day. Chemical bonds could wait. They meant nothing to the young defensive end, who was instead thinking about stopping the ground and pound offense of North Haven. The day dragged on for hours. I fought long and hard not to look at the clock during classes but continuously found myself calculating how much time was left in each period. Finally, when 1 pm hit, we were dismissed from class so we could board the coach bus for our one-hour ride to North Haven High School.

The urban, affluent communities around Darien quickly phased out as we drove into the heart of Connecticut, trading in the views of grand houses to views of farmland and rolling hills. We were entering unfamiliar territory, something that didn't seem to bother the varsity guys who were laser focused.

While I dazed in and out, the bus suddenly stopped about half an hour from our destination. We pulled into the parking lot of a small restaurant, where Trifone informed us we would have our pregame meal at that time. We sat in the restaurant, divided by grade as the other sophomores and I stuffed our faces while the varsity guys ate in small portions, not wanting to throw their bodies off-balance. After about a 30-minute meal, we boarded the bus once more and hit the final stretch of road before arriving in North Haven.

When we arrived, it almost appeared as if we were in the middle of nowhere. It was different for us because we had seen nothing like North Haven's Vanacore Field. Situated right outside North Haven High School, it didn't seem too special. Vanacore stood still with its grass surface; it's big lights surrounding the otherwise underwhelming area. There were small grandstands on the away side with one large grandstand connecting to the press box on the home side. I stepped off the coach bus and made my way onto the field and thought to myself, "well this is slightly disappointing." I looked at there stands and figured they'd be lucky to get them half full by the 7 pm kickoff time.

We were escorted then down the street, about a five-minute walk to their middle school, which would be our locker room, another seemingly underwhelming experience. We got dressed and went out to stretch early, making the five-minute walk to Vanacore Field once again, where the stands remained relatively empty. Disappointed, I returned to the locker room about an hour before kickoff. I looked around as I usually did before the game, taking note of the varsity players and their pregame warm-ups. Nick Kunze, Tommy Gasparino, and the other lineman huddled around coach Tom O'Neil, the run game coordinator. Silas stood close to Coach Ross, discussing the plays that would be called during the opening drive. The mood was tense, the stakes were high, and the lights were about to shine.

We left the locker room 15 minutes before kickoff, accounting for the time it took to get back to Vanacore Field. As we walked in the dark towards the stadium, we saw the lights shining from a distance. When we got nearer to the stadium, the sound of a crowd suddenly began to become faint in our ears. As we came close with the noise getting louder, my heart began to pound. By the time we were a minute away from the field the sound had grown so loud that I couldn't hear myself.

My initial beliefs of Vanacore were utterly wrong. The place was packed with fans all around the stadium, who stood tightly next to each other wearing the maroon and white of North Haven. Those who couldn't get a seat in the stands surrounded the gates and the fence around the perimeter of the premise. I then realized that getting onto the field would require pushing through the crowd, which in return made my heart explode in my chest.

Spotted by the North Haven faithful, we were greeted by a sea of boo's that crashed through my ears. We pushed through the crowd, and the student section began to make its presence felt. I kept my head down while pushing behind my teammates when all of a sudden, someone's voice called out, "Hey 44!" Surprised, I looked up at the stands. "I FUCKED YOUR MOM!" Wide-eyed and taken back by the statement, I lowered my head back down and pushed to the end of the crowd.

The team then sprinted onto the field to the sound of a continuous eruption of negativity. I looked behind and saw the crowd, in awe of the size and sound of it. Behind the two end zones situated closer to our sideline were two firetrucks parked, which to me seemed a bit odd. I learned of their use pretty quickly after the national anthem ended when their horns blared through the night straight towards our sideline. Silas Wyper was one of few people unfazed by the atmosphere, taking in the noise of the North Haven crowd. "I always enjoyed playing in front of away crowds; I fed off their energy. It was always more fun for me. And really, what's more fun than hearing a large crowd roar is hearing a large crowd be silent."

We won the toss and deferred to the second half, and on the field for the kickoff were fellow sophomores Bobby Trifone and Rock Stewart. With the crowd thundering down on the kickoff squad, Stewart remembers the moment like it was yesterday. "I started running down the field on the kick and just remember seeing fireworks go off. I just knew right there that they were here to play."

North Haven did come to play, holding Wyper and the offense to a field goal in our first drive of the game. North Haven then drove down the field and scored on a 4-yard touchdown run. As soon as North Haven crossed the goal line, the firetrucks lit up their sirens along with a roar from the home crowd, something that was incredibly demoralizing to our sideline. North Haven got the ball back and scored again to the sheer joy of the North Haven faithful, extending the lead to 13-3 by the end of the first quarter.

Midway through the second quarter, the offense had scored, cutting the deficit to 13-10. North Haven answered again however and regained the ten point lead. After the North Haven score, Nick Lombardo returned the kick 84 yards for a touchdown, silencing the crowd in the process. Trifone sent the offense out for a two-point try but failed, leaving the score at 20-16. He would get the ball back before halftime and got a touchdown out of Jay Harrison, giving Darien it's first lead since early in the first quarter.

The second half started with a stalemate, but Wyper and the offense scored a pivotal touchdown in the middle of the third, extending the lead to 29-20. The teams would exchange punts until the fourth quarter when North Haven ran a rare passing play that resulted in seven points. 29-27 Darien. The game was close, and the crowd started to become alive.

Freezing in my white hat on the sideline, I watched intensely as one of the best football games I had ever watched unfolded right before my very eyes. With a two-point lead,

Wyper and the offense took the field with eight minutes to go in the game. The crowd began to roar once again, causing a false start on the Darien offensive line. Another penalty followed soon after. Alex Gunn grew frustrated and walked up to Silas, telling him, "It's too loud! I can't fucking hear you!" The noise continued to play a factor, forcing Trifone to shift Silas to under center to use a silent count. Even then, the North Haven fans grew restless, hungry for one more shot at scoring.

All of a sudden, one of the referees blew his whistle and threw a flag. Trifone lost his mind, believing they would be calling another penalty against the offense, who had been collecting flags left and right from the start. The call wasn't against Darien though. The crowd looked around for an answer as the refs huddled and settled the situation. It wasn't even against a player or a coach on either side but instead against the North Haven Band, who was playing while the ball was in play. Our sideline looked dumbfounded, never having seen anything like that. After about ten seconds of confusion, my teammates and I celebrated the 15-yard penalty while the North Haven fans serrated the refs with jeers. A few plays later, Wyper would hand it off to Lombardo for a 20-yard touchdown run, sealing the victory for us. The final score was 36-27, clinching the first playoff berth for Darien in three long years.

The ride home was an absolute party, with players jumping from seat to seat celebrating the historic win. No one on the team had experienced playing in the December playoffs, and that feeling was felt for the entire hour-long ride home. I leaned against the window, tired from the day but reflected on what is still to this day my favorite high school football game ever.

The party and celebration on the bus, however, wasn't for everyone. Following a hellacious battle in the trenches, Mark

Evanchick sat down next to fellow sophomore Andrew Clarke. Exhausted and battered, Evanchick looked at Clarke, and asked him a single question between breaths:

"Did we win?"

"What, are you serious?" Clarke responded, stunned by the question. Concerned, he asked Mark some follow up questions.

"I couldn't even tell him what day it was."

Timmy Graham calls in a play while Colin Minicus (far right) looks at his wristband (November 15th, 2013)

The North Haven side at Vanacore Field (November 15th, 2013)

CHAPTER THREE

Ram Country

The Cardiac Kids

The glamor of the North Haven win along with the aura of the state playoff berth lasted only for a couple of hours since we had a personal foe waiting for us in 13 days. The annual Turkey Bowl on Thanksgiving Day against neighboring New Canaan High School was on the horizon, the biggest game of the year for any Darien High School football player, past or present.

The Darien-New Canaan rivalry is the biggest one in the state of Connecticut by far. What's interesting is the two towns could not be more alike, which is the root of the rivalry. Both towns are affluent communities in southwest Connecticut who boast rigorous academic standards and are incredibly prideful of their athletics as well. The towns share nearly the same history as well; New Canaan was settled in 1731, while Darien was settled in 1737 under the name Middlesex Parish. The towns also share the same infamous history of being anti-semitic and are both historically known as sundown towns. New Canaan, like Darien, is 91% white while only 1% of the population is made up of African Americans.

Athletically, the two communities go back and forth year round on the high school fields, spanning from lacrosse games to hockey games all the way to sometimes intense volleyball games. The bragging rights don't get any bigger though then when the teams clash on the football field. If you win on Thanksgiving, who gives a shit about baseball, lacrosse or any other sport? Winning the annual football game is more significant than a state title, it's bigger than anything you could imagine. You could lose to New Canaan in every other sport, but as long as you beat them on the football field, then the athletic season is a success.

The first game between the two schools was played all the way back in 1928, which resulted in a Blue Wave victory on the grounds of Ox Ridge Hunt Club in Darien. The two towns played up until 1949 (with one year off in 1930) when the rivalry was put on hold after New Canaan dropped Darien from its schedule following three consecutive losses by a combined score of 144-0. The teams finally met again in 1956, but Darien continued its winning ways against the Rams. In fact, from 1956 to 1964, Darien won nine straight games against New Canaan, with the 1962 win being by a score of 70-0. New Canaan answered that winning streak with one of their own, dominating Darien in the years 1967 to 1976.

Then, starting in 1994, the two teams began to play each other annually on Thanksgiving morning, resulting in the famed Turkey Bowl that still goes on to this day. The rivalry reached its full potential when the game was moved to Thanksgiving since it gave the towns a chance to show up in massive waves to support their teams. Besides all that, it's an opportunity for the two student sections to go to war with one another with hellacious chants, while the players are physically battering each other on the field.

Early in the 21st century, a favorite of the New Canaan section was chanting the name "Alex Kelly!", who is a Darien

High School graduate convicted of raping a 16-year-old girl in 1997.[1] Over the years, the chants got a little more specific, with Darien starting the infamous "Everybody knows, NC blows!"chant soon after. By the time the 2010s rolled around, the students were hurling colorful "Fuck New Canaan!" and "Fuck you Darien!" chants left and right. Eventually, the chants got so vulgar to the point where both schools had to place administrators near the stands at games to control the student's behavior.

In recent years, Darien has reloaded with chants and signs that utilize the town's wealth as something they're overly proud of, especially that of being located on the water while New Canaan is landlocked. Signs that read "Boat Days" and chants of "Waterfront property!" are staples at games nowadays for the Darien section. It's a fascinating sight, but a pathetic one as well, depending on which side you are on.

From a player perspective, the Turkey Bowl was something you watched as a child and dreamed about every season. Playing New Canaan during youth football was our mini version of the Thanksgiving game, and it was something we took seriously, even though we didn't know why we hated them.

Even with the sole reason behind the rivalry being that the two towns border each other, it is beyond safe to say that the two teams/towns despise one another. Unfortunately, what began as a friendly rivalry has turned into something more, with off-field issues becoming sort of a tradition of Darien during the previous seasons. In 2010, five Darien players were suspended after spray painting parts of New Canaan High School (their field and logo on their tower) blue the night before the Turkey Bowl.[2] New Canaan would stomp Darien at Darien High School 42-14. Two years later in 2012, Darien would walk away with a 36-23 victory (our first Thanksgiving Day win since 2001), but the win would be tainted by a group of Darien alum who entered the New Canaan locker room and urinated on their equipment.[3]

Due to those actions, Darien had rightfully become the villains in the eyes of many. The events in 2013 following a player arrest and a coach arrest only made matters worse, giving the New Canaan crowd plenty of ammunition against us. The remaining senior captains knew the history and knew the hostility, so they understood the need for leadership in such a big game. This wasn't just any other game, this was *the* game, a game these seniors and the rest of the players watched growing up, and it was now their time to take the field on the biggest stage.

In the weeks prior, the 2013 version of the Turkey Bowl was turning out to be a real classic before the game had even kicked off. Entering the game, New Canaan was 11-0 and held the #1 ranking in Connecticut. They were averaging 47.5 points per game on offense behind the play of dual-threat quarterback Nick Cascione, who was tearing it up on the field week after week. The senior was averaging 173.9 passing yards per game while throwing for 25 touchdowns and put together an average of 7.0 yards per carry on the ground. Against St. Joes, the only team to beat us leading up to the Turkey Bowl, Cascione torched them in two games for a total of 520 passing yards, 142 rushing yards, and ten total touchdowns.

On the defensive side of the ball was a pairing much scarier than Cascione, with respect. Senior defensive lineman Connor Buck, who stood at 6'5 244 pounds, and junior outside linebacker Zach Allen, who measured at 6'6 258 pounds. Together they formed an unstoppable duo that struck fear into opposing offenses and quarterbacks. Nobody was as colossal as them, and they knew it. The pair pounded opposing quarterbacks while stuffing running backs at the line of scrimmage, which forced offenses to almost give up only minutes into the game. The goal was simple for Wyper and the offense; get by Allen and Buck, then we would have a puncher's chance.

New Canaan had a short time to prepare for the game, however, which Trifone took advantage of. The Saturday before the Turkey Bowl, New Canaan beat St. Joe's for the FCIAC Championship but forced the Rams into a relatively quick turnaround. Preparation for this game was massive for Trifone, who held film sessions late into the night following every single practice for the varsity guys. Trifone also created an entirely new scout team made up of mostly juniors and varsity players, leaving the sophomores with less on-field work and more off the field duties. So, my memories of Turkey Bowl week are quite the opposite of those who played on the scout team.

In the days leading up to the game, Pagliarulo and I spent our practice time in the equipment room (commonly known as the Cathouse, named after a former Darien coach) getting gear ready for Thanksgiving. One of our duties was breaking in new footballs for Silas Wyper, which we did pretty poorly. After hours of molding the leather of a new football, we proudly presented our work to Wyper. When we gave it to Silas, he felt it and told us after laughing that "This is absolute crap." He then told us not to worry about it and ran back onto the field, leaving Pagilarulo and me with a crappy football and a couple of hours of our lives wasted. Still happy with our work, Pagliarulo and I took the ball home with us, dubbing it the "Silas Ball" of 2013.

After our blunder with the game balls, we were assigned another job. So while Silas Wyper studied the New Canaan defense, and Alex Gunn went through his footwork with the rest of the offensive line with a fire in his eyes... Marcus and I stood in the locker room in full pads during practice, mopping and sweeping the floors while jamming to "That

Was Crazy Game of Poker" by OAR. Afterward, we were then sent up to the warm press box in our pads with Giorgio and Schmidt, where we filmed practice while singing along to the lyrics of "The Scientist" by Coldplay on one of our phones.

It wasn't how I had envisioned my first Turkey Bowl week, but I couldn't complain. The majority of the team stood outside in the freezing weather while I stayed warm inside. When we finished, we joined the team inside Trifone's classroom where he set the schedule for the next day. Arrive at 6:45 am; buses leave for New Canaan soon after. At 10 am, someone's ass was going to get kicked.

The music bounced off the locker room walls early in the morning. Alex Gunn sat on the (freshly mopped) locker room floor stretching, three hours before game time. Silas Wyper sat alone near his locker, locked in and pushing away any distractions. It was a different tone on the other side of the room though, as fellow sophomores Hudson Hamill, Bobby Trifone and Colin Minicus sat nervously as well after being informed that they would have a significant role in the game later that morning.

We arrived at Dunning Stadium next to New Canaan High School at around 8 am, where the weather was nearing 30 degrees plus massive wind gusts. The stadium was empty, but you could feel the atmosphere already. I breathed heavy, taking in the entire experience of my first Turkey Bowl. New Canaan was nowhere to be found, yet you could feel the presence of the top team in the state.

I had no chance in hell of entering the game, with my only real task was to make sure I called in the plays correctly, but I remained laser focused. I ignored the cheers of support from the Darien tailgaters, keeping the focus on the outside but taking it all in on the inside. We went out for warm-ups an hour before the game, with still no sight of the New Canaan

Rams. Returning to the locker room, the Darien fans who had made there way to the stands roared in approval.

When the time came for us to leave the locker room for kickoff, Trifone again delivered one of his signature speeches. Directing it towards the senior class, he reminded them of how they had been counted out time and time again, and this game was no different. Nobody was giving Darien a chance, since New Canaan was too talented, in fact, one of the most gifted teams Connecticut football had ever seen. He paused for a second and looked at his team. "BULLSHIT!" he exclaimed, exciting the entire locker room. The mood changed almost immediately as adrenaline pumped through the bodies of every single person in the locker room. We jumped to our feet and started moving towards the exit. Game time had arrived.

The feeling I felt as I ran out of the locker room and onto the field at Dunning is indescribable to this day. The cold smacked my face, but I was more enamored by the Darien crowd losing its mind while the New Canaan fans booed us hard. The entire time while running onto the field, I gazed up into the stands in awe of the sheer amount of people in attendance. We then proceeded to our end zone for last-minute warm-ups when all of a sudden, something terrifying happened.

A tornado siren began to blare through the speakers all around the stadium. Slightly startled, I turned to see what was happening. "Don't FUCKING look at them!" senior Myles Ridder screamed. Then, the scoreboard at Dunning lit up with highlights of the season while "Promontory" from the film *The Last of the Mohicans* played. I kept telling myself not to look, but then the New Canaan crowd came alive. I turned towards the New Canaan locker room where I saw Connor Buck ripping through the entrance banner with the rest of the New Canaan Rams. Ridder repeated his previous statement, but I ignored him. My jaw dropped as the massive defensive lineman led his team onto the field at full sprint. Sledgehammer in hand, Buck stopped at the 50-yard line and slammed it to the ground.

I had stopped warming up entirely and just turned to Pagliarulo and muttered the only thing I could think of.

"Holy shit."

The game got underway with New Canaan starting on offense. The defense took the field after 13 days of breaking down film on Cascione, knowing they could stop him dead in his tracks. On the first play, Cascione hit junior wide receiver Alex LaPolice for an 80-yard touchdown, deflating the Darien crowd in the process. Silas Wyper stood on the sideline, remembering the moment. "You felt a sense of 'it's over' from our stands, but we didn't feel that on the field." As the Rams celebrated in the end zone, Trifone walked up to Wyper and said a single phrase to him.

"Hey, let's go."

With that, Wyper took the field alongside the rest of the offense, ready to take on the massive New Canaan defense. Buck and Allen lived up to the hype in the game, dominating from the start and not allowing Wyper and the offense to move the ball at all in the first quarter. Midway through the second quarter, Wyper led a drive that went all the way down the field, getting Darien to the 1-yard line. Coach Ross and O'Neil decided to feed Wyper the ball behind the powerful line of Kunze and Gasparino, leading to a touchdown from Wyper. As he entered the end zone, a New Canaan defender cracked Wyper straight in the head, resulting in a helmet to helmet penalty. Wyper stayed on the ground for a second but pushed himself to his feet, telling his teammates and coaches that he was okay.

The quarterback powered through, and the game seemed to be heading for a halftime tie, but Cascione led a drive all the way to the 2-yard line with only seconds to go. He plunged his way into the end zone to the approval of the Dunning faithful, giving the Rams a 14-7 lead heading into the half.

Doing better than most expected, Trifone was pleased with the effort and knew that we could come back in the second half after making changes. The offense did just that, driving down the field and getting another 1-yard touchdown run from Wyper, who was taking an absolute beating from the New Canaan defense. The Darien defense then stopped a Cascione drive, which resulted in the Rams punting on third down. New Canaan punter Bobby DiRocco took the snap when all of a sudden Mark Evanchick ripped through the line and blocked the punt. The Darien crowd exploded as Evanchick went to pick up the ball. He missed, and a panic for the ball ensued. Finally, Evanchick jumped on the ball, giving Wyper possession at the New Canaan 15-yard line.

It only took a couple of plays for Wyper to find the end zone, resulting in a third rushing touchdown from him, giving Darien a 21-14 lead over the undefeated Rams. After one of the field goals, junior guard Sam Bowtell got his leg caught in a pile, resulting in a scare for the Darien guard. On the sideline, Spencer Stovall stood shaking, terrified of the prospect of going in, due to one single reason: Connor Buck.

Standing there petrified, junior tackle Jack Griffiths came up to Stovall to try to reason with him. "I remember JG coming up to me and yelling and screaming a bunch of things like 'YOU'RE GOING IN STOVALL... BUCK ISN'T TOUGH... STOP BEING A PUSSY; YOU CAN BLOCK HIM.' I then started doing kick back drills on the sideline and was freaking the fuck out."

Thankfully, Bowtell reentered the game when the offense got the ball back, relieving Stovall. Looking back, the situation still goes down as haunting for him. "That was definitely the scariest moment of my football career."

New Canaan managed to get a field goal before the third quarter ended, bringing the score to 21-17 Darien with 12 minutes left to play. Wyper, who was beaten after taking six sacks going into the fourth, got the ball to begin the final quarter. Wyper dropped back to pass on the first play, seeing senior John Reed streaking across the field. He went back to throw the ball when suddenly, the ball was taken from his hands. The crowd erupted into cheers, confusing Alex Gunn. Turning around, Gunn saw Zach Allen in the end zone, giving New Canaan a 24-21 lead.

Confused, Gunn turned to Wyper and asked, "Silas, what the fuck happened?"

"He took the ball," said Wyper, still recovering from the hits he had sustained all game.

"What do you mean he took the ball?" Gunn said, shocked.

"He took the ball," repeated Wyper while walking off the field.

On the sideline, the stress of the game was killing me. We were down three points with ten minutes to go with a quarterback who was concussed and broken from the beating he was taking. Coaches kept asking him if he was alright, and he nodded in approval. "It was senior year," Wyper says. "I was not going to let my teammates and my best friends who I had been playing with my entire life down. It's cliche to say, 'they're going to have to carry me off the field,' but I was not going to leave that field under my own volition."

Nothing happened in the ten minutes following the Zach Allen touchdown. Darien fans stayed extremely nervous while the New Canaan crowd got louder and louder in support of their Rams. Nerves, however, weren't on the battered mind of Wyper, who had confidence in his teammates from the start. He got the ball back with a couple of minutes to go with a wild New Canaan crowd cheering against him. My hands shook as I held up the play to Wyper, mostly from the cold but also from the moment. Slowly but surely, Wyper got Darien to the 1-yard line with 58 seconds left in the game. New Canaan stacked the box, expecting Wyper to attempt to get in for his fourth rushing touchdown. Instead, he handed it to Jay Harrison who bowled into the end zone.

We erupted on the sideline, overjoyed to retake the lead with under a minute left to play. Wyper, relieved and happy, returned to the sideline. Nerves finally started to weigh inside of him, however, as it was all on the defense to win the game now. He was helpless on the sideline, which he remembers as one of the worst feelings from the entire game.

With a quarterback like Cascione getting the ball too, Wyper had every reason to be worried. Cascione drove right down the field immediately, getting New Canaan within ten yards of the end zone with a couple of seconds left. Both crowds got on their feet, ready to witness the final play that would decide the game. Cascione dropped back to pass as time expired, looking for the target at the corner of the end zone. He saw it and fired the ball. The pass was perfect and was headed straight into the hands of the New Canaan receiver. Junior cornerback Griffin Ross jumped the route at the last second though, forcing the ball to the ground and effectively ending the game. The biggest upset in the state of Connecticut had occurred. Darien 28 New Canaan 24.

We rushed the field and swarmed Griffin Ross, having won back to back Turkey Bowls for the first time since the 1997 and 1998 seasons. Christian Trifone found his dad, relieved of the incredible win. "That win gave us our mojo," Christian remembers from his father after the game. The mojo laid on the shoulders of the seniors, who had been counted out since the beginning of August. Just like that, we were the proclaimed "Cardiac Kids," known for our come from behind mentality that showed week in and week out.

The trophy presentation was the real party for the team, as we gathered around Trifone after he received the trophy for the second year in a row. The team had a similar message following the win, constantly saying, "the turkey is going to taste so much better tonight!" It's true, for guys like me. Not having been through a physical battle, I enjoyed the rest of Thanksgiving Day basking in the win.

In the end, the game was due to the heroics and play of Silas Wyper, even though he would tell you otherwise. Wyper dropped back to pass 30 times in the game and was sacked seven times. The offense ran the ball 26 times; Wyper had 22 of those carries. The game took a toll on him physically, and he knew it. While other teammates enjoyed the Thanksgiving dinner afterward, reminiscing about the game, Wyper struggled to remember it at all.

"I remember getting home and having Thanksgiving dinner," says Wyper. "My mom asked me about the drive in the third quarter where I fumbled but recovered the ball… And I had no recollection of it. I looked at my mom and said, 'I don't know what you're talking about.'"

Silas Wyper gets cracked after throwing a pass late in the Turkey Bowl (November 28th, 2013)

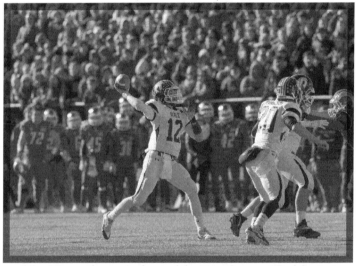

Silas Wyper throws in front of the New Canaan "Red Sea" at Dunning Stadium (November 28th, 2013)

The team storms the field after the win (November 28th, 2013)

A battered Silas Wyper accepts the Turkey Bowl Most Valuable
Player award post-game (November 28th, 2013)

CHAPTER FOUR

State

All Hail Dale

Like the North Haven win, the team did not have more than 24 hours to celebrate the Turkey Bowl victory. We were instructed to arrive bright and early at the high school to begin preparations for state playoffs, which started five days following Thanksgiving. We had clinched the #1 seed in the Class L State Championship tournament with the win, giving us a first round match-up against state powerhouse, #8 Daniel Hand High School.

Hand had snuck into the playoffs with an 8-3 record, but still posed a threat to our dreams of reaching the state title game. Hand was the two time defending Class L State Champion and had 11 total state titles since 1976. Like many of our games that year, Hand was the favorite to win even though we were the top seed. The seniors didn't take real notice of it and prepared like it was any other week, even when they knew it wasn't.

As for us sophomores, the "all-star" scout team remained on the field, leaving us with mindless waiting around or busy work assigned to us. While Wyper (who was still fighting off the pains of the Turkey Bowl) and the varsity guys prepared for Hand, I along with the rest of my sophomore teammates began to make the off-field and game day necessities, assembling everything from the ball warmers to helmet kits that would be needed on the sideline. In fact, we spent more time off the field during practice than on the field during the entire build-up to Hand.

In my mind though, I didn't care, because I was still on a state playoff team that would be playing football in December. Frustration, however, began to build. Sam Giorgio, tired of mistreatment from juniors calling rank over him, got suspended for the state quarterfinals after tackling a junior teammate who told Giorgio that he needed his game pants. Giorgio, after hearing the junior say to him that he was useless, took the player down in the hallway and started throwing punches. After my other sophomore teammates and I stepped in, the fight was broken up, and Trifone laid down the hammer, suspending both players for their actions.

After the so-called "Brawl in the Hall," we traveled to Brien McMahon High School on Tuesday, December 3rd in neighboring Norwalk to host Daniel Hand (Darien was still without stadium lights). In the bitter cold, I watched from the sideline with my play cards as the offense struggled mightily, with a still recovering Wyper throwing three interceptions throughout the game along with a pick-six returned 35 yards by Daniel Hand. The score was 14-3 Hand at the end of the first, putting our Cardiac Kid moniker to the test once again.

In the second quarter, the offense found its rhythm while entering the red zone on multiple occasions. While Wyper drove down the field, Timmy Graham stood next to me as we called in the play. On a designed quarterback run, Wyper made his way towards the end zone before being popped by the Hand defense. His helmet flew off, and Graham's eyes widened. Wyper had to leave the game for one play due to high school football rules, leaving Graham to make his varsity debut in a state playoff game that happened to fall on his 16th birthday. Standing on the field, Graham looked to Ross for the play call. He was calling for a goal-line pass, which took a second for Graham to confirm. Nervous but excited, Graham called the snap count with Gunn at the center position. Dropping back to pass, Graham looked to Griffin Ross in the corner of the end zone, seeing an opening in the Hand defense. Graham fired the ball in Ross' direction, but the pass fell incomplete. Still, Graham ran to the sidelines as Wyper re-entered the game, happy with the play and how it all went down. "Feeling the confidence from the coaches helped," Graham remembers, "It was definitely a cool experience."

The offense was able to put together 16 points in the second quarter, while the defense shut out the Hand offense, putting the game at 19-14 heading into the half. In the third quarter, Hand drove down the field and converted a two-point conversion, while Wyper led the offense to another score. When Hand got the ball back, senior linebacker Matthew Vossler caught Daniel Hand's running back in the end zone for a safety, giving us a 28-22 lead.

The tides turned again during the final 12 minutes of the game. Hand dominated the fourth quarter, taking a 29-28 lead with only minutes to go. Wyper, similar to the Turkey Bowl, stayed confident. "I knew that if we were to get the ball back, we could drive down the field, I didn't really have a doubt in that." In a quick series of plays, Wyper put everything on the line to get within scoring range. Trifone elected to send out senior kicker Daly Hebert for the chip shot game winner, hoping to clinch a spot in the state semifinals for the first time since 2008. Hand called timeout, hoping to ice Daly. The kick was not even 20 yards, but the pressure built. Watching from the sideline, I went to the opposite side away from everyone and laid on my stomach, praying for the kick to go in. Kyle Gifford, holding the kick (he recovered from his concussion, but wasn't allowed to play a contact position) called for the snap.

Hand sent pressure off the edge and laid out for the kick. Hebert connected his foot to the ball, straight through the uprights. For the second game in a row, we came back from a deficit and managed to win it in the final seconds. The Cardiac Kids were in full effect.

There was no time to celebrate and gloat over Hebert's game-winning field goal since it was another quick turnaround for the state semifinal game. Four days after the Hand victory, we were back on the field for a semifinals game against Middletown High School. After a nearly hour and a half drive on the coach buses that we traveled on, we arrived at Pomperaug High School for the neutral site game against Middletown.

We sat in our locker room for quite some time during the lead up to the game, with most players sitting in silence while waiting for the signal to go out and begin our pregame routine. Things took a quick turn for me though, which was something I was not expecting due to my tiny role on the team at the time. As we prepared to take the field for warm-ups, I heard someone scream from behind me. "Mother FUCKER!" I turned quickly and saw Matthew Vossler tearing through his bag. He looked at me with desperation. "BARTHOLD, I need your girdle."

"What?" I said, interacting with Vossler for the first time all season.

"I left mine at home; it has all my pads in it. I need yours."

"But then what I'm I gonna wear…" I responded, realizing how stupid I was for saying that since there was no chance I was going to play anyway.

"Take my sweatpants and sweatshirt, just tell Trifone you got hurt," he told me, taking my girdle.

I didn't even tell Trifone, because I don't think he noticed or cared that one of his junior varsity guys was not dressed. In the 30 degree weather, I called the plays in from the comforts of Vossler's sweatpants and sweatshirt as we escaped with a 13-7 victory; led once again by Silas Wyper, who played the game on a sprained MCL after suffering a knee injury during the quarterfinals. The bus ride home, like any other, was an absolute party. Pagliarulo & I sat together, sharing a pair of headphones while listening to "Separate Ways" by Journey, excited over the win but more importantly, excited over the chance to win a state title. We had clinched our first appearance since 2008, although the game would be coming against a familiar opponent.

White Out

Awaiting us in the Class L State Championship game were the New Canaan Rams, who had rolled through their opposition in the playoffs. The game was set for one week after the semifinals on December 14th at Boyle Stadium in Stamford (where the 2008 Turkey Bowl between the two towns had been played). From the minute we learned New Canaan would be our opponent in the championship, we knew that they would be out for complete revenge after we spoiled their Thanksgiving on their home turf.

When game day arrived, the town of Darien came out in waves of support through social media and good luck signs downtown. What Coach Trifone wasn't expecting that day, however, was the forecast. The game was set for an 11:05 am kickoff, and by 9 am it was pounding snow at Boyle. Unfazed by it, Trifone stuck to the game plan in hopes of recapturing the magic of Thanksgiving Day. Before leading us onto the field, Trifone reminded the team one last time of what we were playing for; a state championship, something that had not been done since 1996 at Darien High School. The senior class had an opportunity to make history, and they were set on doing it.

The first half was a snowy mess, and even someone on the sideline like me couldn't see across the field. The card system was abandoned almost immediately, as the players could not make out the numbers or colors in the blizzard. Freezing, I watched New Canaan dominate from the opening kick, taking a 17-0 lead going into halftime. Emerging in the snow for the second half, the Darien faithful who had made the trek for the game grew loud in support for the Cardiac Kids, hoping to see one more comeback effort. I had faith as well, knowing that Silas and the offense could easily get going with one big play. Wyper did just that, sprinting in the deep snow for a 35-yard touchdown, cutting the deficit to 17-7.

My hopes of a comeback were dashed almost immediately after that. Quarterback Nick Cascione hit Alex LaPolice for a 49-yard touchdown and didn't look back. To make matters worse, New Canaan continued to pummel Wyper as they did on Thanksgiving, totaling 9.5 sacks by the end of the game. Midway through the fourth, the Rams had a 31-7 lead when Wyper found the end zone again on a 6-yard run. Cascione answered with a 41-yard touchdown dagger, sliding into the end zone as his teammates joined him in the snow.

Colin Minicus, who had played a considerable role by stepping up and contributing as a sophomore during the state playoff run, stood helplessly on the sideline. "My forearms were completely frozen, and I could barely feel my hands," Minicus recalls. "Meanwhile, Silas, Jay, Gunn and all them were still just giving it their all and fighting the weather. That is something that will stick with me forever."

The prolonging fight in the seniors motivated some, but in the end, nothing was going right for us, even on the sideline. Mark Schmidt stood freezing near the heater alongside fellow sophomore Burke Blatney, not even thinking about the result of the game. Schmidt and Blatney couldn't feel their feet, so they stuck them into the heart of the heater when all of a sudden, Blatney's shoe caught on fire. "I turned and just yelled, 'HOLY SHIT,'" Schmidt remembers laughing. "Meanwhile, there's a game going on, and I'm standing there trying to put out this shoe fire."

Blatney's spark did little for the offense. The following drive, Zach Allen picked off Wyper and returned it for six points, pouring salt into our wounds and putting the score at 44-12. Freezing and demoralized, I watched as the clock struck zero. New Canaan was crowned the 2013 Class L State Champions of Connecticut, celebrating their first title since 2009. Coach Trifone, devastated but proud, defended his team when fielding questions from the media. "I said (to the boys), 'I know you're hurt right now physically and emotionally, but don't let this tarnish what has been a magical ride,' especially for a group that people expected to go 6-5."

At midfield, the Rams were presented with their title, but near the end zone sat a small group of sophomores watching. Hudson Hamill, Bobby Trifone, Christian Trifone and Timmy Graham stared at the New Canaan Rams, celebrating wildly. The group looked at each other and then looked at their beloved seniors, some of who were crying on the battlefield. "Never again," they remarked to each other. "We are never going to let this happen again."

One hundred and seventeen days had passed since the first day of Hell Week in August. I stood in the locker room, cleaning it out only hours after the heartbreaking loss. The team then filed into the gym, where one by one, we all individually said goodbye to the 2013 seniors. I walked down the line, saying goodbye to guys to whom I had barely spoken through the entire season. It was then when I reached Alex Gunn, whose face was covered in tears. I looked him in the eyes and broke down myself and embraced him. "Thank you," was all I could manage towards my family friend. I moved down towards Silas, where I managed to hold myself together. A smile ran across his face. He looked at me and hugged me, telling me a simple, but strong message. "Believe in yourself."

I walked out of the gym, recollecting my thoughts from the words of advice Silas had given me. I walked through the doors of Darien High School, leaving behind the 2013 season. The next day, the weight room would be open for members of the 2014 Darien High School football team. Hungry and focused, the words of Hamill, Graham, and the Trifone twins echoed through me. "Never again."

PART II
The 2014 Season
"It's what the 'cool' kids do, and if you're a football player, you're a cool kid. Unfortunately, we grew up learning that high schoolers drink and that's normal. So when we get to that age, we automatically assume it's normal. It feels good; it gets you with girls, it's a distraction from the pressures on and off the field really."
- Sam Giorgio on the drinking culture in Darien

CHAPTER FIVE

For the Love of the Game

The Other Side

For guys like Timmy Graham, Hudson Hamill and the Trifone twins, the loss to New Canaan in the 2013 Class L State Championship was a fiery motivation that lit a spark under them. The sheer hatred of New Canaan boiled over, something that would motivate them all the way up until the start of the 2014 season. Their connection to the 2013 seniors also fueled them forward, which is something Colin Minicus reiterates years later. "That whole senior class was such a special group. I still to this day try to take attributes that they had; their ability to lead while also stepping into roles they're not used to."

However, not all reviews of that year were overly positive. Other sophomores, like Mark Schmidt and Marcus Pagliarulo, had different experiences following the season that led to them having to make a decision before the 2014 one began. Following a grueling schedule that lasted from early August to mid-December, Mark Schmidt was starting to contemplate whether or not he was going to remain on the football team for the next season. He didn't think unrealistically; Schmidt knew he was undersized, he knew he wasn't the most talented, and Mark was fully aware that there were no plans for him going forward within the coaching staff. Even having been coached by Coach Trifone since third-grade, Schmidt felt that he had taken a back seat to other players and that enough was enough. Knowing that he still was an athletically gifted individual, Schmidt started to think about possibly using his gifts on a team that had a purpose for him.

It took Schmidt awhile to come to a decision, but he finally came to terms with one. In February, two months after the season ended, Schmidt entered Coach Trifone's office after setting up a meeting with him. He sat down, and let the head coach know what his plans were for the following season: baseball was now his sole focus in the athletic sense, football could wait. "He pretty much called bullshit," Schmidt says years later. "I think it's because he knew I could do both (football and baseball), and he definitely thought I was making the wrong decision."

To Schmidt, he was making the right decision. Sophomore year had been a rollercoaster for him from beginning to end. The physicality of playing scout team along with playing two games a week (sophomore & junior varsity) took a toll on Schmidt's body, and he knew it. Alongside that, Schmidt felt targeted by the upperclassmen, particularly some seniors on the team. "Some of those seniors were laying big hits on me during practice, which I honestly think were completely unnecessary," he says.

When playoffs came, Schmidt grew more impatient with the idea of being on the team. "For me personally, I didn't need to be on that team. I stayed an extra month in playoffs running around with Daly Hebert catching field goals for him all practice long," says Schmidt. "I contributed nothing to the team that year."

Apart from the friend group consisting of Marcus, Sam

Giorgio and me, along with a couple of others, Schmidt was an outsider looking in, in his eyes, somebody who meant nothing to the older guys. "We were misfits, and none of us seemed to have a future in playing on that team at the time. At the moment, it was such a waste of time, because I was getting the shit kicked out of me with no actual contribution to the team. I honestly did not feel like I was a part of that team."

Marcus Pagliarulo reiterates the same ideas, along with Schmidt's, against the seniors, saying "they didn't even know my name at the end of the year. I remember we had six captains that year, yet only two of them ever really spoke to me." He did have some positive experiences with a couple of seniors though, for which he is still thankful. "Guys like Silas Wyper, Alex Gunn, Nick Kunze, the entire senior line was great to me," Pagliarulo says. "The rest? I wasn't wild about them, and by the end of the season, I had even lost respect for a few of them because of their off the field actions."

For me, I was upset to lose a close friend on the team but was still focused on getting myself ready for the 2014 season in the weight room. I always had great friends in Sam Giorgio and Pagliarulo, who had reluctantly decided to play in 2014, so I wasn't crushed by Schmidt leaving the team. Besides, I had a mission in my head; I was going to become a meaningful player in the upcoming season.

I met with Coach Trifone before spring practice that year to discuss my potential position within the team for the next year. Trifone had always been a supporter and fan of me, knowing my family for years due to my eldest brother playing on the team, way before I had even started playing for him in DJFL. Coach Trifone always gave it to me straight, and he did exactly that when we met in his office. Looking at my 6'3, 170-pound frame that I had been bulking up in the weight room, he told me there was no chance in hell I would continue to be a lineman at the varsity level. Looking up to me with my height, he said I should give wide receiver a shot during the spring to see if I could become a target for Timmy Graham.

I accepted the challenge and went way out of my comfort zone to mold myself into a wideout. Having never even been close to catching a football, I began to transition myself into the position. I started running, and practicing get offs in my backyard after weightlifting, hoping to get a head start going into the first spring practice of the year. By the time it rolled around, I felt comfortable with the position, although I knew there was a lot to learn in the next two weeks.

The first practice was remarkably similar to the first practice of 2013. We were given our helmets (although I had my own since my brother had purchased a custom helmet back in 2011 that magically fit my head as well), assigned our numbers (I stuck with #44 for another year), and were thrown out onto the field. I looked around and noticed the number of players in our grade had dipped significantly. However, the rest of us had made it to the second year of spring, and the glory of this spring was the loss of sophomore duties, which as "juniors" (academically, still sophomores), we got to throw onto the new batch of younger guys. Unlike the year before too, I was thrown right into the mix with the varsity group, giving me a newfound sense of confidence that I did not have the entire previous season.

During this first practice, Coach Ross gave me the sarcastic nickname of "Gator," because when I went to catch a ball, my hands clamped down on it similar to an alligator. I explained, and he understood that I was never taught how to catch a football properly because I had been a center/tackle ever since the fourth grade. He laughed at it but told me that I had the potential to be a good receiver if I continued to work hard down the road. I walked off the field extremely happy and pleased with myself, feeling a sense of direction that had been missing from my game since the end of my freshman season.

The sense of direction though didn't flood into everyone's mind, especially Pagliarulo's, who decided he had enough after the first spring practice. Pagliarulo wasn't a part of the Trifone clan of players who had been on the same team since the third grade. He played one year in Darien in elementary school before moving to a tiny town in Pennsylvania. There, Pagliarulo continued to play the sport he loved on a team of only 12 players. He enjoyed the smaller team setting since he felt a sense of organization and brotherhood that he hadn't felt anywhere else. "It was a very relaxed system," Pagliarulo says of his former team. "We never really won anything nor did we really care. We sat back and had fun playing football."

He moved back to Darien going into freshman year because of the educational advantages Darien held, yet on the athletic-front, he noticed the change in competitiveness from Pennsylvania almost immediately. "It was a much tighter system," says Pagliarulo. "I wasn't used to that." Still, in love with playing the game, he made it through sophomore year and decided to give it a shot for the 2014 season. Looking around at the first practice though, Pagliarulo noticed something. "I was way too small to play lineman, so I wanted to make a change." Approaching Coach Trifone, he asked if Trifone thought he should change positions. "He looked at me and told me to go work with Coach Grant and the linebackers." There was one problem though; Coach Grant coached the safeties and cornerbacks. Pagliarulo, feeling like Trifone didn't give a crap about where he played, came to terms with himself that he didn't have the skill level of most on the team. After that realization, he decided to call it quits the next day.

In similar fashion to Schmidt, although with drastically different results, Pagliarulo walked into Trifone's office where he kept it short and sweet. "I handed him my helmet and said, 'Coach, I'm out.' He looked at me and calmly said, 'Okay, that's fine,' like it was no big deal. It actually made me feel a lot better about my decision."

The decision to leave never haunted Pagliarulo, nor will it ever in his mind. "I was happy; I had time to do other things I liked. I really don't regret it."

The team moved on, due to bigger aspirations taking over the minds of a lot of the players. One of those minds was Sam Giorgio's, who, after losing two of his best friends to quitting, decided it was his only goal to make sure he ended up as a big time-contributor on the team as soon as possible.

Varsity Dreams

Sam Giorgio came close to quitting football once in the third grade. Unhappy with the game, he told his mother that he didn't want to play anymore. She relayed the message to Sam's grandfather, a football coach for nearly 35 years, who immediately sat Sam down for a chat. "He just looked at me and said, 'You're not quitting,'" Giorgio says. "Thank God he told me that." Ever since that day, Giorgio has not once thought of leaving the game that is his religion. Similar to Pagliarulo and Schmidt, "Sammy G" wasn't a contributor, but his love for football kept him on the team.

In 2013 as well, Giorgio wasn't the only member of his family playing for Darien High School; his brother Ben, #33, was a senior on the team but wasn't like Wyper, Gunn or Harrison. Ben was a sideline guy for the entirety of his football career, a scout team player for three straight years. What bothered Sam the most, though, was Ben's almost complete acceptance of his role without really caring. He was content with his sideline position, which baffled Sam during that 2013 season.

Sam remembers the 2013 state title game clear as day,

watching his brother stand on the sideline while his teammates took a beating. He recalls the buzzer sounding and seeing the seniors weeping on the ground, but not Ben, who kept the same stoic look he always had on his face when on the field. "I don't think (that loss) affected Ben that much," Sam says. "Maybe it was because of his role on the team."

Ben's role on the team continued to bother Sam a lot during the months leading up to spring football, due to his unconditional love for his brother. "Going through Ben's four years, watching him never hit that field, never be a starter, it got me upset," he says. "I wanted the world for him, and to see him not be able to contribute during his senior year really did hurt me." That spring, Sam decided he wasn't going to let his career go down that path. When picking out a number for his junior year, he decided to switch from #83 to a more personal number: his brother's #33. His reasoning for the choice was clear. "I wanted Ben to be able to live through me almost, and I wanted that number to earn its field time," says Giorgio. "It was pure motivation."

Sam, however, faced an uphill battle. Criminally undersized at 5'6 with a 135-pound body during sophomore year, Giorgio did not give off the look of a typical linebacker, or any position on the football field for that matter. He wasn't speedy, he wasn't flashy, but he had one thing going for him which is something Christian Trifone remembers to this day:

"He had the heart of a lion."

Giorgio made it his goal to become a starter, even in the face of profound adversity. If he wanted something, he was going to go out and get it, no matter what people told him. Sam was a sideline guy through youth football, due again to his size, but was a raging bull on the field when he was put in. Players lining up against him expected a fearful player who wasn't going to hit hard. To their surprise, Giorgio would fire off the line and smack them back a couple of yards. By the time Sam arrived at Darien High School, he wanted nothing more than to be a varsity starter, and he was going to do everything in his power to get that job.

Meanwhile, newly minted captains Will Hamernick, Tim Lochtefeld, George Reed, Griffin Ross and Jack Tyrrell took over the reigns of leading the players on and off the field. All five of the players had experienced heartbreak the year before and were the most determined out of anyone else on the team to lead Darien back to the state title game. Expectations rose as well going into the new year. In 2013, the team wasn't supposed to get anywhere close to the state championship. In 2014, it was expected that Darien would contend once again, throwing a plate full of pressure onto the shoulders of the five captains.

I wasn't worried about the idea of returning to the playoffs but was still trying to create a name for myself. By the end of spring, however, I had fallen to the back of the line on the wide receiver depth chart. My height was my only advantage, but speedy players like Hudson Hamill, Colin Minicus, Christian Trifone and even Rock Stewart were the future of the position in my grade. In the annual end of spring Blue vs. White scrimmage, I was given one drive at the receiver position where I broke free on a post route, but backup quarterback Brian Peters was forced to scramble. Frustrated, I stormed off the field after the game, thinking about the possibility of maybe leaving the team.

I had worked tirelessly to gain some traction with the coaching staff but failed for the second year in a row. What it came down to was this; I knew I wasn't talented enough and didn't need sympathy from others. I wasn't buried in sadness or feelings of "poor me" during that time. Still, I didn't think another summer of weight lifting and camps was worth my time and money, just so that I could sit around watching others get reps ahead of me. It would be a waste of my time. So, I decided to schedule another sit-down with Coach Trifone, not knowing whether I would quit or still be on the team by the time the meeting ended.

At the meeting, I asked Trifone if there was any shot of me playing wide receiver my junior/senior year, in which he once again stayed candid with me. Looking right at me, he said that the talent around me was fierce and that it would be a battle to get reps. I knew I was nowhere near as good as the other guys, so I sat back and looked up, realizing that maybe I had reached the road's end. Still clinging to some hope, I asked him one final question: "If there is any position that will give me a chance to play, where is it?"

He looked down at his depth chart and gave me his insight. There were six senior linebackers for the 2014 season, but he only had one junior linebacker — Sam Giorgio. He offered me a plan, telling me that patience would be crucial in the entire process. If I switched to linebacker, I wouldn't see the varsity field at all in 2014. If I spent the season, however, learning and adapting to the position while also adding more weight, I could be a contributing player my senior year. I looked at him with a smile, knowing I could take the challenge and decided to switch positions for the second time in less than four months. I had never played defense in my life, not even in youth football since I was afraid of tackling, but knew that if this was my only chance to live the dream of being a varsity starter, I had to take it.

Timmy

The biggest story leading up to the 2014 season had nothing to do with Giorgio or me. All eyes were instead directed at Timmy Graham during the spring and summer, with hopes and expectations soaring for the newly minted starting quarterback following the departure of Silas Wyper.

With expectations came a little bit of pressure, something Timmy was used to from the first day he ever stepped on a football field.

The moment Timmy Graham arrived at Darien High School his freshman year, everyone knew that he was going to be "The Guy" by the time he reached his junior year. The idea of being the starting quarterback for Darien was all he ever thought about as a kid, especially while watching his father, Pete Graham, coach quarterbacks at Darien High School. Seeing guys like George Benetiz, Matty Wheelock and Henry Baldwin play had an incredible effect on the young Timmy Graham, who saw no other choice than that position. "Basically my whole life, I wanted to be a quarterback," Timmy says looking back. "That was all I cared about."

The pressure of being a quarterback started early on Timmy, way before he took over the job after the graduation of Silas Wyper. Timmy came from a football family, where his father was a highly recruited quarterback out of New Jersey. Several schools came calling, but Pete decided to enroll at the University of Notre Dame. There, Pete would play under Lou Holtz while also winning a national championship during the 1989 season.[1]

With those accomplishments, Timmy created his own mountain of expectations. He was a workhorse through DJFL, continually working with his father and watching film so he could create the best version of himself. Timmy didn't gloat after touchdowns passes, he didn't take reps off, he didn't point his fingers at other players. Everything weighed down on him, and he accepted that.

For me, I got a first-hand look at what Timmy was like since from sixth through eighth-grade, Timmy and I were a quarterback/center duo. Although a quiet kid who wasn't extremely social, I was the only player on the field who could manage to get a shotgun snap to Timmy without rolling it on the ground or launching it over his head. With that, Coach Mercein and Coach Graham made it impossible to break us up; where Timmy went, I went, no matter what. "You have one job," I remember Coach Mercein telling me as a kid. "Get Timmy the ball, and make sure nothing happens to him." From that day forward, I took it upon myself to not let anyone get near Timmy. I was his protector, and I lived and died by that when I was a kid.

On the field during his youth, Timmy was tough on himself in practice and during games. He rarely blamed others for mistakes but instead would yell and scream at himself when a turnover occurred that was his fault. He would talk with his father, who would guide him through his mistake, then the following drive Timmy would execute everything to perfection, leading to a touchdown.

What was so fascinating about Timmy for me in DJFL was his wildly superior football IQ. My job was simple. All I had to do was snap him the ball and make sure he didn't get hit. Timmy's was different, but he excelled. He was a field general, a wizard with a football in his hands. There were times he knew the opposing team better than the coaches, which resulted in arguments over a play call or how the offense was being run. The best part for me though was the silent relationship Timmy and I had. In school, we were on different spectrums. I don't remember once talking to him during class or in the halls; in fact, I don't ever really remember seeing him that much. It didn't change once we got to practice, because the most he would say to me is, "bring the snap up a little" or "we're going on 'set' here."

There were two instances where I remember Timmy directly using my name during our eighth-grade season. The first is when we were playing against Fairfield, and we were on the 1-yard line. Timmy looked at me in the huddle and said, "Britton, I'm coming off your ass here." He then proceeded to take the snap, grab the back of my jersey and plow into the end zone. The second is one of my favorite memories as a player. Against Ridgefield late in the season, we were up by 20 points. Coach Mercein pulled me from the game, hoping to give another player a chance at center. I stood on the sideline when the backup center fumbled the snap on the first play. Timmy recovered the ball but was visibly upset, signaling for me to come back in. After the drive, Timmy was still pissed off and yelled on the sideline, "WHY WOULD YOU TAKE BRITTON OUT?"

In the shoes of the young quarterback, it was hard to live his life on the football field. The pressure Timmy felt was indescribable as he tried to live up to the expectations of being the son of a Notre Dame quarterback. It was impossible to match it, although Timmy pushed himself to that exact impossible limit every single day on the field. Even through all the expectations and the constant pressure, Timmy still had a blast playing the game. It was always fun for him, but he began to realize there was more to it than just fun in his eyes. Following our monumental upset of New Canaan in eighth-grade, Timmy remembers how football changed for him at that moment. "I realized that this was now a job and that I wanted to play college football."

By the time high school football arrived, Timmy was up for the challenge. The first hurdle, at least in his mind, was the speed of the game. Not being thrown right into the varsity mix was helpful though, similar to the way his mentor Silas Wyper developed. Timmy spent his sophomore year working his craft at the junior varsity level, which he credits to his success later on. "Being able to go against kids who are older and bigger than you really helped me mentally and physically, just knowing that the next year these guys will be even faster," Timmy remembers. "Just being in those situations helped." When the 2014 preseason had arrived following months of camps, 7v7 tournaments and offseason workouts, Timmy was ready for all the challenges that came with being "QB1" at Darien High School.

For me, the start of fall camp in August was another fresh start, a new opportunity to learn and hopefully gain traction. I was up to 180 pounds for my junior year, 15 pounds up from the previous August. Coach Forget, the defensive coordinator/linebackers coach, took immediate notice of Sammy G and I as the lone junior linebackers and took us under his wing. The senior linebackers, starters like Tim Lochtefeld, Charlie Travers, Colin Cochran, while reserve players, Peter Grant and Jack Feeley, welcomed us with open arms. Any questions we had, whether it be technical or scheme related, they were there to answer.

The leadership found in the linebacker group helped immensely, especially during Hell Week. The second year of Hell Week was just as grueling as the first, even though this time around we knew what was coming. John Carlozzi toyed with us, pushing us to limits that we didn't think we could be driven to. Timmy Graham, with a mix of nerves and physical illness, vomited on the field during the first practice, collapsing from the exhaustion Carlozzi had put us through.

When he wasn't running though, Timmy Graham was wowing the coaches with his presence in the pocket. His style differed than that of Wyper's from 2013, but the loss of mobility was made up with Timmy's ability to read and react while making pinpoint throws. The hype around the team was substantial too, a complete turnaround from the previous year. GameTimeCT went on record to pick us as the FCIAC favorites,[2] along with almost every media outlet in the state of Connecticut. Still, the goal, in the end, was the elusive state championship, which Trifone knew he needed to solidify his program as a top contender year in and year out.

For so many of us, football was the sole thing on our mind.

12

Nothing else mattered except the pursuit of a state championship and a perfect season. As football players, we were to remain tough guys in the eyes of everyone else, because that was what football expected of us. Football players weren't supposed to cry; football players weren't supposed to be emotionally connected to something or someone. That changed, however, in August.

CHAPTER SIX

The 12th Man

A Friendship is Born

Coach Trifone first met Jim Mulhearn, 66, during the summer of 2013 before the season while Trifone worked at Roton Point, a summer membership club in Rowayton, Connecticut. Never having a chance to sit down and talk with Mulhearn, Trifone would say hello and shake his hand whenever he saw Jim around the club. That changed in that summer, however, when Trifone saw Jim sitting up on the hotel porch at Roton, wearing a hat that he didn't approve of. "They were having a little luncheon, and he had a Greenwich hat on," Trifone remembers with a big smile. "So I come over and start teasing him because he knows that I coach in Darien. He looks at me and goes, 'Until you give me a hat, I'm wearing this one!' It just so happened I had one in my car."

During the rest of the summer, the friendship with Mulhearn grew, not because of the collective passion for the game of football, but because of Jim's astonishing outlook on life while he lived with Amyotrophic Lateral Sclerosis (ALS; informally known as Lou Gehrig's Disease). The disease, which is incurable, cripples the victim over time, with there being no active treatment to slow the process. Gradually, the victim loses their ability to use their limbs, their ability to speak, and eventually, leads to death.

Having been diagnosed with the disease in 2010, Mulhearn pushed through the battle with an incredible amount of positivity in everything he did. Even while in a wheelchair with little to no mobility, he laughed and joked with Trifone, who was amazed by Jim's positive messages while suffering from the terrible disease that was slowly killing him. "Here's a guy who's dying of ALS," says Trifone. "And yet there's nothing but positive thoughts, comments, and conversations that come out of his mouth."

Eventually, Trifone decided to invite Mulhearn as a guest onto the sidelines for the 2013 Darien vs. Greenwich game, hoping to introduce him to us as a team that afternoon. However, a massive storm rolled into Darien on the day of the game, which forced Mulhearn to stay home and not attend. The win didn't matter for Trifone, but instead, a moment after the game that sticks with him to this day. "What killed me was that a couple of the seniors, after beating Greenwich, which is a miracle sometimes because they're such a big damn school, but the only thing they talked about was the fact that he wasn't there and wanting to meet him," Trifone paused. "I sat there and said, 'Oh my God. Here are these 17-year-old kids, and they totally get it.'"

Trifone stayed in touch with Jim though, especially during the summer months at Roton Point, but made it his mission to get Mulhearn to meet the team before the 2014 season. Approaching Mulhearn at Roton, Trifone talked to him, telling him, "Look, you got to be there. The kids were all asking about you, and they want to meet you."

It was then when New Canaan head coach Lou Marinelli took the ALS Ice Bucket Challenge in August of 2014 and challenged Coach Trifone to do it as well. Trifone saw the opportunity as a golden one to introduce Jim to us, and that's exactly what he did. During the first Saturday of Hell Week, Trifone had Mulhearn come to practice to watch us partake in the Ice Bucket Challenge. Trifone pulled out all the stops, bringing firetrucks in to dump ice cold water on the entire team. In a remarkable moment, we stood on the track at Darien High School and got drenched with the water, while Jim looked with a smile on his face. Afterward, Trifone had all of the players shake Jim's hand and introduce ourselves, and it impacted almost every single one of us the minute we first spoke to him.

"He was just so positive for a guy who was having such a challenge in his life," Timmy Graham remembers of meeting Jim in 2014.

"He was happy to be there," Mark Evanchick says of Jim. "He was happy to be around us, and he was such a big inspiration to keep fighting, no matter what you were going through."

For me, meeting Jim for the first time was almost sort of a wake-up call. For all the struggles I thought I was going through on the field, it compared nothing to what he was going through in his life. Even still, he always maintained a smile on his face, and always asked how you were doing, no matter what the situation.

Trifone saw the impact that Mulhearn was having on us 16/17-year-olds, so he made Jim an offer to become the official 12th man of the Darien High School football team. From that point on, Mulhearn was on the sideline with the team, no matter what. Mulhearn provided motivation and ease to the 2014 version of the Blue Wave, as the pressure that wasn't evident in years prior seemed to be piling up rather quickly. Questions concerning Timmy Graham's readiness at the varsity level began to rise, although the media concerns didn't seem to bother Graham. Instead, it seemed to motivate to the new starting quarterback. "It fuels you," Graham says of media negativity he saw. "The hatred fuels you to be the best player you can be and to beat whoever you want."

The 2014 season would start off the same way as the 2013 season did; against the Hillhouse High School Academics. The hype surrounding the game was not nearly as high as the previous year, due to Hillhouse coming off a 5-6 year, their first losing record since 2004. We were favored by a landslide, but Trifone knew to keep the heads of the starters screwed on tight, knowing that Hillhouse had reloaded and would be out for revenge following the beatdown in 2013.

The opening game atmosphere for me was incredible. It was almost an entirely new experience knowing that I didn't have to set anything up or load the buses anymore now that I was a junior. I took the moment in a lot more and felt a sense of team togetherness that I did not feel as an unnoticed sophomore during the prior year. This year too, we would be playing up in New Haven on the home field of the Academics on a Friday afternoon, which led to another early dismissal from school for the team. I knew the chance of me entering that game were slim to none unless we got up by a ton of points, but I still was excited for another season of high school football. Along with that, I was excited to watch Tim Lochtefeld and the other linebackers play, hoping to pick up a thing or two from their game day tendencies.

For a lot of kids in my grade though, this would be their varsity debut. Timmy Graham would be starting at quarterback, Shelby Grant would be getting carries at running back, Hudson Hamill (now wearing the #22 after switching from #9) and Colin Minicus were heavily featured receivers, while Bobby and Christian Trifone would be running the secondary on defense. Years of hard work had paid off for those guys, and they were about to be given a chance to prove themselves as Coach Trifone's "Golden Boys" on the varsity level.

Unfortunately, the team fell into the trap that Coach Trifone was hoping to avoid. The first half was a disaster, as Timmy Graham struggled to get going in his first start. The Academics sent pressure on Graham constantly, forcing the quarterback to make uncomfortable throws and passes he knew he shouldn't be pushing. On the defensive side of the ball, Hillhouse torched the defense, scoring 18 first-half points which infuriated Coach Forget. At halftime, Hillhouse led by a score of 18-14, creating a scare and sense of doubt within those watching around the state.

Like 2013, being down was part of the drill for us, so I didn't worry. I had no reason to believe we would lose, due to the notion that we were a second-half team that made adjustments like it was nobody's business. The changes worked since Forget and the defense didn't surrender a third-quarter point while Timmy Graham led the offense to two touchdown drives. The onslaught didn't stop heading into the fourth, as Graham put up another 12 points against the struggling Academics squad.

To make things worse for Hillhouse, junior Tyler Grant (who is not related to Shelby Grant) intercepted a red zone pass in his first varsity game, taking it 99 yards for a touchdown to the absolute joy of our sideline. The final score read 47-25 Darien, and despite the slow start, Timmy had thrown for 204 yards, three touchdowns, and only one interception while completing 64% of his passes. In the end, the debut had gone well for Graham, who admits to being nervous at first but calming down the moment after taking his first snap. Graham's debut was a high profile affair for the team, but the following Monday, another debut was coming that didn't make any news or headlines; the beginning of Sam Giorgio and me as a linebacker duo.

* * *

A New Era

The months leading up to September were tough on Sam and me, mostly because we had lost so many friends to quitting that really, we were the only friends each of us had left. Sure, we talked and laughed with our other junior teammates, but Sam and I were already different than most of our teammates by the time of the Hillhouse game. Sam and I were the only juniors playing on the junior varsity team, except for guys like Rock Stewart who occasionally came down when he wasn't needed on the scout team for varsity.

Being the only two regular juniors on the team upset us, not because of the limited numbers, but for a different reason. There were other juniors who weren't getting varsity time; for some reason though, they didn't want to play on the junior varsity team, as if it were an insult. Coach Trifone never forced players to go and play in the J.V. games, but it was clear that the attitude towards the "lower" team was negative, hence the minimal amount of juniors on the team.

Still, Sam and I stayed reasonable, knowing that playing on the J.V. team would give us a lot more experience than staying up at practice, rotating on the scout team while spending the majority of the time standing around. Instead, playing in the J.V. games as juniors gave us essentially unlimited reps since juniors always got the most playing time out of anyone on the team. For me, that was huge, since I had never played linebacker before and needed all the game experience I could get.

We traveled back up to Hillhouse that Monday, with Sam and I leading a group of 26 sophomores into battle for the first time. The sense of responsibility in helping lead the underclassmen fell hard onto Sammy G, who felt a personal connection to his new junior varsity teammates before the first game had even kicked off. "I definitely thought we needed to be role models to the kids because I figured there would be a lot of them, who just like us, might be stuck on the J.V. squad as juniors," Giorgio says about his role. "I just didn't want to see those kids quit. I wanted to see them stick it out like us. We lost two terrific friends of ours leading into junior year, and I didn't want to see any of those kids quit and regret it down the road."

When we got there, things went haywire from the beginning. Hillhouse had an older and more experienced J.V. team compared to ours, resulting in fumbles, turnovers, and miscommunications at every turn. Sam and I held the fort down defensively, but neither of us played offense, leaving that in the hands of sophomore quarterback Brian Peters. My transition to linebacker wasn't as smooth as expected either, because the only experience I had in live tackling was when I was a lineman trying to chase down someone who intercepted Timmy. In fact, I was never really taught to tackle growing up.

By the third quarter, my uneasiness about laying down a hit came to an end. Hillhouse dropped back to pass and threw a lob towards our secondary. The ball was picked off, and I immediately turned into a lead blocker. We made it 20 yards down the field when all of a sudden, Hillhouse's quarterback laid a hit on our guy, causing a fumble in the process. I was about 15 yards from the spot of the fumble when a Hillhouse player picked the ball up and started running. He ran down the sideline but had no idea that I was coming down from an angle. He looked back, thinking he had beaten our entire defense, when out of nowhere, I lowered my shoulder into his neck and floored him, causing a fumble. I hit the ground and saw the ball, clamping my hand down onto it for the fumble recovery.

It was years of built up anger and disrespect that had reached its boiling point. The hit let off a surge of steam in me, and my reaction afterward was proof of that. I stood up after recovering the fumble, ripped my helmet off and stormed off the field with a scowl on my face. At that moment, I knew linebacker was meant for me. My fear of laying a hit on someone had disappeared, and I played like a madman for the rest of the game. We ended up blowing the Hillhouse team off the field, continuing the unbeaten streak of the Darien junior varsity team.

The news of Sam and I leading our sophomores to a win didn't make any waves at the varsity level since Trifone was preparing the starters for a date with the Greenwich Cardinals Friday night. Timmy Graham was also getting prepped for his first Friday night lights start, something he had dreamed about since he was a kid. Nervous, due to the magnitude of the game, the atmosphere and the rivalry with Greenwich, Timmy was able to find a way to deal with it quite naturally. "Being a junior, I had the seniors to lean on, and they really helped prepare me for that experience."

Mentally, Graham felt ready. Greenwich didn't care though, physically taking Graham to town on the first drive. Fumble after fumble occurred for the offense, angering Trifone on the sideline, who couldn't believe that Greenwich was outplaying his team. Out of nowhere though, the attack was picked up by Shelby Grant, who in his second varsity game averaged 13.9 yards per carry to go along with two touchdowns. At halftime, we were down 18-17, trailing at the intermission for the second straight game.

Graham came out firing in the second half like the previous game, nailing Colin Minicus on a 51-yard touchdown bomb. Tyler Grant continued his incredible out of the blue junior season, intercepting Greenwich for the second time in the game late in the fourth quarter, giving him his third interception in two games. At that point, Graham took a knee to run out the clock and escape Greenwich with a 33-26 win.

Even in the win, Trifone wasn't pleased. The offense had played horribly, having coughed up five fumbles in the course of the entire game. Defensively too, the team was not playing up to the high expectations that surrounded us early in the season. It was different than 2013 expectation wise, but Trifone didn't give a crap about that. He wanted success; he wanted dominant wins. He wasn't getting that during the first two games, and he was fully aware the media would be in attack mode following another close victory. Knowing the team needed a spark heading into homecoming, Trifone looked at us and in a serious tone, asked us a simple question:

"When is the real Darien going to show up?"[1]

Homecoming

Following the Greenwich win, we returned to Darien with a relatively easy upcoming game. I wasn't thinking about that though, because Sam and I had to worry about our second junior varsity game of the season which was against the Cardinals of Greenwich that following Monday.

In a complete 180 degree turn from Friday night, both teams went stagnant, not scoring until the fourth quarter. Greenwich reached our goal line, where Sam and I led a stand that went all the way down to the final minute. Greenwich prevailed, however, scoring with only seconds to go, crushing Sam and me. The nearly three-year junior varsity winning streak was over, and it fell solely on our shoulders. Broken and devastated, we returned to the varsity squad the next day when we realized something about the junior varsity loss; nobody cared. The loss went unnoticed by everyone, understandably. The varsity team didn't associate with the junior varsity guys, so it didn't mean a thing to them. In fact, most of them didn't realize we had a game or were missing from practice, and never mentioned how the game went or how we played. The "real team" was 2-0, and that was all that mattered.

Sam and I still took the experience as a learning one, but also knew that something bigger was coming up on the real schedule; the homecoming game against Bassick High School. Bassick was a bottom feeder in the FCIAC, which was something big for guys like Sam and me, who were hoping to get in during the game to register real varsity minutes in front of the biggest home crowd of the year.

That week of practice, Coach Forget let us know exactly that, telling both Sam and me to pay attention a lot because the chances of us going in during the second half were super high. I remember that week going to the film sessions that I usually wasn't attending, only because I wanted to take hold of the chance I was going to be given on Saturday afternoon. Through all the homecoming spirit days and pep rallies (where we infamously made one of our two African American players reluctantly dance to "Hot N*gga" by Bobby Shmurda to the roar of the rest of the high school population), the only thing on my mind was the chance I had to play that weekend in front of the biggest home crowd of the year.

When Saturday came, I woke up and prepared myself a lot more than I had done for the previous games. I arrived early at Darien High School and got my jersey and pads all laid out and ready for game time. Along with that, I went into the training room and got my wrists and right ankle taped, something I rarely did, only if I knew that I would be playing that day. I stayed as focused as possible, wired into my music as "Whole Lotta Love" by Led Zeppelin blared into my ears. This was my one shot to impress the coaches, and I wasn't going to blow it.

The crowd was loud and alive that day, roaring when we broke through the tunnel for our first home game of the year. The stadium was packed, with fans lining up on the roof of the cafeteria at Darien High School to watch us take on Bassick. I looked around still extremely focused on the game, but couldn't help but smile inside at the idea of all these fans coming to watch us play. I looked back down on the field, where I also saw Jim sitting with his daughter in his wheelchair by the 20-yard line. Before the game, players went up to him and shook his hand, looking for any advice Jim could give before kickoff. Anything helped, especially from the incredibly gifted mind of Mulhearn.

The game was a slaughter. We led by 30 points at halftime, where I remember sitting in the locker room when Coach Forget looked at Sam and me and said, "Get ready." My heart stopped, excitement flowed through my body. I ran out of the tunnel and looked up to my mother, sitting in the stands at the 50-yard line. I stopped and gave her a thumbs up, signifying that I was about to make my on-field varsity debut.

Our offense started with the ball, but went three and out and punted to Bassick. They held the ball at their 30-yard line when Forget signaled for me to enter the game. Trying to stay calm and poised, I jogged onto the field and looked back at the crowd as I heard the stadium announcer say, "Britton Barthold in for the Blue Wave." From the view on the field, the crowd seemed 10x as big as it did from the sideline. I collected myself and looked at Forget for the call. Read and react. Bassick ran the ball down the middle, where Sammy G stuffed them at the line. Bassick huddled, and I looked to Forget again. Same thing, read and react. Another run right down the middle happened, resulting in the same stop by Giorgio.

Third down came, and I looked to Forget. He signaled.

"Blitz." He slashed his hand. "Off the edge, hard."

My eyes widened as I crept up to the line. Bassick's quarterback took the snap and saw me blitzing from a mile away. He rolled to my left, and I overshot him. I planted my feet and went after him, leaving any blockers behind. I pushed hard and closed in on him. I dove after him and grabbed onto his hips, forcing him to the ground.

The sideline and crowd erupted, and the adrenaline took over my entire body. I stood up, looked straight to the sideline, and for some reason, screamed something that just came out of my mouth without any thought.

"YYEEAA MOTHER FUCKERS!!!"

I then flexed my arms and mimicked Cam Newton, tearing away to reveal that I was actually Superman, which created an even louder response from my teammates. I jogged off the field, slightly embarrassed by my outburst and reaction, but was greeted with a smile and smack on the helmet from Coach Forget.

The offense went three and out again, resulting in another punt. Still feeling the adrenaline rush from the sack, I jogged out onto the field and tried controlling my breathing. I got set for the play after getting the read and react call from Forget, ready for whatever was to come. Bassick's quarterback dropped back to pass again, forcing me to shift into the zone I was covering. I stayed low, masking my height when all of a sudden he threw the ball right above me, hoping to hit the slant route. I jumped into my full height and intercepted the pass to the roar of the crowd and my teammates. I brought the ball down and tucked, seeing the end zone in front of me. At the moment though, the shock must have taken over, because I only ran two yards before getting tackled.

I didn't scream anything stupid this time, but instead stood up and sprinted to the sideline while yelling at the top of my lungs as if nothing could stop me. I was greeted by a hug from Hudson Hamill, followed by a laughing Forget giving me another hit on the helmet. The captains one by one came up to me and congratulated me, almost as if I had just won us the Super Bowl. After, I looked to the crowd where my mother was waving to me with complete and utter joy. I smiled and shrugged, suggesting that even I didn't see this coming.

I then looked to the end of the sideline as well, where I saw Jim sitting with his daughter with one of his signature smiles on his face, laughing and giving me a thumbs up.

The game ended with a final score of 41-0, and I was named Defensive Player of the Game. We huddled around Jim, where Trifone presented him with the homecoming game ball. Jim accepted the ball with complete grace and looked at the team to tell us how proud he was of the win.

Afterward, I was all smiles, and before I headed straight for the locker room to celebrate with my teammates, I thanked Jim for coming out to support the team. He laughed again and said to me, "You were awesome."

The rest of that day, I kept replaying the sack and interception in my head, not because of the plays themselves, but because of the roar of the crowd. It was *addicting*, and the more I thought about it, the more I wanted of it. Heading up to Coach Trifone's office after to turn in my jersey, I tried to play the moment off as completely normal. I put my jersey quickly in his room and tried leaving, but he stopped me. He looked at me and said, "Keep doing what you're doing, and you'll be making those plays every game next year." I nodded and thanked him, leaving to see my parents following the game.

Before that, however, I ran back down to the locker room, where I saw a group of Darien players standing alongside the Bassick players outside of their locker room. Instead of gloating in our victory, I saw our group of players invite the opposition into our locker room to eat some of our post-game food. I smiled as I joined the Bassick players and my teammates in the locker room, where we stood together and celebrated what was for both teams, win or lose, a fun day of football.

The following week, I was on the practice field with my teammates again, willingly taking the backseat to the starting linebackers to learn once again. The performance against Bassick did earn me some merit since coaches put me on the scout defense more and more in the weeks after homecoming. I moved on from it pretty quickly but used it as motivation for the rest of the year. I wanted more of that adrenaline rush that I had felt when I pulled their quarterback to the ground and intercepted that pass. I knew I would have to wait until the next year to be able to chase those feelings of joy and excitement again. In the meantime, learning under Tim Lochtefeld and playing junior varsity defense was all I could do, and I was okay with that.

Everything seemed okay on the football field to me. I had tasted success myself, but more importantly, the team was winning and firing on all cylinders. The team was impressive and was rising the ranks in the Connecticut state polls. Our football lives were incredible; it seemed like nothing could stop us on the field. Off the field though, life was beginning to become different. Everything that seemed to make Darien a perfect town was halted, as the glaring issues of academic and social pressure made a screeching stop outside the doors of Darien High School and the houses surrounding it. On the field, we were superstars. Off the field, we were fighting for our academic and social lives, day in and day out.

Coach Trifone talks with Jim Mulhearn after giving him a souvenir Blue Wave football jersey (August 23rd, 2014)

Captains Jack Tyrrell, George Reed, Tim Lochtefeld, & Will Hamernick stand with Jim Mulhearn following the homecoming game (September 27th, 2014)

CHAPTER SEVEN

Inside the Halls, Inside the Homes

Darien Athletic Academy

"I think some teachers were out to get us honestly," says Sam Giorgio. "Not all of them, because there are great teachers at Darien High School who are nice, genuine people. But don't get me wrong, there's a few of them that were against us."

The treatment of athletes has always been a subject of controversy, not only in Darien, especially when narrowing it down to the high school level. In Darien, academics and athletics are the staples of the community, which causes pressure on both sides to come crashing down on students during all four years of high school. Some parents want their children to be the smartest of the students and get into the best college possible, while others want their children to be the most athletic out of all the students and to earn a scholarship to a prestigious school somewhere. In some cases, parents wish for both, and when it comes to that, the combination is lethal on a teenager's body.

For someone like Timmy Graham, school wasn't something he thought about, due to his unbreakable bond to the game of football from such a young age, and it is understandable. As a 16/17-year-old kid, the last thing you're worried about is what is being taught in class, and Graham remembers that vividly. "You show up to school and go to class, but you're not really thinking about what the teacher is saying. All you're thinking about is practice or the fact that we have a game later that night." Still, Graham understood the necessity to perform well academically in order to pursue his dream of playing college football. Football, though, was his true love, just like a lot of other players, and teachers and students alike began to take notice.

For me, it wasn't the easiest of jobs being a high school football player, especially during the time between 7 am to 2 pm when I was in school and not on the field. I earned good grades in high school but struggled the most in the fall season when football was my primary concern. The fall season was always the worst in-school period for me because I felt targeted by teachers who didn't think my priorities were straight. I wasn't the only one, as Mark Evanchick experienced the same issues, although his case was a little different than most. "I felt the worst of it during lacrosse; I remember I did have problems with a teacher because of lacrosse," he remembers. "It was really because of my early commitment (during sophomore year)."

The UPenn commit had a tough road ahead with a target on his back. During our sophomore year, Mark and I sat together in chemistry class. One Friday morning while wearing our jerseys to school before a Saturday game, we both received a bad grade on a quiz we had taken earlier in the week. When handing back our quizzes, our teacher looked at both of us and remarked, "I guess football strikes again, huh guys?" That was only in my sophomore year, so for the rest of my high school years, comments like that were just typical to me. I had to accept the fact that being a football player and athlete made me different in the eyes of my teachers, good or bad.

It spread like wildfire around the team, even towards good students. Rock Stewart's mother asked him to not wear athletic shirts to school so he would avoid such treatment. For Sam Giorgio, he endured lectures from a Spanish teacher who would spend half the class period berating athletes and the school, going on to tell the students that they attended "the Darien Athletic Academy." For Giorgio, it was pretty evident throughout his high school years. "I don't think some of them like how much the Darien High School community revolves around sports."

It wasn't just the teachers, but some students as well took a stance against athletes in the classroom on a regular basis. During my junior year, Timmy Graham, Sam Giorgio and I shared an American Studies class where both American History & Literature were discussed in a seminar-style environment. Time after time, when one of us tried making a point in a discussion, students would ignore or feel as if our information was invalid, just because we were athletes who couldn't be smart at the same time. We were stereotyped as lazy and uneducated, which for almost every single football player in the school, isn't true. When we did get A's on projects and did make valid points in debates, it was almost like a victory in our minds. "We had to balance between football and school, and we exceeded at both because of the work ethic we learned from both," Timmy Graham says about the situation. "It proves to people that were not these dumb jock athletes; It's the opposite, we have the ability to work on and off the field and be successful at both."

Graham's idealism strikes an excellent point about the hidden lives of football players in Darien. From 7 am to 2 pm, we would be in school, learning and preparing for tests later in the week. From 2:30 pm to around 6:30 pm, we were strictly around football and only football. Practices and drills exhausted us physically and emotionally, while film sessions and game planning after practice would drain us mentally. By the time we returned home, we were spent, but had a mountain of homework and studying to do on a brain and body that was running on fumes while parents told us we needed good grades to get into college. The next morning, we would rinse, wash, repeat.

For former Darien High School English teacher Elise Dardani, recipient of the Darien High School Teacher of the Year award in 2015, her viewpoint saw a balance from both sides. Having coached soccer at the high school and played Division-I soccer, she understood the pressures of being an athlete and the grueling time that goes into it, on and off the field. "Darien is just one of those towns in lower Fairfield County in which there seems to be an exorbitant amount of pressure on kids," says Dardani, now working at the Center for Global Studies in Norwalk. "The culture is such that each student is under pressure to be excellent in a number of areas. They are expected to perform at a high academic level in every field of study; they are expected to bear an overwhelming extracurricular load; they are judged harshly if they do not have full social calendars."

In the end, no matter the viewpoint, when school ended for us it was time for the real work in most of our minds. Everything that had happened that day beforehand was out the window because all that mattered was football practice afterward. I never worried about a test I had the next day at practice or a paper that was due later that night because, on the field, those things don't matter.

The football field was an escape for me starting my junior year; an escape away from the pressures of getting good grades and getting into a good college that I felt down my neck every day from my parents. Those pressures couldn't reach my teammates or me on the field, which is what made the escape to the turf that much more special every single day. Some players dealt with in on the field, getting any frustration from the school day out on the turf. Others, however, took a different path when coping with the pressures surrounding them.

A Drink for Darien

What happens on the field though, rarely translates to what happens off the field. The athletic department at Darien, like any other school in the country, has a strict commitment policy that all athletes must sign before partaking in a sport at the school. In regards to drug/alcohol use, the Student Handbook states:

"For all students at Darien High School, any use or possession of illegal drugs, alcohol, or any form of tobacco, nicotine, including vaping, at any time during the period of participation in an extracurricular activity or athletic team, in school or at a school-sponsored event, will result in appropriate disciplinary action."

For a first offense after using drugs or alcohol, the punishment is as follows:

"The student will be suspended from membership and participation in all activities related to that extracurricular or athletic team (including team practice) for fourteen calendar days."

A second offense?

"If the second offense occurred within the same season as the first offense: The student is suspended for the rest of the season."[1]

The policy is crystal clear in the Handbook, and well-written for anyone who breaks commitment. As a student, the first time commitment was brought up it loomed over my head as I feared to do anything that would come close to breaking it, but I soon realized the reality of the situation.

"It's a complete joke," says Mark Schmidt, remembering it during his time playing both baseball and football.

During my junior year, it was evident that after games during the weekend, a small number of senior football players and their friends on the team would go out and throw parties week after week. I didn't think too much of it and didn't go along with it, because my parents threatened me if I was ever caught drinking during the season. I also knew that if I lost football after being caught in the act that my life would be over because football was *my* life. So for the entirety of my junior year, I avoided it at all costs.

However, we still had players who broke commitment on a weekly basis in 2014, whether it be through the use of marijuana or drinking alcohol during the season. It wasn't anything new, especially for a town like Darien. From a young age, I knew about it and just thought it was a regular part of life. Binge drinking in the town had become widely accepted or ignored at this point, with the justification being that "high schoolers will be high schoolers." The town addresses the issue from time to time when a speaker or survivor of alcoholism comes in and talks, but the guilty feelings about the binge drinking go away pretty quickly following these talks for some.

The statistics are what is alarming in Darien, though. In a study done by the Darien Community Fund, it was found that the average age for youth to start drinking in town is 13.7 years of age. In fact, the study shows that 25.6% of high school seniors consume alcohol more than six times in 30 days.

There are even more alarming statistics found in the study: 51% of teens in Darien don't think their parents have any issue with their binge drinking. The 51% are somewhat right, at least from the perspectives and experiences of certain students. Students know of parents in the town who tend to turn a "blind eye" to the drinking problems, uttering the infamous phrase "just be careful" right before their 16-year-old child throws a party in the basement or backyard of the house.

The statistics only get worse. 58% of high school juniors had consumed alcohol within 30 days of the census, according to the study, and 67% of seniors had been drinking in that same span. The United States average for binge drinking for kids between 12 and 17 years old is 14%. The percentage of 12 and 17-year-old kids binge drinking in Darien? 26%... Nearly twice the national average.[2] High schoolers will be high schoolers, sure. But almost double the national average? There might be an issue.

People debate back and forth about why the percentage is so high, and while there may be other factors, one seems to be pretty evident in the eyes of Darien teens: Pressure. Academic pressure. Athletic pressure. It takes a toll on the body and spirit, and Schmidt remembers it. "It is definitely because of the pressure. The school pressure is pretty intense, but they call us the Darien Athletic Academy for a reason. Sports play a huge role in it too." And priorities seem skewed, too. The following phenomenon is not an unusual scenario: Some parents in town lose their mind if their son/daughter gets a C on a test, but those same parents don't seem to mind when their child comes home at 3 am drunk on a Saturday morning. Where's the balance in the mind of a 15/16/17-year-old kid?

From my experience, there is none. The recreational leash on some of the towns high school athletes and students, in general, is beyond long, giving them the freedom to do virtually whatever they want to blow off steam as long as they don't get caught. That was it really, as I remember being told as an athlete by coaches and other players... just don't get caught doing anything stupid.

Good luck carrying that message to a high school aged kid, which was evident by the mistakes made by the 2013 captain who had his captainship revoked. Good luck sending that message to the five 2011 Darien players who spray-painted New Canaan's field,[3] and good luck sending that message to the two players suspended in 2010 before the Turkey Bowl for throwing an underage party; while at the same party, a former Blue Wave player was arrested after assaulting a student, causing nearly fatal injuries.[4] Good luck with that.

There are no boundaries when you are surrounded by your friends, especially when consuming alcohol. That's what it does; it makes you feel good inside when surrounded by other people. Sam Giorgio remembers it, and looking back understands why it appears to be such a big problem in Darien. "It's what the 'cool' kids do, and if you're a football player, you're a cool kid. Unfortunately, we grew up learning that high schoolers drink and that's normal. So when we get to that age, we automatically assume it's normal. It feels good; it gets you with girls, its a distraction from the pressures on and off the field really."

Elise Dardani goes along with the message of this statement but also points back to the pressures of academic, athletic and social pressure as a mix. "Any additional pressure that scholar-athletes feel surely stems from their own desire to be acknowledged in an area (figuratively and literally) that most people in the town place a high premium on. It's part of the culture, and the recognition feels good." So, to succeed in Darien, the message is be exceptional: in class, on the field, and at parties.

The blame can go either way, but living a day in the shoes of a student-athlete can show why drinking is something they gravitate towards. When expectations take over your life and go through the roof, the feelings of alcohol are an escape for a young mind. When intoxicated around friends, the last thing you are worried about is your parents breathing down your neck about a scholarship opportunity. It's an escape for kids, notably in a town like Darien. On the football team, in 2014 in particular, I saw the pressure from the athletic standpoint. After an out of nowhere year in 2013, the 2014 seniors were predicted to do amazing things left and right by members of the media and by coaches. After a week of physical abuse and mental limits being pushed, the ability to go and drink away pain and worries is hard to say no to. In their mind, they earned the right to go out and enjoy themselves after putting their bodies on the line and after a week of rigorous academic work.

Dardani also sees the danger in the attachment to the partying and the devotion to the sports in which the athletes play, something that can be attributed to the pressure around being an athlete. Whether it be in sports, academics or in their social life, when certain aspects of life are mounted onto kids, they become connected to that thing, which can cause even more damage down the road. In the end, Dardani looks at it in this way:

"Kids are expected to be excellent in all things, which of course is impossible, but the effect seems to be that they cling to the thing that they do best and internalize it (football, lacrosse, art, music... partying), it becomes too aligned with their identity. When that thing ends, or when they aren't competitive enough to compete professionally, they experience a real identity crisis. They don't know who they are because they haven't spent enough time developing their whole person in a healthy way. When a person doesn't acknowledge and develop all of these parts, they lose their balance. As a teacher, I see it all the time. Common results (of this inability to "measure up") read like the side effects of prescription medications: depression, substance abuse, anxiety, anger, suicidal thoughts or even suicidal actions. It's not rocket science; it's actually fairly obvious. But it is really hard to change a culture."

CHAPTER EIGHT

The Men in Black

Midseason Push

The month of October wasn't anything special for the team following the homecoming win against Bassick, although it did start off with a bang. We stayed home the following week to host St. Joe's, hoping to avenge our only regular-season loss from the previous year. The game had monumental implications as well since we were the #3 team in Connecticut while St. Joe's held the #5 spot.

The game, like the previous year, did not go according to plan from the start. Mufasa Abdul-Bassir, the running back who dominated in 2013, was back for more and continued to do damage against our defense, rushing for 135 yards with 4.7 yards per carry. By the middle of the third quarter, St. Joe's was up 17-0, and Timmy Graham was once again struggling to find his groove after throwing two interceptions and losing a fumble. In a fit of frustration, Graham entered the locker room at halftime with nothing to show after the drubbing against Bassick. Maybe he was a fluke; maybe he wasn't cut out for the job; perhaps he couldn't follow the lead of Silas Wyper. The thoughts tried entering Graham's head, but he refused to believe it. All he needed was to focus on his game and make one big play, that was it.

Fearing a second straight loss to the Cadet's that would be catastrophic to our FCIAC hopes, Trifone needed a spark to get the team back into it. He got it from bruising senior running back Peter Archey, who bulldozed into the end zone from five yards out to begin the second half. During the following St. Joe's possession, Hudson Hamill picked off the Cadet's quarterback to give the ball back to Graham in St. Joes' territory. A boost of confidence was needed for Timmy, and he knew it too. Dropping back, he saw senior receiver Todd Herget streaking down the sideline towards the end zone. Timmy launched the ball towards him as the 6'4 Herget leaped up and snagged the ball, falling in for the score.

Fortune kept coming our way when St. Joe's fumbled after Bobby Trifone laid out their running back, creating an opportunity for Hamill to recover the ball. Two plays later, Graham hit Colin Minicus for a 35-yard touchdown, giving us a 21-17 lead with less than ten minutes to go in the game. "We knew we were going to win that game, because the seniors kept telling us that, even down 17-0," Graham says. The defense held St. Joe's scoreless in the fourth quarter, giving us a massive comeback victory that Trifone credited as his best comeback win to date.[1]

By this time as well, Sam Giorgio's hard work on the scout team had paid off, as he was awarded a spot on the kickoff team during the season. The stocky junior took pride in the role, saying, "It meant a lot, it was like all the hard work I was putting in was paying off a little bit at least." He knew the role was small, but also knew that with it, he was officially on the radar of the coaches who would be watching him on every single play. The kickoff spot was everything to him, and he knew with one single screw up, he would be off in it a heartbeat; he couldn't let that happen.

Still, Giorgio and I held down our roles as leaders on the

junior varsity squad, winning every game since the loss to Greenwich. We began to notice the effect we were having on the sophomore class too. Rather than ask senior captains, seniors or varsity juniors, the sophomore players seemed to gravitate towards Sam and me more when in need of something, or if they had a question. The varsity guys were untouchable in their eyes, almost scary to some. However, they found ease in conversation with Sam and me, something we took to heart, especially Sam, who felt the need to protect those who were on the brink of leaving the team similar to Schmidt and Pagliarulo.

The remainder of the midseason was easy work for the varsity team, punishing Fairfield Warde 42-14, and following it up with a 42-0 drubbing of Trinity Catholic the following week. Six days later, we marched into Ridgefield for a Friday night showdown at Tiger Hollow Stadium. Graham, who struggled in his first Friday night game, had another rough start with two interceptions given to the Tiger defense. Like his previous Friday night game though, Timmy emerged in the second half with two touchdown passes to Herget, who received 119 of Graham's 200 passing yards. Up 50-6 going into the fourth quarter, the junior varsity defense and I entered, surrendering 17 points, but still walking away with a 50-23 win under the lights.

After the game, the statistics did not lie. Graham was struggling on Friday's, compared to the work he did during day games or on Saturday afternoons. In day games, Graham was thriving with a quarterback rating of 97.0 (a calculation that shows the performance of passers; in professional football, a perfect rating is 158.3). During the night shift, it was different, where Timmy had a rating of only 86.0, nowhere near his daytime average. Maybe it was the bright lights, the intense build-up, or perhaps it was just a fluke to begin the season. However, Graham didn't think about it at all since he remained focused on the bigger goal, which was reaching the FCIAC Championship.

Still, Graham received another shot to right his wrongs under the bright lights on Friday nights, playing against Wilton High School, the last of a three-game road trip. In the cold October night, Timmy put on a clinic, completing 19 passes on 23 attempts for 208 yards and two touchdowns. His quarterback rating was 137.6, his highest of the season, dwarfing his previous season high of 114.8 against Trinity Catholic.

He then continued his Saturday afternoon dominance, throwing for three touchdowns in a dominant performance against Harding High School, pushing the team to a 9-0 record. Even with that record, the team wasn't in a position to play for the FCIAC title, due to Brien McMahon High School holding more "points" in the standings. By virtue of the controversial power points system, McMahon held 2nd place behind New Canaan with 128.57, while we had 126.25. The next week would be huge, because if McMahon beat St. Joe's, they would clinch a spot in the FCIAC Championship against New Canaan, no matter what our result. A McMahon loss and a win for us, however, Thanksgiving morning would then be home to the FCIAC Championship game.

The Turkey Bowl was far away in every single person's mind, including Trifone's. The next game seemed to worry Trifone more than any game so far that season and for a good reason. In a rematch of 2013's classic November showdown, North Haven would be making the trip to Darien High School for a battle between SCC and FCIAC teams. It wasn't just the Indians plan for revenge that scared Trifone, but the idea that North Haven wasn't going to be traveling alone.

Talking to the media, Trifone made a claim that made waves in North Haven, stating, "They'll bring a thousand fans." Fearing the worst, Trifone then called out the town of

Darien:

"I just don't want the away stands to be more filled than the home stands."[2]

Trifone had every right to worry about the possibility of North Haven bringing more fans than Darien. Ever since the St. Joe's game, I had started noticing smaller and smaller crowds due to the blowout fashion that most of our home games were ending in… And the last thing we wanted as a team was to be shown up by North Haven on our home turf.

Throughout the week, social media blew up about the North Haven game, with many wondering if North Haven would take on the challenge of trekking down to Darien for the game. Those people got their answer pretty quickly when North Haven announced on their Instagram page that students would be riding down to the game on a bus. The Indians didn't stop there, posting almost every single day to hype up the atmosphere of the rematch. On our side, we were trying equally as hard to beat North Haven at their own game. The students at Darien High School began to post all over social media as well, trying to get every single non-football player to show up loud and proud in the student section for North Haven. On the practice field, the big fight atmosphere was everywhere. The Indians were locked into sight, to the point where coaches started making scout team players, like me, wear feathers in our helmets.

Like the previous year as well, North Haven week presented Trifone with an opportunity to give us a little present; which was new uniforms. For the North Haven game, we would be debuting black jerseys, something that had been rumored for weeks. When Trifone pulled them out during a team meeting, the room exploded into cheers.

Seeing that #44 jersey with the name "BARTHOLD" across the back was remarkable to me because the first thing I thought about was a home crowd seeing the names and numbers, and associating #44 with me. That was a dream of mine, to make my number mean something. I hadn't achieved it yet, but after wearing it for two years straight with a chance of starting the next year, I was on the right trajectory.

The day of the game had arrived just like that, and all the preparation, the hype, and the social media battles were about to be settled on the fields of Darien High School. Set for a 1 pm start, Timmy Graham arrived at Vavala's Deli before heading to the high school, where Mark Evanchick was getting his same sausage, egg, and cheese (never forget the hot sauce) for pregame like usual. Timmy's meal was a little different than Evanchick's; A turkey sandwich with bacon and lettuce on a roll. He'd take the bag and head out, but not before grabbing a blue Gatorade, just like he did every single game.

He arrived in the locker room and went through his game day gear. Headphones over his head, "Ain't Worried About Nothin" by French Montana blared into his ears. I never liked hanging around the locker room during pregame, so I would usually put my jersey on, leave the locker room and sit outside looking onto the field before the stadium started filling up. This day was different though, because almost two hours before kickoff while sitting, I looked to the parking lot…

The North Haven faithful had arrived.

Tailgating in our parking lot, the Indian fans were in full force and began to file into the stadium way in advance before our fans had even shown up. Slightly intimidated by their presence, I retreated into the safety of our locker room away from their fans, notifying my teammates that they had arrived. I couldn't hide in the locker room forever though, because the time came for us to leave and take the field. Donned in our new black jersey's, Trifone gave us a status update for the game: the place was packed on both sides. Goosebumps ran over my arms as we made our way through the halls and towards the tunnel. We paused at the tunnel, while Timmy hopped up and down, ready to go in front of the screaming fans. Smoke then began to fill the tunnel while the crowd grew louder. On cue, the seniors led the charge, storming through the smoke and onto the field as the crowd erupted at the sight of their new "Black & Blue Wave." Running out to midfield, we saw the sheer mass of North Haven fans who had made the trip. They overflowed in the stands, forming around the fenced area surrounding the field.

The captains moved to midfield for the coin toss, joined by Jim Mulhearn, who was named an honorary captain by Trifone earlier in the week. Jim sat next to the senior captains at the 50, smiling his signature smile while the referee explained the toss and the proceedings that would follow. Both sides of the stadium grew louder as tensions rose, with our fans and the North Haven fans dueling to see who could create more noise before kickoff. Looking around at our fans and theirs, I knew that this game was going to be a good one.

I was wrong, again. A couple of minutes into the game, Shelby Grant broke loose for a 78-yard touchdown run, giving us the lead right out of the gate. A couple of drives later, Graham found Hamill on a short pass, resulting in a 14-0 lead. By halftime, we led by a score of 21-0. It wasn't even a contest since the defense was dominating the North Haven offense, with Evanchick leading the way with two sacks and Hamill getting an interception as well.

The second half was a little slower than the first because both teams went scoreless in the third. Feeling desperate it seemed, the run-heavy North Haven offense started throwing the ball in the fourth quarter, hoping to catch fire with a small spark. On an attempted wheel route, Bobby Trifone read the route like a book and intercepted it for a 60-yard dagger.

The game ended with a win for us by a score of 31-0. North Haven ran the ball 49 times, averaging only 3.3 yards per carry. Senior linebacker Charlie Travers totaled 11 tackles on defense, while Timmy Graham had another solid outing by completing 20 of his 26 passes for 248 yards.

During the game too, it was announced that St. Joe's had defeated McMahon 33-17. For the first time on Turkey Day since 2008, when we were in fifth-grade watching Matty Wheelock and Brian Kosnik, Darien and New Canaan would meet at historic Boyle Stadium for a chance to win the FCIAC crown. Thanksgiving just got a whole lot more interesting.

Thanksgiving Week

With the FCIAC Championship overlapping with the annual Turkey Bowl, it made the game and weeks leading up to it a whole lot different than the previous year. Having not won an FCIAC Championship since 2010, the team felt a sense of urgency of needing to win to show that we were the dominant team in Fairfield County. Almost always in the shadow of New Canaan, a win would do wonders for the program. And as if the FCIAC Championship aspect wasn't big enough for us, the game also boasted New Canaan (9-0) as #2 in the state and us (10-0) as #3 in the state.[3] The game wasn't just a county affair, it was a state affair, and everyone would be watching. For me, after spending the 2013 Turkey Bowl week sweeping the floors of the locker room and not even being on the field during practice, the 2014 week was a breath of fresh air. Taking a beating on scout team was still awful, but in my mind, I had the feeling that I was contributing to the varsity guys before they took the field on Thursday morning.

The situation was different for other juniors, mostly Timmy Graham. Mark Evanchick, Hudson Hamill, Colin Minicus, Bobby & Christian Trifone all had some experience from the previous year, but Graham was making his Turkey Bowl debut playing a position that all eyes would be on.

In the week leading up to the Turkey Bowl, Graham thought about it non-stop. "I remember going to Boyle Stadium (in 2008) when Wheelock and Brian Kosnik were playing. You dream about that as a young kid, running out of that tunnel in front of both towns. There really was nothing better than Thanksgiving morning." Timmy understood the pressures surrounding the big game, and it only got more significant when game previews began to surface. Throughout the entire year, he was compared to the play of New Canaan's junior quarterback Michael Collins, who stood at 6'5 210 pounds, compared to Graham at 6'4 185 pounds.

Coming into the game, Collins was on an absolute tear. Completing 55% of his passes for 216.8 yards per game with 24 touchdowns and only four interceptions. Graham was having an equally good season, completing 65% of his passes for 190.2 yards with 18 touchdowns, but eight interceptions. At the end of the day, for Graham, the statistics didn't matter, only the game result did.

There was other business to attend to before the Thanksgiving morning, because the Monday before was the junior varsity game against New Canaan, obviously dubbed the "J.V. Turkey Bowl." This was the biggest junior varsity game of the year, understandably, because it's when all the varsity guys show up to watch the younger guys play the only time all year. Sammy G and I didn't care about that though; all we were thinking about was having one final game to show the coaches, who would be watching, that we were talented players who could contribute to the varsity team next year.

Giorgio and I played probably our best junior varsity games that day. New Canaan had nowhere to go when trying to run down the middle since Sam met their running back in the hole nearly every play. On the outside in the slot, New Canaan's receivers were shorter than me, allowing me to take over my whole zone and remove any chance of them throwing across the field.

The game remained close, and New Canaan ended up with the ball down a touchdown with only a minute to go. We got them to fourth down, where they needed 10 yards to continue the game. They went 2x2 (two receivers on both sides), and I lined up over the slot, staying with the same "Cover 6" coverage that had worked all game. On the snap, the slot ran a switch route with the wide receiver on the outside, but I stayed back, knowing the outside receiver would be crossing by me any second. He did just that, and the quarterback released towards him. I had gone too deep into my zone though, forcing me to come down on the receiver to make the play. I stuck my hand between his arms, disrupting the ball's path to his hands.

The ball fell to the ground, and we had won the junior varsity Turkey Bowl for the third straight year. I celebrated hard as I watched Coach Trifone in the bleachers stand up and head back into the high school after watching the game with a small smile on his face. That was one of my final shots of 2014 to show him what I had, and I nailed it.

The Monday win was fun for Giorgio and me, but the fun stopped when Sam got the news that he was dreading to hear, but the news he was expecting. "I was removed from the kickoff team before every big game," says Giorgio on the situation. In a sense, he felt almost "used" by the coaching staff. "It made me feel like I was just trying to be kept satisfied (by the coaches) and kept on the team." It happened against St. Joe's, it happened against North Haven, and it was happening for the biggest game of the year. Devastated by the news, there was still, however, a silver lining for Giorgio. He was being counted out once again, even after an incredible junior varsity performance. He understood the reasoning behind it, even looking back four years later. "What it came down to it really, I was still not good enough to play at the varsity level."

By the time Wednesday rolled around, Giorgio wasn't the only person being counted out. In fact, our entire team was being counted out when major media outlets began to pick New Canaan as the overwhelming favorite against us. It wasn't like this was abnormal though. In 2013, New Canaan was the heavy favorite. In 2012? Same thing. Trifone reminded us of that, and it stuck with the group during the final walkthrough on Wednesday evening. Even then, the media was ignored by players like Hudson Hamill. "I tried to focus only on us because those New Canaan teams were damn good."

When Wednesday evening came, the team seemed prepared on both sides of the ball. There were fewer nerves and more excitement from the starters, ready for whatever the Rams threw at them.

The coin toss against North Haven (November 15th, 2014)

Sam Giorgio & I leave the field during the "J.V." Turkey Bowl
(November 22nd, 2014)

CHAPTER NINE

Thanksgiving Day

Boyle Stadium

It was after midnight when the quiet grounds of Boyle Stadium were interrupted by flashing car lights. In freezing weather, a Darien parent along with a relative stepped out of their car and snuck onto the field. Keeping quiet, the two pulled something out of a bag: It was incense. The two adults lit a match and burned the incense and began to wave it around the field, hoping to rid the demons of bad luck at Boyle for the Darien football team. Following losses at Boyle in 2008 and 2013 against New Canaan, the exorcism was necessary to some. After completing the ritual, the adults left in their car, speeding out of sight as Boyle once again fell into silence.

There was just something about playing at Boyle, something different. Home of the Stamford High School Black Knights, Boyle had grown to become a legendary venue over the years. The stadium first opened in 1937[1] and has hosted some of the biggest football games in FCIAC history, including the annual Westhill-Stamford contest. The big draw of the stadium though is its capacity, which can go over 10,000 people on game day.

Darien and New Canaan had a small amount of history at the stadium, starting back in 2008 during the FCIAC Championship/Turkey Bowl. New Canaan won *that* Boyle showdown 28-20. Five years later, we met again in the 2013 State Championship, although the crowd was barely half the size of the packed house in 2008.

The two towns were expected to fill the stadium once again on Thanksgiving morning, six years after the initial battle at Boyle. The FCIAC was predicting upwards to 10,000 people to show up for the championship game, creating an unbelievable atmosphere that no other stadium could replicate in the area. On the team, we had heard the buzz about the 10,000 fans, but that wasn't the priority. Still, the night before, I thought about it. Only about 4,700 people were at the 2013 Turkey Bowl at Dunning Stadium, and that was about to be doubled.

The morning of the FCIAC Championship/Turkey Bowl was calm for me, especially now that I (correction: thought I) knew what to expect after my sophomore year in the Turkey Bowl. I woke up about an hour before the report time and started to pack up my bag that I would be taking from Darien High School to Boyle Stadium later that morning. I neatly folded everything I needed into the bag, careful zipped it up, placed my headphones on my head and went out my door.

Walking into the locker room, there was the annual tradition of letters posted on the walls from former Blue Wave players wishing us luck in the game later that day. It was something I loved, especially in 2014, when I got to read letters from guys I looked up to, like Silas Wyper, Alex Gunn, and Nick Lombardo. After reading, I turned the corner into the central part of the locker room, where Timmy Graham was sitting next to junior lineman Spencer Stovall. Graham was leaned over, eye black already on with his Beats headphones pressed against his ears. Similarly, Mark

Evanchick sat in front of his locker with no expression on his face, just pure focus. Colin Minicus, staring into the mirror in the bathroom, prepared his eye black in a way that was different than most. "I only did one (line) of eye black, that's just something I'd always do." Weird looking? Yes, but "Mino" didn't care. It wasn't superstition or anything, because he didn't believe in superstition. It was just something he did, and it worked.

I didn't do anything special, but I still stayed focused. I knew the chances of me going in during the game were slim to none, but there was still a chance (a special teams injury or God forbid, the entire senior linebacker core went down). Unlike the previous year too, there were no sophomore duties, so I sat in front of my locker just waiting for the announcement that the bus would be leaving. The dreadful part was the wait. I sat anxiously at my locker, trying to think of anything to pass the time leading up to the game. The only thing I could do was wait patiently, which killed me on the inside.

After what seemed like an absolute eternity, Coach Grant announced that we had five minutes until the buses left. Gathering our stuff, we made our way out of the locker room and onto the buses parked outside, ready for the 20-minute journey that would take us to Boyle.

Just like in 2013, the cold had taken over early in the morning. The wind wasn't as bad, but there was light snow in the forecast. Arriving at Boyle, I stepped off the bus, marveling at the sight of the stadium. Two stone grandstands lined the east and west sidelines, giving a rustic feel to the historical field. Camera's were already surrounding the stadium since the game would be broadcast live to those who couldn't make it. The FCIAC was expecting an overflow of fans as well, so metal separators lined the end zones so that fans wouldn't step onto the field.

An FCIAC official then led us underneath the New Canaan stands, where locker rooms for both New Canaan and us were located. Settling in, everyone took their spots and resumed the complete silence that had carried over from Darien High School. We had about thirty minutes until warm-ups, so I waited in the quiet locker room awaiting instruction.

Thirty minutes later, we exited the locker room for our warm-ups on the field at Boyle, where pockets of fans began to form in the crowd. The focus was on the game though, especially when New Canaan came out of their locker room for their warm-ups, screaming and yelling at the top of their lungs. By the time warm-ups ended, Boyle was still filling up with about 30 minutes to go before game time.

Returning to the locker room, we began to put our shoulder pads and jerseys on, locking in before it was officially time to leave. About five minutes before though, hints of the crowd started emerging from above us. Located right below the New Canaan student section, a faint chant could be heard from where I was sitting…

"hhaaiill NC."

It was quiet but noticeable. A couple of minutes later, Trifone gave us the order that it was time to go. The team crammed towards the exit, which was an upwards stone ramp, and Minicus remembers it vividly. "I still remember walking up the stones, those slippery stones. You can't run, so you're walking, and I remember it was steep enough so you couldn't see anything but the sky. So I'm looking up towards the sky while also looking at my feet so I don't slip, but I remember coming out of that tunnel and looking around. The place was packed."

Sifting through the 5,000 strong in the New Canaan stands, the jeers and insults were deafening in our ears. I kept my head down, avoiding any confrontation with fans when all of a sudden, we broke free and started running on the turf. I looked up. A sea of 5,000 people wearing blue and white erupted at the sight of their hometown team arriving. Timmy Graham, who always left the locker room last, came face to face with the crowd. Seeing the 5,000 fans on our side on their feet cheering, Graham looked around and said to himself, "Holy shit."

The adrenaline was like a straight punch to the face. The noise of 5,000 of your townspeople cheering in approval got me going like nothing else. I remember hitting the sideline and looking up and around, my heart thumping at the sight and sound. The joy of the moment only lasted for about a minute though, because the faint chant that we heard in the locker room had become a full-on war-cry once we stepped outside.

"HHAAIILL NC!"

A pause, then again…

"HHAAIILL NC!"

Goosebumps covered my body as I looked at Sammy G and said, "This is fucking insane!" Light snow began to fall as well, which the crowd approved of with a massive roar. I looked around. Two undefeated teams in front of 10,000 people were about to go to war in the FCIAC Championship during the annual Turkey Bowl.

It was fucking insane.

It's the Turkey Bowl

Sitting on the far side of the sideline was Jim Mulhearn, who had made the trek to Stamford to cheer us on. Before the game started, each starter made their way to Jim to let him know how much it meant that he was there. Jim sat smiling, happy to be there while still spreading positive messages minutes before the biggest game of our lives.

After the coin toss, Timmy Graham made his way out for

his Turkey Bowl debut, surrounded by the screaming fans from both sides. Graham took a deep breath after looking around at the crowd. In his mind, he was telling himself one thing: "Just get the first snap off." Looking back, Graham still agrees with his mentality. "Once that first play is over, it's just clockwork after that."

The first drive was unsuccessful for Graham, but nothing terrible happened. He had gotten his first real look at the New Canaan defense, once again anchored by the returning Zach Allen from the previous year. He returned to the sideline calm and collected, ready for a second chance at the defense. He would get it rather quickly after Michael Collins hit receiver Michael Kraus on a 46-yard touchdown pass. New Canaan would get the ball back almost immediately, and Collins wasted no time hitting Alex LaPolice for a 32-yard touchdown with six minutes to go in the first quarter.

It didn't stop in the second. Right off the bat, Collins hit Kraus again for a 38-yard touchdown to put the score at 21-0 New Canaan. I stood helplessly on the sideline, constantly looking at the scoreboard and the time on it. I would then look up to the fans on our side, most of whom were shaking their heads in disapproval of the way we were playing. It was pretty evident that New Canaan was pissed off and motivated after the last year, and by midway through the second quarter, we were playing catch-up with a Rams team that was on fire.

The debut half for Timmy Graham could not have gone any worse, either. He fumbled early in the first and then threw two interceptions to New Canaan. Looking up into the stands towards his father, Timmy came off the field, stunned and upset with himself. The second interception set New Canaan right within our 10-yard line, where our defense held on for dear life, knowing that a touchdown would be the dagger. The Rams would have to settle for a 26-yard field goal attempt, which was missed by New Canaan kicker Peter Swindell. With only a couple minutes to go, Graham was able to get into a rhythm to drive down the field. With just several seconds left on the clock, Graham hit Minicus, who dove into the end zone to the absolute joy of the Darien crowd. Heading into the half, New Canaan led by a score of 21-7, although we had momentum on our side with getting the ball to start the second half.

In the locker room, Graham sat with his receivers and went over the first half mistakes. Wanting to do whatever he could to help his team, he knew he had to step up to give his team the best chance of winning. I stood and looked around, knowing that if we could score during our opening drive that we would be in control. Guys like Mark Evanchick and Jack Tyrrell were containing and putting pressure on Collins, and with both those guys, the longer the game went on, the better they got. I had hope, but more importantly, the entire team had confidence. We stormed back onto the field to the roar of our town, ready to put together another signature comeback that we had become known for.

The hope was quickly dashed to start the second half when Graham was intercepted during the opening drive, his third of the game. Our crowd died at the moment, but Graham stayed faithful to his teammates. "They had stepped up all game long, and I knew they were going to step up again."

On the first play after the interception, Collins fumbled after being hit. Evanchick recovered the fumble on the New Canaan 22-yard line, setting the offense up perfectly for a chance to score. Five plays later, Peter Archey bowled into the end zone from a yard out, cutting the score to 21-14. Archey's touchdown sent me into a frenzy, and I turned to the crowd and fired up the section I was in front of… We had ourselves a ball game.

The rest of the third quarter was a stalemate, with both

teams looking for an edge. I stood on the sideline when I looked into the Darien student section. From the other side, a New Canaan student had snuck into the student section and stole the Darien flag. He ran across the outside fences and returned to the New Canaan section, where the flag was passed around and torn into pieces by the students, who roared in approval during the entire situation. Shocked, I tried turning my attention back to the field but couldn't help but stare back toward the section every minute or so.

The action picked up early in the fourth quarter, when Collins connected with Kraus for 38 yards, setting the Rams up three yards from the end zone. Stressed out of my mind, I went to the opposite side of the sideline, hoping and praying the defense could hold. They didn't need to hold, because New Canaan fumbled and we recovered, again causing an eruption from our sideline and crowd. Graham led the offense back onto the field following the turnover, looking to tie the game midway through the fourth.

On third down, Graham dropped back to pass deep in our territory when Zach Allen stripped him. New Canaan got the ball back ten yards from the end zone. Stress and anticipation filled me again. I crouched down on the sideline, praying again that a miracle would happen.

All the praying seemed to come in handy because it appeared as if God was really on our side. New Canaan lined up in the wildcat formation with LaPolice at quarterback and Allen at tight end. Allen ran a fade route, and LaPolice lobbed it up to the 6'6 linebacker. Out of the blue, Hudson Hamill picked the ball off, giving us possession with four minutes left. Now, Graham was faced with the daunting task of driving 94 yards against a New Canaan defense that had bullied him all game.

Unsuccessful on the first play of the drive, Graham launched a deep ball to Will Hamernick on second down, who caught and ran for a 56-yard gain. A couple of plays later, Todd Herget made a circus catch 37 yards down the field all the way to the 2-yard line. The next play, Archey bulldozed his way into the end zone, tying the game at 21 with only minutes to go.

The game would go to overtime, which was like a kick to the groin to me. I had a massive headache from screaming and yelling all game and didn't know if I could handle overtime from an emotional standpoint. Poor me.

New Canaan won the toss and elected to defend first. Graham defiantly made his way out, ready to create his everlasting Turkey Bowl moment. Trying to catch New Canaan off guard, Graham, who wasn't known for his speed, ran the ball up the middle for a 4-yard gain. Graham hit the ground hard though and got up clutching his left shoulder as the crowd grew silent. He looked to the sideline and waved to Trifone, signaling that something was wrong.

I stood there and immediately looked at Brian Peters, the backup sophomore QB, and Cooper Drippe, the senior safety who had played QB junior year. Both of them looked to Trifone, who made an executive decision. Instead of Peters or Drippe, Trifone went with Hamill and the wildcat offense. We hadn't used this offense all season long, so Trifone knew that New Canaan would be surprised. They were; because, on the first play, Hamill faked a handoff and drilled Griffin Ross in the end zone for seven. Ross calmly looked to the crowd and bowed as we took our first lead of the entire game.

Collins took the field next, needing to score to keep the game alive. On the first play, Collins looked to Kraus on a screen play that gained no yards. On second down, Collins again looked to Kraus on a slant, but it was broken up. On the sideline, I was shaking uncontrollably. With third down coming up, I turned to the crowd and began to throw my arms in the air to get them to become louder. The crowd raised to their feet and started to yell. I wanted more, so I started screaming and yelling for them to get louder and louder. The noise level grew, as Collins got the play from his sideline.

On the field, Christian Trifone stood close to his brother Bobby, talking about what to expect in the next play. Christian took notice of LaPolice on the outside, and Kraus lined up in the slot. Lining up with his brother, Christian recalls the moment. "I looked to Bobby and said, 'we got this, only two more downs.' Sure enough, they ran a crossing pattern. Kraus ran a corner and LaPolice came under him with a slant." Christian saw the route coming and came down on the Rams receiver. Undersized against the bigger LaPolice, along with his broken fingers wrapped up, Christian put his helmet to LaPolice as soon as the ball reached the receiver.

The ball slipped out of the hands of LaPolice. I stood on the sideline watching the football as if it was moving in slow motion. It laid in the air when all of a sudden Bobby Trifone grabbed it and fell to the ground. Darien 28 New Canaan 21.[2]

The crowd stormed the field as Bobby Trifone was swarmed. I threw my arms up and started running around the field in circles, not even thinking about where I was going. Timmy Graham had a similar experience to me after the game too. "I wasn't thinking; I started running around the field trying to find someone to hug," says Graham. Funny enough, I saw Timmy and ran up to him, nearly jumping onto him before realizing his shoulder was hurt. I stopped and looked at him, saying the only thing I could think of… "HOLY SHIT!" I then continued my run, celebrating with fans and people I had never even seen in my life. I didn't care though, because we were winners.

In a humorous twist, Christian Trifone sat on the ground after the play, unaware of what happened. "I was on the ground, and everyone was storming the field. I ended up finding out that Bobby had intercepted it a couple of minutes later." When he found out, he was overwhelmed with joy. "I just remember repeating, 'Holy crap; we did it.'"

For the first time since 2010, we were FCIAC Champions. At midfield, we were once again presented with our Turkey Bowl trophy but also presented with the FCIAC Championship trophy and medals that were given to each player. The minute after receiving the prize, we made our way over to Jim, who was ecstatic. We gathered around our 12th man, handing him the FCIAC trophy and posing for a photograph. He was all smiles; *we* were all smiles. Nothing else mattered that day, and for a 16-year-old, that's a pretty awesome feeling to have.

New Canaan lines up while their crowd watches (November 27th, 2014)

Timmy Graham throws towards the end zone during the second quarter (November 27th, 2014)

Hudson Hamill before throwing the winning touchdown pass in overtime (November 27th, 2014)

Jim Mulhearn with the FCIAC/Turkey Bowl trophies after the game (November 27th, 2014)

CHAPTER TEN

The Road to Redemption

Rising Emotions

After the FCIAC Championship and Thanksgiving Day win, we clinched the #1 seed in the Class L-Large CIAC State playoffs. It was going to be a bit different than 2013, where only four state tournaments took place. In 2014, the CIAC decided to expand the field to eight tournaments, meaning you played one semifinal game and if you won, you were in the state title game.

Awaiting us were the 9-2 Naugatuck High School Greyhounds, who were the #4 seed in the L-Large bracket. The game was hosted at Darien High School on a rainy afternoon on what was a forgettable day from the start. Not only was the weather awful but the atmosphere at Darien High School was dead because the entire state of Connecticut knew that we were going to punish Naugatuck. Leading 35-0 at halftime, the game was over, and we had clinched a spot in the Class L-Large State Championship game later in the week, but we still had to show up for the second half. That's when I made my state playoff debut, getting to play the majority of the second half at outside linebacker, something I didn't expect. The entire second half was still a great learning experience for me, getting to play in a state playoff game with another opportunity to show off my skill set to the coaches.

Everything was going great until late in the third quarter when I crashed down to stop a run up the middle by Naugatuck's running back. I lowered my head, which was not the right thing to do, and hit right into his helmet. Shaken up a little, I got up anyway, living by the mantra I was taught since the fourth-grade of "man up" and play through the pain. I remember getting back to the sideline, walking slowly over to Coach Forget to tell him that I was done.

He looked at me confused, asking why I wanted out with a quarter to go. Not wanting to mention the word "concussion," although I wasn't sure if I had one, I just told him that a sophomore deserved some time in the game. Still looking at me weird, he agreed and pulled me for the rest of the game. I stood on the sideline the rest of the game, not putting my helmet back on because when I did, it felt like something was pressing up against both sides of my head. I ignored it and played it off as needing to hydrate more, not thinking it was a big deal. It was a part of football after all, and that was my mentality at the time.

The game ended by a score of 42-12, giving us our second straight state title appearance, the first back to back appearance in nearly a decade and a half. There was no celebration of the clinched title appearance, no party in the locker room, nothing like that. Instead, we made our way into the Darien High School cafeteria, where Jim was waiting to congratulate us on clinching a championship berth. Never talking about himself, Jim had made no mention that it was his 68th birthday that day, a fact that Coach Trifone had secretly shared with us before the game. After congratulating us, we broke into song for Jim, singing happy birthday for our 12th man. Soaking wet in our pads from the game, we celebrated his birthday alongside him, where he showered us with "thank you" through the entirety of the song.

I remember that celebration being exceptional and tend to give credit to Coach Trifone for what I got out of that moment. Having just clinched a spot with a chance to win a state championship, we weren't celebrating that; we were celebrating the birthday of one of our biggest fans and inspirations. For the second game in a row, this wasn't about football, but instead about a man who was fighting for his life. It wasn't about individual performances and not even a team victory, but a family victory. That's what was important; being a family, something that was bigger than athletic success or championships, which is something hard to come by in the town of Darien.

The ease of the pressure while celebrating Jim's birthday lasted only a couple hours because later that day we found out who our opponent would be in the championship game; none other than the Rams of New Canaan, who had defeated Weathersfield High School 27-14. Three weeks after battling for the FCIAC Championship, the rematch was set for the Class L-Large State Championship.

The week leading up to December 13th was like any other week, which was a signature of Coach Trifone. He never wanted to change things up just because of a game, sticking to the same practice agenda to keep players comfortable and away from thinking about the magnitude of the game. It was different than 2013 too because the previous year was the first time anyone had ever been around state playoffs. This year, the senior and junior classes had the experience from 2013, giving it more of a sense of "we've been here" mentality. Unfortunately, the mentality seemed too strong for some players, including a senior captain who showed up late to a practice, causing an outburst from Trifone that was directed straight at the captain. Livid, Trifone stormed back towards the rest of the team, sarcastically saying, "Outstanding leadership."

After a week of preparation, the night before the game was somewhat of a nerve-wracking experience. We went up to Trifone's room for a final team meeting, where waiting was a member of the 1996 state championship team. Trifone had arranged for the guest speaker to talk to us, so for almost 30 minutes, the former Darien player, who had spent years as a Navy SEAL, spoke to us about his experience in the military and how it all went back to his days as a Darien football player. He reminded us of the thing that haunted him to the day, even after winning the state title in '96; the team finished with one loss, which sat at the back of his mind.

Looking into our eyes, he challenged us to bring the title home. We had a chance to go undefeated for the first time since 1979, and re-establish Darien as a football town. He then started to walk away. He stopped though and turned back towards the team. Without speaking, he pulled his Special Warfare insignia (commonly known as the SEAL Trident) and slammed it onto the table. He then walked out the door as the team sat in silence.

Never Again

We arrived at West Haven High School, the site of the Class L-Large State Championship about two hours before kickoff, which was slated for 10:30 am. Stepping off the bus, we were met by Jim who had arrived earlier that morning. He did his signature pose, giving us a thumbs up as we walked up to him, shaking his hand and thanking him for making the long trek.

It was relatively warm for a December morning. The sun was shining down on the field while we walked up the hill into the high school where our locker room was located. Well, not a locker room, but a basketball gym. The location of the locker room didn't matter to a single player, because the sole focus was the New Canaan Rams who were situated across the hall from us.

The mood in the gym was interesting, contrasting once again between the seniors and my class. Timmy Graham bounced up and down on his feet, throwing a ball whenever he got the chance. Mark Evanchick sat with his teammates, locked into his music and staring blankly across the gym.

Following warm-ups, seniors like Peter Achey sat up in the bleachers of the gym alone, away from everyone else. I kept looking to the seniors, curious about what was going on inside their head. Were they thinking about this being their last game ever, or were they just wired in on beating New Canaan and finishing undefeated?

I wasn't able to get an answer, because I sat alone with Sam Giorgio and kept to myself. Trifone then entered the gym and gathered the team. He kept his message short and simple, but it was effective as always. Looking at the team, he ended his talk with words alluding to the 2013 State Championship loss:

"Don't let it happen again."

We then bowed our heads and linked our arms, praying the Lord's Prayer for one final time during the 2014 season. We stood up and exited the gym, ready for the long walk down to the stadium. The crowd was nowhere near the size of the Thanksgiving crowd at Boyle, but both towns made a solid appearance at the game, especially the student sections. We sprinted out onto the field, ready for an opportunity to make history and cement our legacy. Reaching the sideline, I did what I always did before a game; I looked up into the stands, found my mother and gave a thumbs up. She smiled and waved as I turned back, ready to watch what was promised to be a great football game.

The game started slow, with punts traded back and forth during the first four minutes. It didn't stay like that for long, because after recovering a fumble on the 15-yard line, Collins hit Kraus a couple of plays later for a 15-yard touchdown.

Graham struggled to find any success in the first quarter, once again pressured by the dominant New Canaan defense that stifled him all game on Thanksgiving. A fumble and an interception stopped drives short for the offense, but it didn't matter, because Evanchick and the defense held their own against New Canaan the rest of the quarter.

In the second quarter, the offense woke up. Seven seconds into the quarter, Graham hit Hamernick on a 30-yard touchdown pass, tying the game at 7-7 with nearly 12 minutes to go in the half. When Graham and the offense got the ball back a couple of minutes later, they drove 44 yards in four plays, ending with a direct snap to Hamill for a 3-yard touchdown run.

With two minutes to go, Graham led another long drive which ended with an 11-yard touchdown pass to Griffin Ross. The next play, senior kicker Stephen Walker lined up for the extra point, where Hamill was awaiting the snap. Looking back on the moment, Hamill remembers it like it was yesterday. "The snap was a little outside, but definitely something I could've handled. It was the first time I had to make a 'fire' call in a varsity game, but I picked it up, turned the corner and thought I was going to get in. I went to jump and got my leg clipped at the one-yard line."

At halftime, we rushed back to the locker room with a 20-7 lead over our hated rivals with excitement flowing through our veins. The defense was dominating the Rams, sacking Collins six times and only allowing 53 yards of offense for New Canaan, along with an incredible -22 rushing yards for the Rams.

I ran back into the locker room telling myself that it was over, that we had pretty much clinched the state title. Coach Trifone put those feelings quickly to bed, however, reminding the team of who they were playing against. He told us with once again a simple but effective phrase: "We did it to them on Thanksgiving, now they're going to want to do it to us."

The Rams received the ball to start the second half, and constructed a four-minute drive down the field. After taking shots downfield with deep balls during the first half, New Canaan adjusted to using short passes to catch the defense off guard. When Collins and the offense reached the red zone, our defense stiffened, forcing a fourth down on the 17-yard line. New Canaan decided to go for it, putting all the marbles on the shoulders of Collins. He didn't disappoint, lobbing a pass to junior receiver Kyle Smith who caught the ball over Hamill, cutting the score to 20-14.

Momentum was starting to shift, and on the sideline, I could feel it. On the kickoff, the Rams pulled off an onside kick which they recovered, giving them the ball once again. Sam Giorgio and I stood there watching, with nothing we could do from the sideline. "You feel helpless in those situations," Giorgio says. "Standing on the sideline, there was nothing I could do to help my team."

The defense held its own against the Rams, forcing consecutive punts the remainder of the third quarter. The New Canaan defense did the same thing to Graham and the offense, keeping the speedy receivers at bay on our side. Entering the final quarter, New Canaan regained possession with 11 minutes to go. On third down, the defense stopped the Rams, but an illegal substitution penalty gave New Canaan new life, which proved fatal to us. More short, quick passes from Collins to his receivers allowed for time to come off the clock while also getting closer and closer to the end zone. Finally, with a little over six minutes left, Collins found LaPolice for a 24-yard touchdown, giving New Canaan a 21-20 lead.

My heart sank hearing the New Canaan crowd break into

cheers and seeing their sideline celebrate. Graham stayed composed though, knowing he could get the team down the field for a chance at a field goal at least. He had plenty of time too, so there was no rush in his mind. The offense got the ball after the kick and started to drive down the field. Penalties began to hurt the Rams, who had personal fouls called on back-to-back third downs, giving us hope that we could inch closer and closer to Stephen Walker's range.

With a little under four minutes left, the coaches decided to take a shot downfield, putting the fate of the game in Graham's hands. On the play, Hamernick was wide open down the field with his man beat, and Graham launched the ball towards his direction. New Canaan's Mike Cognetta caught up to Hamernick though, and picked the ball off, resulting in Graham's third interception of the day. Stunned, Graham slowly walked off the field, looking up at his father, who stood atop the grandstands. He reached the sideline, where every player was feeling the same sheer shock. Up 20-7 at halftime in the state title game, we had fallen behind 21-20 with only a slim chance of getting the ball back. I stood with my eyes full, staring at the clock on the scoreboard, trying to figure out how much time we would have if we got the ball back.

New Canaan was able to milk the clock down to the final seconds, due to us having no timeouts in the later part of the game. Collins lobbed up a bomb on the last play to let the clock hit zero, and just like that, the New Canaan Rams were the Class L-Large State Champions, defeating us for the second consecutive year.[1]

New Canaan rushed the field to celebrate their 10th state title in school history while we stood on the field, still trying to figure out what had just happened. Hudson Hamill, realizing the one point deficit fell on him, stood on the field and found his father, burying himself in his arms. "At the time, I thought that game was completely my fault. To this day, it's probably one of my biggest regrets and definitely something I'll remember for the rest of my life."

Timmy Graham stayed on the turf with his head held down. Mark Evanchick, staring at the scoreboard, collected his thoughts. "That loss was everything; it was absolutely everything. There's no worse way to lose a game then by one point, and there's no worse team to lose to."

The mood on the field was devastating, as seniors broke down in tears at the lost opportunity of a lifetime. A CIAC cameraman approached a crying senior captain, who scolded at the cameraman loudly and needed to be pulled back by coaches and other players. On the other side of the field, Charlie Travers sat on one knee in tears, something that Sam Giorgio noticed from a couple of feet away.

"Charlie and I were never that close personally," Giorgio says on the moment. "But I looked up to the guy like he was the world. He played inside linebacker beautifully, he wasn't the fastest, he wasn't the strongest, but he just played and played well, and that's who I wanted to be. Watching him cry and break down on that field, I just lost it."

I stood alone on the field with my eyes fixed on the scoreboard. I don't remember thinking, but just staring for minutes at the scoreboard while New Canaan celebrated on the field. I came to it and looked to the opposite end zone, where I saw Jim Mulhearn being wheeled up the hill towards the buses by his wife. Without thinking once again, I started slowly jogging past my teammates towards the busses while New Canaan students yelled at me, shoving the loss into my face. I ignored them though, keeping my helmet low and picking up my pace to catch up to Jim before he reached his car.

When I got up to him, I put my hand on his wife's shoulder. She stopped and turned Jim around, who looked straight up at me. I composed myself, and I grabbed his right hand, saying the only thing I could think of at the moment:

"I'm sorry."

Through the little strength he had, he gripped my hand and started to talk. I remember it clear as day, as he said to me, "Don't apologize. Don't be sorry; you have nothing to be sorry for. But I have something to say to you, and that is thank you."

There's a terrible misconception that football players aren't supposed to cry. I was taught that from a young age by my mother, who always told me that football players don't cry. I had lived by that up to that moment, but the minute he said 'thank you,' I lost it. Through a wave of tears, I looked at him and thanked him, leaving him to console the other players heading up after me.

A Farewell, But a New Mission

The ride home from West Haven was dead silent. The occasional sniffle from tears came up, but that was about as loud as it got. Most players just sat in their thoughts, replaying the game over and over in their heads. Christian Trifone sat quietly on the bus, thinking about what had happened, but also thinking about Jim. "In my mind, we let him down. He believed in us, he was there for us, but we fell short. We let him down."

Christian did try to stay positive on the ride home, as his thoughts drifted towards the 2015 season only an hour after the 2014 season had ended. "I felt I had more control (going into 2015), there was only so much in our power when we were juniors. But everything had been building up to our senior year. It was all lining up perfectly."

Arriving back at Darien High School, we carried on the yearly tradition of saying goodbye to the senior players in the gym. Tears of sadness poured through their faces, but all I could think about was the Monday following the game. The only thing that was on my mind was my senior season, and redeeming all that had gone wrong in the state title game. I stood in the gym after saying goodbye in my shoulder pads and jersey, keeping my thoughts to myself while the rest of the team finished their farewells. Afterward, returned our equipment to Trifone in his classroom, where I saw my coach since I was a child with his head up. He looked me straight in the eyes and said, "See you Monday Brit."

On Monday, the material being taught to me in school meant absolutely nothing. I was only thinking about the weight room after and starting my journey to become a starting outside linebacker for the Darien High School football team, while also redeeming the two straight state title losses. I had been dreaming about it since a kid, but a dream only goes so far. I knew that from this point forward, I had to work my ass off, and the 2014 state title loss was the perfect motivation for me to do it.

In the middle of the day during my free period, I went down to the library and logged onto a computer. A couple of minutes later, I printed out a piece of paper with a photo on it. I went down to the dark and empty football weight room, where the door was unlocked. I went inside and stepped up on a bench, taping the piece of paper onto the wall where it was visible to all.

When the final bell at 2:20 pm hit, I went down to the weight room where the 2015 team was gathering. Guys like Timmy Graham, Mark Evanchick, Sam Giorgio, Bobby & Christian Trifone and I, along with a host of others seniors stood in the weight room, awaiting Coach Trifone to make his way down. Trifone entered and looked up, noticing the paper on the wall.

A picture of the scoreboard from the 2014 title game was taped to the wall, with a phrase written across it: "We're

Coming Back." Coach Trifone smiled and delivered one quick sentence.

"It's time to get to work."

We didn't need a pep talk or a motivational message. We knew what we wanted, and we knew it had been building up since elementary school. We were the "Golden Boys," the "Chosen Ones," it was up to us to go undefeated, to go to the state title game, to win the first state championship for Darien since 1996. Anything else would be considered a failure.

I plugged my headphones into my phone and went to work. Playing on my phone was "The Man Comes Around" by Johnny Cash, a song that sent waves of pain, loss and pure motivation. The words of Cash rushed through me, especially the closing line of the song. Using lines from the Book of Revelation, the last book of the Bible that describes the second coming of Jesus through the apocalypse, Cash sings...

> *And I heard a voice in the midst of the four beasts.*
> *And I looked, and behold a pale horse,*
> *And his name that sat on him was Death,*
> *And Hell followed with him*

Time was running out. It was do or die... And we knew it.

PART III

The Road to 2015

"Unfinished Business. That was our motto. We weren't going to let anyone stand in our way of what we wanted to accomplish as a team."

- Timmy Graham on the lead-up to 2015

CHAPTER ELEVEN

A Non-Stop Affair

John Carlozzi

The morning following the 2014 state title loss, John Carlozzi sat quietly during the early hours of the morning in his gym. Unlike the angry, hatred-fueled motivation us players felt, John had a more optimistic and humorous way of dealing with the state title loss. On his phone, John decided to send a few more words of encouragement towards the 2015 football team. Not via a group text or anything like that but instead on Twitter, where he tweeted:

"THE WAVE WILL RISE IN 2015"

For those who were close to Carlozzi, they weren't surprised by the tweet or his mindset. It was those who didn't know Carlozzi that were taken aback by the actions of the strength trainer. If you didn't know John, you saw an extremely quiet individual who would rarely talk to someone about something other than football. Parents would try to converse with him, but they would be met with one-word answers or a conversation that ended before it even got started. From the outside, Carlozzi was a mystery, a magician who was churning out athletes left and right through his extreme knowledge in the field of personal training. That was his image, at least from the perspective of the parents and people who never got a chance to talk to him personally. From a player perspective though, John was a completely different person.

"I mean, John is everything," says Timmy Graham on Carlozzi. "You can ask anyone." Almost all players credit Carlozzi to the reason behind any success they have athletically because of the work he puts them through, including me. His creative workout regiments are unlike any other, and to players, that is what makes him so unique. To go along with that too, Carlozzi isn't just a stereotypical meathead trainer who makes you lift and go home; he is also a great role model and mentor to the players around him. Whether it be lifting at the high school, lifting at Carlozzi's gym or standing on the sideline during practice, John had an impact on us wherever we were.

John Carlozzi had been around Darien High School for a while, with his first experience coming after graduating from Southern Connecticut State University. While working as a coach at a youth soccer camp at Darien High School and then working as a student teacher in Waterbury, Carlozzi was contacted by the Darien High School staff to start helping out after school with athletic treatment from the hours of 3 pm to 5 pm. As time passed, he found himself working the weight room with athletes as well, something that he hadn't thought about as his primary goal in life. While continuing to work with athletes and specifically the football team at Darien High School, Carlozzi came to terms with his passion around the sport of football and high school athletes following a game back in 2008 between Darien and Greenwich. "I remember that game at Darien High School, where Trifone was speaking to the team prior to the game," Carlozzi says. "Greenwich had been the powerhouse for some time, but he told them, 'Greenwich has had their time... Now it's yours.'" Carlozzi watched as the 2008 Blue Wave upset Greenwich 31-25 behind Brian Kosnik's 127 receiving yards along with Nikki Dysenchuk's two touchdowns, seeing the turn of the tides as Darien started to become an FCIAC threat.

Carlozzi continued his work around Darien sports as an athletic trainer, leading up to the first time my teammates and I encountered him in eighth-grade. John was working as an on-field trainer during our home games in DJFL, aiding any players who were injured or in need of assistance may it be through taping or covering up an opened cut. While still working as an athletic trainer, he continued to push towards working more in the weight room where he felt more comfortable. Players began to gravitate alongside Carlozzi, who created a less stressful, more laid back environment which in turn, created better results in the gym. Seeing the change, Trifone started to direct players towards Carlozzi to continue to create a new culture within the Darien High School weight room. It seemed to have worked because by the time we were sophomores in high school in 2013, John was working with the football team and training staff around the clock during the offseason and in-season as well.

The relationships that Carlozzi formed with the players were incredible and started building right off the bat once he began at Darien High School. Players would listen to him carefully, asking his advice on anything that had to do with their lifting program and asking for tips on form and other performance questions. A rapid improvement was seen in the entire program from every single player associated with Carlozzi, which the trainer credits to one thing... Trust. "Everything comes down to trust," Carlozzi says on his relationship with players. "The more they trust in you, the more they will trust in the process as a whole."

Carlozzi, of course, is infamous for his Hell Week conditioning sessions. Players would jokingly tell John to go home or in a more playful sense, to "fuck off" whenever he showed up at the end of an August practice. Carlozzi is a firm believer in cardiovascular health and in conditioning being a major part of a football players life, but also believes that conditioning should be a slow build to create that peak state of health. "For me, conditioning starts as a general physical preparation," says Carlozzi. "It is a build up." Even when players feel as if the first conditioning sessions are the worst, it is just Carlozzi creating a threshold to see how well of shape the players are in going into the season. When he finds that threshold, that is what he works around during the rest of the season. The level of difficulty changes on a weekly basis according to Carlozzi, depending on who the team plays that week and if it is a big game. "I mean, I'm not going to physically test the team when we're playing a weak team," he says. "Now if its the week leading up to New Canaan, I want the team to be in the best shape possible going into that game."

By the time the 2014 season came to an end, John Carlozzi was as crucial to the team than any coach or any player. He wasn't just some trainer in our eyes but also a great role model and person to talk to, someone we could trust to make us better players through physical transformation. Carlozzi believed that as well, not being a huge X's and O's guy but instead living by a mentality he instilled when he first started working with the team. "My job is to present Coach Trifone with talented athletes," he says. "After that, it's my job to make sure they remain talented athletes." His motivation going into 2015 seemed to be just that, although bigger than years prior. Carlozzi had begun working with a lot of us following our eighth-grade year, so he felt a sense of do or die as well. He wanted to give Coach T the best athletes possible, and by the looks of his tweet following the 2014 state title loss, he wasn't going to let any of us down.

* * *

The Prophecy

Although my teammates and I were in the weight room with Carlozzi two days after losing the 2014 state title game, the 2015 season "officially" begins following the annual end of year banquet that the team holds at Woodway Country Club. A celebration of the previous season is a big part of the dinner, but this year was even bigger because we were fitted for our FCIAC Championship rings. It was bittersweet though, knowing we were only one point away from a more prominent, shinier state title ring.

The banquet is a celebration of the prior season, but it is also where the seniors hand the keys over to the juniors almost ceremoniously when the captains are announced for the following season. Sitting at the table with my teammates, all dressed up; we watched as the captains from 2014 approached the podium one by one to address the team for a final time. One speech stuck with us hard, and it was from one of the more humble leaders of the 2014 group. Will Hamernick stood in front of the parents and players and looked directly towards my fellow juniors and me, delivering the prophecy of our class straight to us.

"In 2013, we lost two games. In 2014, we lost one. It's all lined up; in 2015, you will not lose a single game."

I remember listening to that and hearing Bobby Trifone across the table say while smiling, "holy crap."

Yea, holy crap. Talk about pressure and expectations, especially weight and expectations that dwarf those in comparison to 2013 and 2014. Mark Evanchick, who was entering his fourth season with a varsity role, understood and saw the hopes and dreams a mile away. "They were preparing us to go in and set out to accomplish what Trifone has wanted all these years." A state title. An undefeated season, a perfect team.

Even in celebrating an incredible 2014 season, the thoughts of 2015 and the relentless pursuit of our dreams and goals stuck inside our heads, especially mine. My time was running out to live my dream and to do something extraordinary, which in my mind, was making history on this team.

My thoughts were interrupted that night by the ending ceremony at the banquet when Trifone stepped up to announce the senior captains for the next season. I knew I had no chance to become a captain; the standard had been you had to be a starter and an exceptionally well-known player on the team. It had become a popularity contest of sorts, which in turn, created some poor captain choices over the years.

The other odd announcement that was made was the fact that instead of five captains, which again was standard for Darien football, there would be six captains. Immediately after that announcement, you could see some parents at the banquet roll their eyes, knowing what was coming. It was painfully obvious what had just occurred, and everyone was aware of it. Trifone announced the 2015 captains, calling them to the front in the country club dining area. Timmy Graham, Hudson Hamill, Colin Minicus, Mark Evanchick and the choice people saw coming a mile away; Bobby and Christian Trifone.

Christian though, couldn't care less about what people, never mind adults, thought of the situation. It was one of the biggest honors he had received, saying, "Being elected captain by all my peers, that was one of the coolest things to ever happen to me my life. It also told me that guys looked up to me and I wanted to set the example along with the other captains."

He knew that people would talk behind his back, parents and students alike, who believed that he was getting his captainship and playing time just because of his dad being the head coach of the team. I always wondered, how hard was it to live like that, and were there moments where either twin hated having their dad around them through every single football season of their lives? "Honestly, I loved every second of it," says Christian. "Really, the only hard parts were when I started thinking, 'Is he starting me over somebody else because I am his kid? Am I really the guy for the job?' I think that was the hardest part, but it only motivated me to prove myself more."

Following the announcement, the captains understood and took their responsibilities and leadership roles to heart. It meant even more to a guy like Hamill, who was still beating himself up for the botched extra point attempt in the state title game. Hudson's mind was on something different after being named a captain, though. After all the drama, after all that happened in previous years, Hamill knew it was time for a change. The unnecessary off the field trouble players were getting into had to stop, the massive post-game drinking parties had to stop. It all had to stop if we had any chance of fulfilling our destiny, and Hudson was the first to come to terms with that.

"All six of us loved to have fun," says Hamill with a chuckle. "But we all came together and said, 'Nobody on this team is going to put themselves in a situation where they are going to get in trouble, where they are going to hurt the team.'" The other captains hammered down the mentality as well, knowing that they were in control and any blame would fall on us as a senior class. Evanchick saw it clear as day, after all that had happened during 2013 following the drunk driving that caused a senior to lose his captainship.

"We took it extremely seriously," Evanchick remembers. "There had been so many issues in the past, and we were trying to fix our image in a way because of what happened. If one guy screws up, the whole team gets branded as a bunch of hooligans."

Luckily, there wasn't any major drama in the election of the captains within our grade. We knew who the captains would be, and didn't care what parents or other people thought. We all needed to step up as leaders given our status within the team and within the program. We had a goal in mind, and we didn't allow for outside interference to come in and destroy that. It was that precisely, that motivated us as a senior class. On top of the pressures of chasing a state title, of going undefeated and satisfying our coach, we knew that Darien had a bad reputation when it came to off the field issues. We knew all eyes would be on us, mainly due to our status as Trifone's boys.

The Kid Inside

There is no offseason when you play football in Darien, especially when it's the only main sport you play. Guys like Rock Stewart, Spencer Stovall, Mark Evanchick and a few others had winter sports and lacrosse to get ready for, but the rest of us were in the gym day in and day out preparing ourselves for the upcoming season.

The workouts led by Carlozzi were grueling, but it was something that we knew, in the end, was worth it. It was also gratifying being around your teammates three days a week in the gym while developing friendships with underclassmen. It took a while to get comfortable in the role of being a senior leader, but once I got the hang of it, it was a special feeling. Besides the excellent benefits of getting to use weights before underclassmen and being the priority in almost everything, it also allowed for me to mature a little more into an adult, knowing that everything I did alongside my fellow seniors would be watched and noted by the underclassmen.

Our lives weren't all about football during the weeks following the end of the 2014 season though. We were given off days on Tuesdays and Thursdays (along with the weekends) to catch up on school work which was piling up in the winter due to impending midterms. It was quite nice, as many others can attest to. The free time we had after school was incredible, allowing us to study and do work that we never had a chance to do during the season because of how exhausted we were after practices and games. In fact, my grades always went up after football season ended because I had more time and energy to put towards the school work that I otherwise did not have during the fall season.

Alongside the time for more academic focus during the winter, the free time also gave us an opportunity to explore and be a part of activities that we never had the chance to partake in during the fall season. For Sam Giorgio and I, that meant volunteering as coaches for a seventh/eighth-grade recreational boys basketball team at the Darien YMCA. Both Sam and I were the equivalent to a dumpster-fire when it came to our basketball skills, but we saw it as a chance to give back and do something fresh with the status we had as football players.

Our status as players, in fact, did help because the kids we coach would only ask about football stories and everything surrounding the game and high school life. Obviously, we couldn't tell them everything that went on in our lives since they were young kids, but you could see the happiness they got being around high schoolers who also happened to be football players on a wildly successful team. It was also something I took extremely seriously because I was once a kid looking up to high school football players as if they were legends themselves. When I was that kid, I would have killed for someone like Matty Wheelock or Brian Kosnik to coach my basketball team, because they were equivalent to Tom Brady or Antonio Brown to me.

It was tough to live the life I was in, given the academic

expectations from my parents who hounded me with the mentality that I was smarter than my grades, which to me just added more pressure onto my back. Then there was my own pressure of wanting to be socially accepted and wanting to fulfill my dream of being a football star; it amounted to a massive mound of it all weighing down on me from all sides. It sucked, and it eventually started to consume me, especially when I began to experience anxiety and waves of depression here and there.

In reality, all I wanted during that time was to be a kid, which I was. My classmates and I weren't adults; we were 15/16/17-year-olds. We were high schoolers who wanted to do stupid stuff and laugh. It was hard to be that person though with everything that went on, and indeed, we all just needed an escape from that bubble that was bound to burst.

As previously noted, some students and athletes dealt with that pressure by going out on Saturday nights and drinking alcohol with their friends. I was a little different because I dealt with that stress by coaching and being myself around those kids. Sam and I were forced to act super mature and like adults when around the sport of football, and for a 16-year-old, that was draining. Then, when we coached that winter going into our senior year, it gave us a chance to be kids again and to get our immaturity out.

It didn't matter if we sucked (which we did, we were terrible our first year as basketball coaches) since there was a more significant meaning behind it all. The kids were having fun (we played dodgeball during the final 15 minutes of practice) and Sam and I were having fun, which was a rarity among the mountain of pressure that sat on us during that time.

Don't get me wrong, football was still entertaining for me, through weightlifting and socializing with my teammates. I knew it was only going to get more fun as time went on, especially when late January hit. Just a little more than a month after our on-field season had ended at the hands of New Canaan, we were back on the turf by taking part in the indoor "7v7" passing league that was held annually for football programs in the FCIAC at Sono Field House in Norwalk. I was a rookie to 7v7, but from what I had heard, it was a blast. It is exactly what it sounds like, seven players on offense against seven players on defense. No linemen are used, and only passing plays are allowed, resulting in a jam-packed 15-20 minute game that never disappoints.

By the time the first 7v7 session had come around in late January, I had been penciled in as the starting weak side outside linebacker on the defense. Sam Giorgio was the starting inside linebacker, and junior Finlay Collins was the starting strong side outside linebacker. The dream was alive, and I was beyond excited to get out with the starting defense and play alongside them.

The adrenaline was flowing, even in the laid-back setting that was 7v7. On the first drive against Brien McMahon, Sam and I got a swift kick of reality. Getting set for the play, we saw Christian Trifone holding his arms out wide and screaming, "CHECK! CHECK! SKY SKY SKY!" Dumbfounded, Sam and I looked for answers out of each other since we had never been taught the varsity coverages during our time on the junior varsity team. After consulting Christian after a couple of plays, we were caught up and were ready to start playing for real. During the second drive, McMahon set up into a base 2x2 set which was my bread and butter. I dropped into my zone (running Cover 6 coverage), eyes darting from the quarterback to the receivers in my area. I passed a crossing wide out to Sammy G while yelling "IN! IN! IN!" to notify my friend of the incoming route. The remaining receivers ran out of my zone, causing me to drop more in the pass situation. The McMahon quarterback saw his slot cut down after a deep crossing pattern and launched it towards him. Christian Trifone had him locked down and caused a tipped pass, allowing me to dive on the turf to intercept the ball.

Unlike my outburst after my interception against Bassick, I tried to stay professional. Still, on the inside I was a complete emotional mess, holding in the excitement and thrill that had come with once again intercepting a pass. The indoor season could not have gotten off to a better start. I didn't make any mistakes, intercepted a pass, and was pretty conservative on the field. Nothing big, nothing bad, it was what I needed and was looking for. I did what I was told, and it worked.

In the end, I was solidifying myself as a viable linebacker option for Trifone alongside Sam Giorgio. We weren't flashy, we weren't superstars, but we did what the job entailed. It worked, and it felt good. I was closing in on fulfilling my goal of becoming a varsity starter, and all seemed to be going to plan, all until out of nowhere, a familiar face started to appear around the team.

CHAPTER TWELVE

The Fight Goes On

An Unexpected Return

One day in late January while the team was lifting in the private weight room, Coach Trifone wandered into the student weight room across the hall when he thought he recognized someone. He thought it was Mark Schmidt, who had left the team over a year ago. It didn't look like Schmidt, at least from Trifone's eyes. The last time Trifone had seen the former player, he was a little sophomore who had came into his office to tell him he was tired of not contributing and wanted to quit. Now though, Schmidt was bigger. He was standing by the pull-up bar, banging out rep after rep with ease while Trifone watched in awe. It was incredible. Over the course of the year, Schmidt had gone from 5'6 150 pounds to 5'10 170 pounds, going from nobody to somebody in Trifone's eyes.

Stunned, Trifone went over to Sam Giorgio in the other room to talk to him about the new version of Schmidt. He hounded Sam with questions, asking what Schmidt had been doing after quitting football. He then asked Sam if he thought Schmidt would be interested in coming back. Telling Trifone that he would talk to him, Giorgio went back to work, brushing it off at first.

Trifone didn't brush it off and was back talking to Sam about Schmidt only a couple of days later. Giorgio again told Trifone that he would speak with Schmidt, but then a couple of days later, Trifone was asking about Schmidt once again. Day after day, it was the same conversation with Trifone, which Giorgio remembers. "I would be in the weight room every day, and Mark would be there too because he was doing shot put for track and training for baseball. Every week or so, I would get Trifone coming up to me telling me, 'Sam, I really need you to get Schmidt to come back to play next year. He's a monster now.' I remember Trifone made it not just his but made it *my* personal mission to get Mark to come back for our senior year."

Sam went back and forth with Schmidt about it, but initially, Mark didn't take it seriously or to heart. Schmidt instead just made it as a friendly conversation with Sam and was not considering it as a serious issue until Trifone came up to him. "What it really came down to was the same reason why I quit in the first place," says Schmidt. "If I could make an impact and actually contribute to the team, I would then consider coming back."

Finally, in February, Trifone decided to confront Schmidt with a serious proposition in hoping to regain the now promising athlete onto his team. "I remember he walked up to me and said, 'Schmidt, you're looking pretty big, I think we need you on the team this year, would you consider coming back?' I looked at him and said, 'Yea, if you think that you need me, then I'll be back.' From that moment on, I realized that I was significantly larger than I was before and that I could actually play." Just like that, Trifone had done the equivalent of signing a five-star recruit to his team. Watching Schmidt on the baseball field and by watching him in general, you could see the talent and raw athleticism. He could be plugged in at any position on either side of the ball and would make an immediate impact.

Unfortunately for me, Trifone decided that Schmidt would best fit as a linebacker. Not just any linebacker, but at outside linebacker. Schmidt arrived at 7v7 later that week with a big smile on his face; holding his cleats in his hands while slapping hands with his old teammates. He grabbed a football and started to throw it around, showing flashes of potential by snagging one-handed catches with little to no effort. Hopping up and down, his vertical was already proving to be absurd, and we hadn't even started playing yet.

Schmidt sat out the first couple of defensive drives to watch Finlay Collins and I play outside linebacker so that he could slowly pick up the defensive schemes we were running. When Schmidt finally stepped onto the field for the first time in over a year, it was all but confirmed that he was the next big thing on the Darien defense. Mark was flashier than anyone else on the field, with speed and agility that was almost unheard of for a linebacker of his size. He was quick to the ball, storming down the field towards any routes that were his responsibility. He didn't even need to learn the defense, because it came to him naturally.

It wasn't a surprise, since Schmidt's love for football did not disappear after he quit following the 2013 season. Schmidt was an NFL fanatic and a New York Giants super-fan, going all the way to naming his dog after Giants legendary running back, Tiki Barber. He dominated in fantasy football, knew NFL offensive/defensive strategies by heart, and was probably the most talented Madden player at Darien High School. It's safe to say that Schmidt's football IQ was off the charts as well. He picked up right where he left off during the 2013 season when on the 7v7 sideline, predicting what each team was doing just by looking at their formation.

By the end of that session, you could see that Trifone had

won the jackpot by luring Schmidt back to the game of football; Schmidt was a bonafide star. Not only that, but he was a playmaker, a star personality to build around, a flashy player who you could point out after every play. The team needed that, and Trifone had found his guy.

It could have been tough for me, because within a couple of weeks, the security that I felt of being a sure thing starter was out the window, although hope was not even close to being dead. Even with Schmidt's return, I remained pleased with my spot on the team and role on the defense. I still had a chance to become a contributing linebacker, even a starter, but would have to work harder than before to achieve that goal.

The Approaching Season

By the time March had come around, guys like Colin Minicus, Hudson Hamill, Mark Evanchick and the Trifone twins were beginning their spring season for lacrosse. At this point, the football weight room had become almost empty, save for a few guys like myself, Sam Giorgio, Timmy Graham and Spencer Stovall, who had just returned from wrestling season. Stovall, who had dropped from 250 to 220 pounds for wrestling season, was tasked with regaining the weight before spring football started in a couple of months. Alongside that, a lack of captains caused guys like Stovall to step up into leadership roles, primarily due to the influx of juniors like Division-I prospect Andrew Stueber and Brian Keating who were rising stars within the program.

The mood inside the weight room began to take a more serious tone too due to the coming season closing in on us. Timmy Graham would sit quietly after each of his sets, lost in his thoughts. There was only one thing on his mind, the 2014 state title loss, where he had three interceptions in a game he knew he could have won. He didn't need to look back at the game film to understand that, in fact, he never actually did see the game film from that day, not wanting to relive the blown lead. "I never went back to that game, never watched the film," says Graham on the situation. "It was a motivating factor. After 2013 where we said, 'were never going to let this happen again,' after that loss, it was more of 'this better not happen ever again.'"

Avenging that loss was all that mattered to Timmy, and was his top priority heading into his senior year. Even with all the recruiting he was going through during the spring, the 2015 season was the only thing that seemed to be on his mind. You could see the drive in Timmy's eyes through 7v7 sessions during the winter and leading into the spring. He took each and every scrimmage like it was the state title game, making precise passes to his receivers and scolding himself at the slightest mistake. He, like every other rising senior on that team, was chasing what appeared to be impossible, and that's perfection. Graham reiterates that by saying, "Going into my senior year, my mindset was I was going to do everything I could to win the state championship for the town of Darien."

I drove myself to that point as well, doing whatever I could to get the team to the level it needed to be at, especially when I realized how much stronger I was getting in the weight room. At the end of my sophomore season in 2013, I was barely able to put up 160 pounds on the bench press. By the time March of 2015 arrived, I was pushing close to 260 pounds on the bench. I had put on nearly 10 pounds as well, putting myself to around 185 pounds on my 6'3 frame. Sam Giorgio felt the effects of Carlozzi as well in the weight room, going from a 225-pound squat to a 365-pound squat in a matter of months.

The success in the weight room was almost the equivalent to the success you feel on the field after a big play or win. It was addicting seeing your bench press numbers go up and seeing them posted on the walls of the weight room. You wanted more of it; you wanted to get stronger because it felt terrific. Leading into spring football, I had felt the best I had ever felt in my life, due to the work Carlozzi was doing with my teammates and I. It was really paying off as well, since I could feel myself playing better on the field during 7v7 and could feel my legs working harder and faster during those sessions.

The weight room was also a necessary escape for me. As a junior in high school, I was being pushed left and right to get my college applications done while maintaining high grades at the same time. It was an incredible amount of stress, so for me, I needed a place to let loose and release. The weight room was that place after coaching had ended for Sam and me, and it's a beautiful place to release, given that you physically exert yourself and can use stress and anger as motivators. It's an awesome feeling, one that was honestly the best way for me to deal with stress and pressure during that time.

From an emotional standpoint too, It was during this time when feelings of senior year began to hit myself and my teammates included. It took a while to get acclimated to being on top of the team and felt weird at events where we were the oldest guys on the team, only two years removed from being the bottom feeders who were cleaning up after seniors. It was weird at first, but you had to embrace it, and once you did, you saw the more significant meaning behind being an older guy on a team made up of mostly younger talent.

I hated that feeling as a sophomore of being a bottom feeder to the senior class, so I made it part of my mission to make sure that I didn't treat any of our sophomores that way since, in reality, the treatment of sophomore students is why we lost so many back in 2013. I first really clung to that ideal during the annual Blue Wave Football car wash fundraiser in early May, when that is in actuality the first time the team is gathered together, oddly enough at a car wash event. Sam and I didn't want to play the role of the jerk senior jocks who were "too cool" for the underclassmen, and you could see that as well with the captains. We didn't stick together as one group, but instead during the event worked alongside younger guys (even freshman who had shown up), to make sure they felt like they were a part of the team. Mark Schmidt took it personally as well, wanting to right the wrong he had felt as a sophomore by reaching out to the younger guys and making them feel regular around us.

We easily could have gone down that route of being "too cool" for the younger guys, but that was not who we were as people. Specifically guys like Sam, Mark and I, we struggled as sophomores to connect with the seniors and did not feel as if we were part of the team during that time. We wanted that to change, and we wanted to be role models; not people that underclassmen hated and despised. This mentality stuck hard with Giorgio especially, after years of mistreatment and after spending his junior year tirelessly making sure the sophomores below him didn't give up on themselves.

Being Sammy

The music of Bruce Springsteen jumped through Sam Giorgio's body as he walked through the halls of Darien High School on his way to his next class. Springsteen resonated with Giorgio, which is one of the many things that made Sam different than his classmates. Ever since a young age when his dad introduced Springsteen's music to Sam, the messages of his songs motivated him and helped keep him balanced through his days.

Baby this town rips the bones from your back,
It's a death trap; it's a suicide rap

We gotta get out while we're young
'Cause tramps like us, baby we were born to run

Walking down the halls, Giorgio remembers a confrontation he had with a coach during the freshman football season. The coach, who saw Giorgio as an undersized, un-athletic player, told the young Giorgio that he would never play varsity football in his life. Sure, he could be on the team, but he wouldn't touch the field as a varsity starter, ever. "You're just not big enough," he said to Giorgio. "It's the truth."

It had been two full seasons since Sam Giorgio had joined the Darien High School varsity football team, and it seemed as if the words of his former coach were beginning to become true. Following his sophomore season, he was an afterthought. Now following his junior season, it seemed as if the coaching staff was forced to give him a chance since he was the only returning inside linebacker. It was just the way it was, which Giorgio understood.

There just wasn't anything spectacular or relatable about Sam, especially in a town like Darien. Outside of football, he was one of the few people in the school who listened to a guy like Springsteen, waltzed to the music of Frank Sinatra and pondered the poetic lyrics of Bob Dylan in the early 1960's. It wasn't only his musical choice, since he also was an avid filmgoer, with his favorites spanning from *Casablanca* all the way to his admiration of Liam Neeson in the Academy Award-winning film, *Schindler's List*. Don't even get him started on Robert De Niro and Ray Liotta in *Goodfellas*, or Orson Welles' superb directing and acting in the iconic 1941 film, *Citizen Kane*. He was barely 17 years old, yet unlike any of his other teammates, he could recite the words of Marlon Brando's iconic speech in one of the opening scenes of *The Godfather*.

* * *

"Now you come and say 'Don Corleone, give me justice.' But you don't ask with respect. You don't offer friendship. You don't even think to call me 'Godfather.' Instead, you come into my house on the day my daughter is to be married, and you ask me to do murder - for money."

Off the field, he was different. On the field, he was different. He wasn't being marketed as the next big thing on the Darien defense; he wasn't up on the level of Mark Evanchick concerning star power, he wasn't even considered a key player on the team. Undersized and underrated, Giorgio was once again used to this role, especially after being practically ignored his entire junior year when he was "demoted" to the junior varsity team. On top of all this, Mark Schmidt was back and being groomed to take over the entire defense.

It was not negative, because the return of Schmidt was a personal and social victory for guys like Sam Giorgio and I. Mark was one of our best friends, and having him rejoin the team while also joining the linebacker group was fantastic. The return of Schmidt seemed to have a small effect on Sam, one that you would not have noticed if you did not know him. He was used to it all. When things were appearing to be going Sam's way, the return of Mark began to overshadow the hard working Giorgio, who had gone through hell and back in to get where he wanted to be. Years spent getting physically battered on the scout team, offseason's spent working countless hours in the gym with Carlozzi, and all of a sudden, it's almost all ignored after Mark's return to the team.

At this point too, Giorgio wasn't guaranteed a starting job, since Trifone was looking at other options outside of his senior. It didn't help that Giorgio was also a rugby player in the spring, something a lot of coaches did not agree with. "It's a dangerous sport," they would tell Giorgio. "If you get hurt, you're done." His commitment to his spring sport caused him to miss an occasional lifting session or 7v7 practice, which coaches didn't take kindly to in the beginning.

It also didn't help that behind Giorgio was rising sophomore Nick Green; someone Coach Trifone had his eye on from the beginning of the offseason. Green, like Schmidt, was a flashier player who had a deadly combination of speed and strength at only 15 years of age. Of course, this would happen, because why wouldn't it? Nothing came easy for Giorgio, but again, he was used to it. It didn't anger him, it didn't motivate him, but instead, it was just there, because he already had a truckload of motivation surrounding him at all times. The legacy of his name stayed with him whenever he was around football, wanting to fix his brother's image and create something out of his family in the Darien program.

Even through the hard work, all of Giorgio's hard work seemed to go unnoticed, even in the eyes of Christian Trifone and Coach T. "Towards the end of our junior season, we'd go home (Bobby, Christian, and Coach Trifone) and talk about who is good and who would be starters, and we started talking about linebackers," Christian recalls. "And Sammy really wasn't ever considered, he was undersized and I didn't know if he wanted it bad enough." Over time though, it became obvious to the captains, especially Christian, that something special was brewing inside of Giorgio. "Sure enough, he started working out like crazy. One day, I said to my dad, 'Hey, have you seen Sammy lately? He's killing it in the weight room.' Carlozzi would tell me the same thing, about how Sammy was putting in the work and how he had potential to be a strong linebacker."

Carlozzi saw the untapped potential in Giorgio and believed in the linebacker from the first day Giorgio talked to John about lifting. "I was going to make Sam the best athlete he could be," says Carlozzi on Giorgio. "And he took off and ran with everything I gave him." Hours with Carlozzi in the weight room started paying off big time, even if Coach T or others were not noticing the results immediately. It didn't surprise Sam; that was just the way things worked in the program in his eyes.

Giorgio knew he wasn't the flashy type, and knew guys like Schmidt and Green were more athletic and better playmakers than him. He understood that he couldn't match them in those regards, but Sam goes back to a conversation that he had with Coach Forget that stuck with him. Forget had always been a firm believer in Giorgio from day one, seeing the potential and heart in the young linebacker that he had only rarely seen before. Talking with Giorgio, Forget told him, "If you don't do your job, you let ten other people on that field down, including yourself and including me."

Giorgio took that lesson and anchored his mentality down. It wasn't about being flashy; it wasn't about getting the most interceptions or scoring touchdowns, it was about one straightforward thing; doing his job. That's all that mattered to Giorgio, and he reminded himself of it almost every day. "Maybe others could go out there and do flashy stuff and still be good football players," says Giorgio. "But for me, I needed to be focused; I needed to be in the zone, I needed to be thinking about the play at the moment. I go out there, and it's another day in the office where I am doing my job."

It was easy to get behind Sam as a leader too, mainly when the other two senior linebackers in Schmidt and I were extremely immature around each other. Sam, on the other hand, was all business on the field, saving his "Three Musketeers" persona for after practice with Schmidt and I. Sam was just a natural leader because of his underdog lifestyle and hard as nails work ethic. Younger guys saw someone like Sam, who wasn't athletically gifted but was still in the hunt to be a starting linebacker as motivation. If someone as undersized as Sam could push himself to the limit, why couldn't others?

The reappearance of Schmidt did nothing to Sam because he had grown almost immune to change at this point. Football had hardened him on the outside into a tough, gritty person who wasn't afraid of any challenge. The fearful young third-grader who was contemplating quitting? That version of Sam Giorgio didn't exist anymore. There was only the underdog Sam Giorgio now, no matter what happened. He could get a Division-I scholarship, be a five-star recruit; it didn't matter though, he was the underdog. That's just how he was built.

Undersized, unappreciated and overlooked. That's Sam Giorgio, but he didn't care. He embraced it and reminded himself of it at every chance he got. One night, up in Giorgio's movie room in his house, I sat with him as we watched a favorite of ours, *Rocky*. Giorgio related heavily to the story of the underdog boxer because Sammy G was pretty much, in a sense, the "Italian Stallion." He wasn't supposed to be where he was, yet somehow, he was. Watching the film, Giorgio became laser-focused near the end, when Balboa is in the midst of his heavyweight title fight with Apollo Creed. Rocky pushed hard to make it all the way to the end of the 15th round, wanting to "go the distance" to prove himself. On the screen, Creed knocked down Balboa late in the 14th, signifying the end of the fight in his mind. Rocky's trainer agrees, yelling at the fighter to stay down and stop the beating he was taking. Giorgio watched the scene that he had watched hundreds of times before, where Rocky ignores the pleas of his trainer and gets up at a nine count to the shock of everyone, including Creed.

Giorgio's face doesn't change throughout the entire sequence. Inside, a fire builds within him. Win or lose, Giorgio didn't care. All he wanted was to prove the coaches and the doubters wrong. All he wanted was a chance. All he wanted was to go the distance.

That's Sam Giorgio.

*Sam Giorgio, Mark Schmidt and rising sophomores Alex Dehmel
and Kevin Grune at a 7v7 scrimmage (April 27ᵗʰ, 2015)*

*Colin Minicus and Mark Evanchick at the annual Blue Wave
Football Car Wash (May 17ᵗʰ, 2015)*

Rock Stewart, Spencer Stovall, Mark Evanchick, Shelby Grant, &
me at the annual Blue Wave Football Car Wash (May 17th, 2015)

Hudson Hamill, Christian Trifone, Coach Trifone, & Colin Minicus
share a laugh at a 7v7 scrimmage (June 7th, 2015)

CHAPTER THIRTEEN

Why We Play

Fun, Fun, Fun

There is nothing more fascinating, followed by the action on the field, then listening to and watching fans and parents in the crowd on a Saturday afternoon at Darien High School. Loud and supportive most of the time, there are instances where parents will yell from their seats, critiquing a play or moment in the game which they disagree on. Sometimes, they'll openly criticize their child after a play, embarrassed by how it happened. That's normal in football anywhere, but there's something different in a town like Darien.

I remember during the 2014 season, spending most of my time looking up into the stands during moments of despair after our team had made a mistake. The father of the player who made the error would hang their head and clap in frustration, embarrassed that it was their kid who messed up. A more clear memory was standing on the sideline during the FCIAC Championship while we were down 21-7. Fans would scream at Trifone, telling him he should do this or that, sometimes berating him with insults about how he was driving the program into the ground. There stood Trifone, ignoring everything thrown at him, just focused on the game in front of him.

Trifone had no choice but to ignore the fans. He was used to it. In a town like Darien, in the age we are in today, parents continuously have their eyes on coaches and assistants alike, which is something almost all coaches in town are not strangers to. In 2012, Lisa Lindley, the head girls lacrosse coach, was the center of attention following an incident where she grabbed a players helmet and scolded her for a mistake.[1] She was suspended for the remainder of the lacrosse season, while the town went back and forth on the issue. To this day, the incident casts an overwhelming shadow over the wildly successful coach, who's one simple "mistake" in people's eyes has overshadowed her positive work and accomplishments within the community.

The incident proved to be a mistake on the part of the Lindley, and understandably. Physical contact with a student-athlete should always be held to a minimum, and should only be used in extreme situations, but even then in limited levels. The argument can be made that these incidents go back to the idea of pressure being on athletes who consider playing a sport in high school a job, and even the slightest mistake results in a lecture or punishment. To be a successful program, any coach will tell you that discipline and action after errors is a must in developing the said program.

But that's precisely the point that comes to question when looking at it in a broader sense. Where are the limitations in adults coaching, especially around a younger age in youth leagues and leading into high school? Where is the line drawn in coaching for success against coaching to make sure the kids have fun while playing their sports, especially with parents watching every move?

In 2010, Darien resident Peter Barston and his brother Stephen embarked on a mission to find out the real reason why kids in a town like Darien played sports. Going through the majority of the youth leagues in town, Barston surveyed kids in fourth-grade through eighth-grade asking why they played the sports they played. The options ranged from "to have fun, to make friends" all the way to "to win, to earn a college scholarship," listing 11 options for the kids to choose from. After surveying about 255 players in the Darien Junior Football League (DJFL), Barston found that the results were overwhelmingly pushing to one side:

"To have fun" won by a landslide. In second place was "to do something I'm good at," followed by "to improve my skills." The option "Winning" didn't even get near the top 10.

Barston saw with the results came a simple message. "It shows kids are out there to get away from their lives and have a good time with their friends. They're not out there just to win."[2]

The results of Barston's survey should have served as a wake-up call in the community, but they were relatively overlooked after receiving public attention for a little bit. It is worth revisiting though because the competitiveness in Darien has only grown, mostly due to the rising popularity and success of the towns high school sports programs. As kids, growing up and watching high school athletes play was equivalent to watching professionals play. It was better in my opinion because the high schoolers wore the same colors and name that we did when we played youth football. We wanted to be like them, whether we knew what it entailed or not.

Even when dreaming of becoming a superstar, the real reason for playing was rooted in one simple word: fun. From fourth through eighth-grade in DJFL, I was always wanting to win a championship and was devastated whenever I lost, but the game was still fun, which is why I kept playing. Being on the field with friends every night during practice, getting to run around and call yourself a football player, playing games on Saturday nights, it was fun. Guys like Timmy

Graham, Hudson Hamill, and Colin Minicus all can agree with that, citing that they played football strictly because of how much fun it is. "It's always been fun, and it always will be fun," says Graham. "It's what gets me through the school day, knowing that I've got football practice. It doesn't matter what it was; football has always been fun."

In fact, the danger of youth sports has nothing to do with the kids, but more in the parents who live through their kids on the field. Especially in Darien, there appears to be a sense of entitlement from some parents who think that their kid is the best, and should be playing more than anyone else on the team. It sometimes reaches extremes, where parents coach their kids from the stands, forcing a young child to choose between listening to their actual coach or their parents. Naturally, they are going to pick their parent, because that's how the mind of a young child works. It doesn't seem to affect them immediately, but down the road, it can lead to disastrous results of a child leaning too much or complaining to their parents to fix a problem they are having on the sports field.

The problem with parental interference on the field has grown over the years, all the way from email complaints to storming onto the field to confront the coach about why their son isn't playing. It isn't anything new, but more or less has become somewhat of a norm in a town like Darien. When it happens, everyone watches it unfold like it's an everyday part of the game.

The danger in too much parental involvement comes down on parents who are coaching as well. In the DJFL along with other youth leagues in Fairfield County, there have been countless issues in which coaches purposely sit a player out to ensure their team gets a victory. Instead of playing a 12-year-old child in a game, you get a 40-year-old father benching him because he won't help the team win in what is really a meaningless game. In these situations, it is when the program loses what could be a talented young player who's love for the game has been tarnished because of the ego of a father who is obsessed with winning a youth football game.

Even adults like John Carlozzi see the sometimes insane measures that parents might go to in order to make sure that their child gets ahead of everyone else. Carlozzi has gotten calls over the years from parents trying to get their 11-year-old child involved in weight training since Carlozzi has been known for creating star athletes. Carlozzi, seeing the danger in the situations, has turned down offer after offer. "I get parents calling into the gym all the time, saying that they want their kid to run, you know, a 4.2 (second) 40-yard dash," Carlozzi says. "I respond, telling them to call me in two years and that in the meantime, have your child ride a bicycle and shoot a basketball in the driveway because that is what normal 11-year-old athletes do."

For someone like Mark Schmidt, he looks back and sees the effects some parents had on his development as a football player and person; specifically, when it came to the New Canaan rivalry. "Darien football conditioned me to hate New Canaan from such a young age. And I mean not just beat them and win, but I mean, I *hated* them. When I tackled them, I wouldn't just tackle them and get up. If I had a free shot, I was punching them after the play was over, and this was me at only 11 years old. I was taught by my coaches to hate them for no reason; it's honestly terrifying."

One former Darien High School football player in an anonymous survey put the parental issues at the forefront of his struggles when playing the game. Stating that he felt the most pressure from his parents when playing, he writes, "As a kid, they were constantly talking about football all the time, like as if I was expected to be good automatically. It's hard to live up to that as a kid and into the high school years."

It appears as if parents in and around Darien will do anything for their child to get an advantage, which is something that eventually leads back to attacks on coaches because of limited individual success. Lisa Lindley, who after enduring all the drama back in 2012, still has trouble today with parental interference. Appearing on *The Ruden Report* podcast, Lindley spoke of difficulties that she experienced during one lacrosse season. "What happened was prior to the start of (one) season, an anonymous letter was written about me," Lindley said on the podcast. "It was filled with complete lies and (was) attacking my character and my morals. Frankly, it was totally mean-spirited, and nothing in it was proved to be correct." Through it all, the reasoning behind it seemed pretty evident to Lindley. "The letter was written, I truly believe, because people were unhappy with their kids not getting national recognition or postseason awards," Lindley continued on the show. "It went beyond playing time. It was more about bragging rights. It's really unfortunate, but that's our situation here in Darien. It's not about playing time; it's about being the best player on the team, it's about making All-American. It's more about the individual accolades than playing for the Blue Wave."[3]

Lindley continued to talk about the issue, pointing at a glaring problem that has seemingly been shoved under the rug in and around Darien. "They want a coach that they can influence," Lindley stated. "And I'm not one of those coaches. So that creates a lot of friction because I'm always going to be truthful and honest; and parents and kids alike are not ready to hear the truth, certainly when it's about someone's ability."

Not everyone, however, goes down that path. Rock Stewart had a different experience than most in town. Afraid of how some parents acted around their children and coaches on the sports field, Stewart went down a separate path to avoid any drama. "I partially chose my sports because I knew my parents didn't know anything about them," Stewart says. "They would ask me from time to time if I wanted them to do anything (to help). I saw how some of the parents in our grade acted and told them, 'No, I don't want you to be like that.'"

Even though parental interference and issues had always been going on in Darien and other communities, it gained national attention back in 2011 when my teammates and I were eighth-grade football players. Our league was made up of two fantasy tiers at the time; New Canaan was on the first tier, every other team was on the second tier. New Canaan was unstoppable. They were undefeated for consecutive years, dominating us and other teams in our league by blowout scores that were embarrassing to look at. It wasn't fun playing New Canaan, because their team was run like a military group. Parents allegedly reported that coaches on the team were emailing them in advance to tell them that their son should not come to the game because it was against a tougher opponent, and they needed to play the best players possible.

When we beat them on that late October night on their home turf, their coaches were livid throughout the game, shouting and berating the refs after each call that went against New Canaan. In the handshake line after calling our coach an "Asshole," it was as if the New Canaan coaches had just lost the Super Bowl; yet these were 13-year-olds.

A couple of weeks later, we played the same New Canaan team in the league championship. Their coach was foaming at the mouth at the chance of revenge, once again, against a bunch of 13-year-old kids. The day didn't go as planned for him though since we dominated and walked away with another stunning victory. Devastated and ashamed, their coaches walked off the field.

That wasn't the end, unfortunately. At the end of the year

team party for the New Canaan eighth-graders, the coaches took the players to a park and encouraged them to throw their runner-up trophies into a pile. The coaches then covered the awards in gasoline and lit them on fire, burning away the failure of their two-loss season in front of a group of eighth-grade children. The actions of the adult coaches caused an understandable uproar, forcing the coaches to resign from the league board and resulting in their immediate suspension from coaching youth football.[4]

Rod Fox, identified as the head coach when the story went national, explained his actions in a statement released following the incident. "Our point was to flush away the disappointment of the team's last game and move on and not dwell on it any further," wrote Fox. "This was an exceptional group of kids who were very successful. It is unfortunate that this event is clouding the great accomplishments of these young men." It is unfortunate that he forgot one thing as well…

The kids were 13.

Where's the Line?

On the DJFL website, the mission statement reads:

"The overall objective of the DJFL program is to provide a positive introductory and development experience in the sport of football for all its participants. The ultimate goal of the program is to stimulate and develop the potential and passion of each-and-every football player in the program."

The statement is short but gets to the point. Without directly using the word fun, the statement gets the idea across of creating a love for the game of football and refuses to mention success, winning, or championships. It instills the ideals of the program, and shoes away any person who believes that championships and glory should be chased during the years of youth development.

The mission statement holds true in even the most extraordinary set of circumstances, including the times I played while being coached by Trifone during my youth years. In the kids' eyes, including that of Colin Minicus, being coached by Trifone was different, something Minicus reiterates years after. "I always thought having the privilege of having Coach Trifone was really beneficial for us because it gave us a way to transfer going to youth football to high school football very smoothly."

Trifone looks back and sees the idea of coaching us from such a young age differently. He was not concerned about us being talented and state title contenders but was worried about something else. "There was no question we had a lot of talent," Trifone says, looking back nearly a decade. "But one of my main goals was not so much focused on making this a state championship team, but to make sure that (you guys) loved football, and that I didn't lose (you guys) to lacrosse and other sports, because it would have been very easy for (some guys) to do that."

When I was in DJFL, it was tough for parents to get angry or mad at Trifone for the way he was coaching, because he knew what he was doing, and everyone was aware of that. His concern wasn't going undefeated and leading a group of fourth-graders to a championship, but more or less creating an atmosphere where football was enjoyable and something we would stick with going to the high school. Thomas Mercein, who coached alongside Trifone during our DJFL years, agrees with that ideal. "Our job was to get as many (players) to the high school program as possible," says Mercein. "That was it."

It was easy to trust Trifone and his process, indeed because of his status within the town and the success he had at the beginning of his high school tenure. While I was in third/ fourth-grade though, upper classes in the DJFL system were continuing to struggle with parental interference, leading to one coach to create a set of rules and mentality that set the standard going forward.

Guy Wisinski coached in the DJFL for years during the 2000s, becoming a vital member of the DJFL Board during that time as well. Over the years of coaching, Wisinski has had plenty of run-ins with parents of players who were wondering about why their son wasn't playing the entire game, or why they weren't playing a particular position. Over and over again, parents and even other assistant coaches tirelessly approached him, and would cause a scene on the field. Wisinski even remembers one time, an assistant coach openly called a fourth-grader a "pussy" right in front of the kid, causing Wisinski to lose his mind at the coach. Incidents like these were pushing him to the edge, which finally resulted in a drastic but effective measure to ensure the madness stopped.

Before the start of a season one year, Wisinski called a meeting with all the parents of his players. It was then when he introduced what he called the "Asshole Rule," which explains itself pretty clearly. "It was pretty simple. If a parent was an asshole, yelling or creating a scene, we would pull their son from the game and send him home. It shut the parents up pretty quickly," says Wisinski.

The new rule worked like a charm, allowing Wisinski to coach freely without distractions. After introducing the "Asshole Rule" to the parents, Wisinski then decided to add a new mantra and lifestyle to the kids he was coaching. The two-word phrase spoke a million words, especially to a group of youth players:

No Punks.

Printing the phrase on stickers and using it any way he could, Wisinski drove the "No Punks" mentality hard into the kids all the way to the point that when they were seniors in the fall of 2011, they were effectively known as the "No Punks Class of 2012" around the program.

Wisinski didn't want any egotistical, self-centered players who cared more about the individual than the team. He drove home the idea always to be good sportsmen and to still show great respect to the referees and other coaches in any situation. It worked, and even though the team didn't win championships, the players came out of it with a lesson of good manners and good sportsmanship, which made Wisinski extremely proud of them.

Still, there were moments where what he was trying to avoid overtook him. He remembers one of his biggest regrets in coaching when his son made consecutive mistakes during practice. Upset, he sent his son to "run the stairs" to set an example for the other kids. Turning his back to his son to pay attention to the drills on the field, a fellow coach approached Wisinski and whispered, "Hey Guy, you're being an asshole."

Realizing that he had broken his own rule, Wisinski pulled his son to the side and apologized. He put his son back out onto the field, vowing never to let his competitiveness get in the way of his son having fun on the field again.

There wasn't any glory or championship success during Wisinski's tenure as a DJFL coach, but there was a personal success in creating a strong-minded group of young men who took lessons off the field into their lives. The class that Wisinski coached went on to be wildly successful at the high school level, winning an FCIAC Championship their junior year in 2010, and putting together a strong season in 2011 as well.

There comes a question too in Darien, especially when parents coach teams, about the line drawn between having fun and winning games. Trifone understands that line as well, seeing the perspective from both sides. "There's a fine line between having fun and winning/having fun and losing.

Winning is fun, and losing is not. In my mind, I wanted to build a program from the DJFL on up that was fun, but was disciplined enough so that we could win," Trifone says. "I knew success was going to breed success."

Timmy Graham looks at it similarly, saying that "I didn't care if I lost a football game in fourth-grade. Now an eighth-grade football loss? That is when it hurt. But in the beginning, it was about having fun, yet once we reached eighth-grade, we knew we had to start winning."

This ideal doesn't just come from Trifone or Graham but is shared in the DJFL, even today. Andy Von Kennel, a father of two in Darien who has spent years coaching in the DJFL system, is gearing up for his final year coaching his son in the upcoming eighth-grade season.

Von Kennel had a different upbringing than most in Darien, growing up in the heart of Texas while playing for Dallas Jesuit and genuinely experiencing Friday night lights during the heyday of high school football. Living through cortisone shots to play through pain, all the way to concussions he never even had diagnosed, Von Kennel has seen it all from a football standpoint. When arriving in Darien though, he saw a similar passion to the game when coaching that he saw when growing up. "I love watching how these boys want the sweatshirts and wear them with pride. They are so 'Blue Wave'; it's beautiful, humorous and probably disgusting, depending on the eye of the beholder," says Von Kennel.

Fun, like the mindset of Trifone and Wisinski, has always been the primary goal for Von Kennel. He never wanted to force the game that he loved onto his son but instead let him pick and choose the things he found interest in. Von Kennel believes in that mentality firmly, saying, "I look at my son and say, 'I don't care what you play, I don't care what you do, I just care that whatever you are doing, you are all in and that

I'm here to support you."

Like Mercein as well, Von Kennel feels the need to get as many players to the high school as possible, and then let the process of elimination occur to separate the men from the boys essentially. But like Trifone said, success was going to breed success, and for that to happen, the boys that Von Kennel coach needed to taste success.

Success though, was "MIA" in the grade that Von Kennel leads. The struggle has been persistent over the years, and Von Kennel seems to understand maybe why the struggles for success have been so consistent. "They need to learn how to win," says Von Kennel. "They need to learn how to play together because that's going to matter down the road." He continues, saying, "There is this assumption (from the kids) that 'we're going to be awesome because we live here (in Darien).' No, you have to work hard, you have to play together, and you have to learn to win together."

As Trifone said, there is a fine line between the idea of having fun but the idea of competing and winning. The problem is this, where do we place the line? In an affluent town like Darien, surrounded almost by a bubble, do we create an atmosphere of winning being what makes football fun, or do we stick to the idealism of it being fun no matter what? Eight years after Peter Barston's survey, the results remain relevant. Out of a group of DJFL players surveyed about the reason behind playing football, "To have fun" dominated the polls.

Fun, however, seems to slowly be taking a backseat to the dreams and expectations of the town itself. Pressure comes from all angles, with one youth player saying in a survey, "I feel the most pressure from the grade above me," he writes. "I feel like I am letting them down when I don't succeed."

For one rising eighth-grade football player, the sole reason behind playing football is the idea of it being fun. He, however, at a young age, sees the danger in adults living through their kids and the pressures that come with being an athlete in Darien. "It's just a bad culture, the 'try-hard' mentality in town is so stupid," he says at 13 years old. "I honestly feel pressure the most because of the need to win; especially in this town where people are so used to winning that they don't realize that losing is a possibility." In his mind, the pressures of winning don't affect him too much now, although it has instilled in him a fear of what will happen down the road. "It's still fun because we don't worry about it too much in our youth years," he continues. "If we aren't winning enough now though, I think it is in the back of all of our heads about what will happen once we get to the high school."

The youth years are the least stressful, the most carefree out of any year playing football, or at least they should be. As Timmy Graham said, there seems to be a turning point where the game is still fun, but it turns into a job and less of an activity; whether that is controlled by the players or adults around it. Is the game still fun? Of course, but there's more to it now. As the pressures creep up to younger ages in town (evident by the rising eighth-grade player), the reality becomes this: There are expectations to live up to; scholarships to obtain; championships to chase. Anything else is below the standard.

Will this all ever change? It is difficult to say. If anything, one thing is known in all this. In the words of Elise Dardani…

It's all quite obvious, but it is really hard to change a culture.

CHAPTER FOURTEEN

The Boys of Summer

One Final "Spring"

After pushing ourselves through college applications, finishing SAT/ACTs; we were given the gift of ten days of spring football; although spring football in June is honestly summer football, but who cares? Spring football was a reward for all our hard work in the classroom, a chance for us to go out for the first time officially as a team before the start of the preseason in August.

Spring football had become sort of a circus act for me during my first two years, since I entered 2013 as a lineman, entered 2014 as a wide receiver, and was now entering 2015 as a linebacker. This year felt different though because I knew I had an opportunity to contribute and compete for a spot on the starting defense, something the previous two years I had zero chance of doing. This spring I had a role, an opportunity to contribute, which in turn made the lead up to the practices enjoyable for me.

Standing around waiting for practice to begin, I went up to the student managers to confirm my number for the 2015 season. There was part of me that was conflicted about possibly changing my number after two years of wearing

#44. There were two other options I was considering, both that were numbers that meant a lot to me. The first was #55, which was the number that I wore in DJFL all the way through freshman year but had been taken during my sophomore and junior years. The other was #18, which is the number my brother wore on the team from the years 2009 to 2011, wearing it in honor of his hero, Peyton Manning. Since I idolized my brother growing up, and knowing that Sam was wearing #33 in recognition of his brother, I came very close to paying fellow senior Tyler Grant an unnecessary amount of money so I could have the number for myself.

Instead of spending all my money on a number, I decided to stick to what I had been in for the entirety of my varsity career and keep #44. My mentality was pretty simple looking back; my brother had made a name for himself in the #18 jersey, and that was his name to keep. Now, it was my turn to do something special with my number. Rarely, do players get to keep the same number for three years, so I took pride in #44 and in wanting to create a legacy out of it. I never really had valid reasoning behind it but found humor in it whenever people asked me why I wore #44. Instead of giving them the truth, which was "I don't really know, it was just assigned to me as a sophomore, and I stuck with it," I would tell them, "Forrest Gump wore it, so that's why I wear it."

Numbers were the last thing I should have been worried about, but I was relatively loose on the first day of practice. I didn't try to stress out over the idea of competing for a job because I knew things would turn out alright regardless. I was in the best shape of my life; I was nearing my final year of high school football, it was just a laid-back moment for me. I wanted to go back to what had made me fall in love with football in the first place, and that was having fun. The first day of practice was an incredible experience since the feelings of senior year were overtaking me. It was the little things that made the biggest difference, at least in my eyes.

Sam, Mark and I drove the linebacker group through agility and tackling drills, guiding them through tips and tricks that we had picked up over the years learning from guys like Matthew Vossler, Charlie Travers, and Tim Lochtefeld. During the first couple of practices though, Mark Schmidt initially struggled to regain his footing within the sport even after months of passing league practice. "Maybe it was the pads or something, but I was like, 'Shit man, I haven't done this in a while," Schmidt says. "I felt out of place at first but knew it was a transition, so I didn't get frustrated or anything like that."

After a successful few days, everything seemed to be going great for the team. Then one day, as we practiced in the June heat, a familiar face which we had not seen since the end of the 2014 season came into sight. Wheeling onto the field was Jim Mulhearn with his wife, wearing his Darien football hat with the biggest smile on his face. We continued to practice, but whenever we had the chance, we would walk up to him, shake his hand and have a conversation. At the end of practice, Coach Trifone gathered the team around Jim to let him speak to us. I didn't get an up-close look at him on the field, but after we gathered around him with the seniors in front, you could see the crippling effect ALS was having on him. He was paler, more fragile than the last time I had seen him. He went to speak, but the disease was slowly destroying his ability to talk clearly.

He sat there with a smile on his face while he was closing in on death, telling us to go out and win a state title, because it was our destiny. Coach Trifone stepped away, fighting back tears at the sight of his dying friend sending his message to us. Jim continued to speak, but eventually became choked up. He collected enough energy to talk once again, when he gave us our team motto for the 2015 season. A lifelong fan of the band Bachman-Turner Overdrive, Jim looked at us and said, "You ain't seen nothing yet."

We surrounded our friend and did the breakdown as a team, including him. For nearly 15 minutes, we spent time talking with him personally and thanking him for everything he had done for us. Staring in the face of death, Jim kept repeating the same humorous motto that also meant the world to us: You ain't seen nothing yet. Afterward, with his thumb up on his chair, he was off once again after impacting our lives as nobody had ever done before.

We wrapped up spring football later that week but ended it differently than previous years. Due to an influx of injuries during the 2014 Blue vs. White scrimmage, Trifone made the call to cancel the annual game and instead do a very low contact, 7v7 type scrimmage between the offense and defense while the lineman did their own competitions. At this point, Finlay Collins and I were splitting time at outside linebacker about 50/50, but to me, it wasn't about it being a competition, because Finlay and I didn't allow it to be like that. I had tremendous respect for him and felt that as the older guy, I had a responsibility to do whatever I could to make him a better player, even if that meant giving him an edge in a position battle.

There was mutual respect, and we learned from each other, with me learning more from him. Finlay was similar to Schmidt in style, but also had traits of Sam Giorgio in his mentality to "do his job" before thinking about making a selfish play. He was an athletic phenomenon as well, being heavily recruited by top lacrosse schools. It was an uphill battle for me to beat him out, but it was also an incredible experience being able to teach and learn from him. We never had any hostility, we learned from each other's mistakes, and we did our best to create better versions of ourselves by helping the other. It did wonders for me and kept me in love with the game. It also worked mysteriously well in relieving any pressure I felt to perform or win the starting job because I knew if I didn't win it that it would be in great hands under Finlay.

At the end of spring football, that was extremely helpful to me. I began to focus more on the team and less on myself, something that I had fallen victim to in trying to become a superstar which I had dreamed about as a kid. I began relating closer to the message that Timmy Graham had been spreading of winning for the town and winning the state title. The individual didn't matter as long as there was a team surrounding him, and we needed to realize that as a team if we wanted to succeed. That was the goal heading into summer, our only goal.

Gone Camping

The end of spring football meant the beginning of the second busiest time of year for the football team, which is the summer season. The summer season was a big time of development for the team since the majority of players who were out of spring practice because of lacrosse now had a chance to rejoin the team and start preparing for the 2015 season.

That included Mark Evanchick, who was spending his early summer days attempting to gain back the 30 pounds he had dropped during the winter. Evanchick didn't only have a massive weight bulk on his plate, but he also had hovering over his head the state sack record, which he was 17 shy of to break NFL legend Dwight Freeney's Connecticut record. The attention was all on Mark leading in, but he didn't let it bother him. "It's nice in a sense, but you don't want all eyes on you, but more eyes on the team and what we planned to accomplish together," Evanchick says, remembering the summer lead up to the season. Evanchick quickly transitioned back into his football persona with hours in the weight room working with John Carlozzi. By the time late June arrived, Evanchick, like the rest of the varsity team, was ready to go for our annual summer football camp.

Every year, Coach Trifone schedules a three-day, two-night trip to a football camp in the state of Connecticut to give players a chance to continue to refine their skills without violating any rules within the boundaries of high school athletics (for a small fee of around $350). For the summer of 2015, we were headed to Central Connecticut State University (CCSU) for an experience that many would compare to the brutalities of Hell Week.

Assigned to the dorms at CCSU, we picked our roommates and began to pack for the three-day trip. I was rooming with Sam Giorgio, and we decided as football players, we only needed the essentials going into camp; baby powder, Advil, foam rollers for sore legs, sunscreen and plenty of food. We arrived at the front of Darien High School early on the morning of the 22nd of June, loaded up the coach bus and boarded, ready for the hour and a half drive to the campus of Central Connecticut State.

The drive was mundane, except for one instance where I found myself needing to relieve myself after drinking an absurd amount of water to prepare my body for the summer heat that would be pounding down at Arute Field at CCSU. Waiting since a fellow senior had walked into the bus bathroom before me, the player stepped out and looked at me while smiling and laughed as he sat down in his seat. Slightly confused, I walked into the bathroom and was met with what I assumed my teammate was laughing about… the smell of marijuana. Then my confusion went away because from what I had heard and from what I knew, a lot of players used marijuana as a pain reliever, sometimes before a game/practice but mostly after. It was a foolproof method because we didn't get drug tested, so there wasn't a risk in smoking when we were in season. I hadn't done it, although I had considered it after some bumps and bruises following junior varsity games in 2014, but managed to stay away from it until later in my senior year.

It trickled back to the idea of an escape for us. There was no way we could drink before a game or immediately after a game to ease the pain, but a quick hit did wonders. Honestly too, the effects felt good on the body and mind of a teenage football player, with college decisions looming and the upcoming season just around the corner. Pressure from parents, pressure from ourselves, it added up, even during the summer time. It was an escape, one that some of us desperately needed.

When we finally arrived at Central Connecticut State University, we quickly moved our stuff into our dorms and took our helmets down to the primary field for a quick team walkthrough before the other teams arrived from all around the state. The hot weather was almost sticking to our skin on the field, a brutal combination of humidity and pure heat. We fought through it since we only were doing small bursts of speed and running in the walkthrough environment. It was still before 12 pm, and we had a full practice later that afternoon, shoulder pads and helmets, so there was no need to exhaust ourselves. We retreated to our rooms and then down to the CCSU dining hall for lunch, where a nice mediocre college meal sat in our stomachs before we took the field for a two-hour practice with the other teams that had arrived.

The day was a hellacious mix of competition and pure adrenaline. Teams ranged from Shelton High School all the way to Southington, who was the perennial powerhouse team in the state after riding a 20-game win streak while also claiming back to back state titles in 2013 and 2014. We would get a chance later in the evening to play them in 7v7, which was an opportunity we relished, knowing that there was a chance we would play them in the state playoffs; especially after Darien High School got moved from Class L to Class LL, the largest class in the state.

By the end of the day, after dinner and right before 7v7, our bodies were nearly broken. We were running on fumes, but we could use any energy we could get since the most crucial part of the day was coming up. We took the field for 7v7, Finlay Collins and I ready again to rotate at our position, something we both were happy about since any break we could get would feel great on our legs. Timmy Graham didn't let fatigue get in his way though, even after a full day of throwing and footwork drills. He knew that everyone would be watching the 7v7 games, and if he could make his mark here, then it would put the rest of the state on notice.

Early on, Graham struggled to connect with his receivers, and it came to a peak when a receiver ran the wrong route, resulting in Graham throwing a costly interception. Graham, who could have easily lost his mind at the young receiver, instead used it as a teaching lesson, remembering the moments during his sophomore year where Silas Wyper would use mistakes as a teachable moment. The following drive, after speaking with his receiver, Graham connected on a long touchdown, drawing a loud reaction from our team on the sideline.

The sun began to fade and night started to fall, which meant the end to a day that felt as if it had gone on forever. Now wholly physically broken, I went back up to campus towards the dorms, straddling my legs like I was a cowboy due to the absolute pain that was in my lower region because of the savage chafing that had overtaken me. Climbing the stairs with Sam Giorgio to our third-floor dorm room, we collapsed onto our beds after a much-needed shower, and I proceeded to put a nuclear bomb's worth of baby powder into the affected region. The remainder of the night, I sat lying in bed, pondering the words of Bruce Springsteen's song "Backstreets" (Sam had turned me on The Boss) while my body berated me for putting it through such a monstrous regiment. I fell asleep by 9 pm, a new record for me personally. It was a successful day, but the next two were going to be just as bad, and I needed as much rest as possible.

Waking up the next day to a resounding "ffuuucckkk" from Sam, I realized what was causing the outburst from my friend. I went to get out of bed, but my legs were having none of it. I went to bend my knees, and again, my body was firmly telling me, "no." I managed to roll onto the ground, where I grabbed a foam roller and proceeded to put my body through more pain as I rolled my legs out slowly. It helped a little, but when I stood up, I also realized that the baby powder didn't do its job, causing me to do my beautiful cowboy walk all the way to the dining hall for breakfast.

The second day was more or less of the same stuff from day one, although we did get a chance to watch film from our scrimmages and 7v7 sessions. That was a much-needed break and allowed for us to get mentally ready for the remainder of the day. By the end of the second day, my body was feeling better, only because I didn't feel any pain since everything had gone numb.

Unlike the uneventful first night where I was passed out by 9 pm, a fire alarm went off at around 10 pm, forcing me out of bed to investigate what was happening. I stepped outside my room, where my teammates and I had learned that a group of players on another team had been smoking marijuana in their first-floor room, not realizing that the smoke would set off the detector. No, I'm not kidding.

We, of course, rushed down to watch what was happening, where we found a couple of police officers walking around the area talking to coaches and the players involved. Naturally, I took the moment as a chance to make a joke with everyone watching, so I went upstairs, got my speaker, and proceeded to play the *Cops* theme song while walking around with Sam.

The third day of camp was again a repeat of the previous day, except a little shorter because we were leaving by mid-afternoon. A couple of drills and scrimmages later, we officially had ended our time at Central Connecticut State University. Sorer than anyone could imagine, we piled onto our bus after packing up our stuff and headed back to Darien. Stories filled with laughter took over the bus ride for the first half hour, but after that, most of us just passed out. Our first test of the summer was over, and we had passed with flying colors. Our offense was firing on all cylinders; our defense was working as one unit; our team was ready. We felt good, we were having fun, and it was just an all-around good time to be a Darien football player.

Grip It, Then Rip It

Before we got the chance to take the field in August for preseason, we had one more bit of business to take care of in mid-July. It was the annual Grip It & Rip It tournament, which meant teams from all around the area (Connecticut, New York, even New Jersey) came together for a chance to go to the national Grip It & Rip It tournament later in August. The competition went over a two-day period, with the qualifying rounds taking place the first day followed by the elimination tournament on the second day.

The tournament was being held at Dunning Stadium and the turf fields surrounding Dunning at New Canaan High School, and similar to camp at Central Connecticut State, the days were going to be extremely hot on the turf. Arriving at Dunning the first day of the tournament, I found our team pretty quickly since we had mounted a giant "Blue Wave Football" tent on the sideline on one of the fields. Stretching and preparation commenced, but like at camp, a rather light mood was surrounding us as players. There was no sense of urgency or anything like that, but instead a group of players looking to have fun and hopefully win a few games in the middle of all that.

Even though I was overly excited and the heat tired me out pretty quickly, I did a good job on the defensive side of the ball. I played what I like to call the "Giorgio Method" now, which was just doing my job and not letting anything bad happen. I didn't make any big plays, but I didn't let up any big plays, so I considered it a success. Defensively, we did outstanding on the first day. We collected turnover after turnover and jumped all over each other after each interception. On the offensive side of the ball, Timmy Graham was throwing dimes to Minicus and Hamill, causing blowout after blowout on the field that day. We were like a well-oiled machine, one cohesive unit, and we were dominating everything that was thrown at us. We cruised into the second day of action with critical wins, clinching us a spot in the tournament.

When the second day arrived, competition got a little tougher on our end, now that we had entered the elimination bracket of the tournament. Finlay and I continued to rotate, but with him being the superior athlete, he was easily more set for the long run than I was. I was nearly dying by the time we reached the quarterfinals, where we were playing one of the top teams from New York out of Brooklyn. The team was bigger and faster than us, but it didn't stop us from putting forth our very best effort. We played them tough early, and it was a blast. Yelling between the routes that were coming towards us to switching out coverages pre-snap, I was mentally and physically drained, but still smiling on the inside because I was playing the game that I loved.

With a little under five minutes to go in the game, I was lined up on their slot receiver in our primary "Cover 6" scheme. I was playing on the weak side as usual, but they motioned the running back towards my side, causing a shift in strength. I didn't panic, knowing my responsibility was to jam the slot receiver and then pick up the running back if he went out for a route. As I expected, the running back did go out, first faking a basic flare route but turning it upfield into a wheel route. I was outmatched, my speed was nowhere near his level, but I kept my distance, allowing me to pursue him from an angle. The quarterback saw the mismatch and threw the ball in my direction. Only a couple of yards behind him, I had him covered but had noticed the quarterback had thrown it just a little ahead of the target, giving him the advantage. With one final ounce of strength, I jumped into the air and used my height to my advantage, getting my fingertips on the ball to disrupt the spin. When I touched the ball, I brought my hand down in a swatting motion to knock the ball down, but the trajectory of the spin and the movement of my hand forced the ball up, falling right into the hands of the running back for the touchdown.

Demoralized, I returned to the sideline where Coach Trifone greeted me and patted me on the helmet, telling me, "Don't worry about that, it was a hell of an effort. 99 times out of 100 that will go your way." Still relatively upset at giving the opposition the lead, I squatted down on the ground and took my helmet off, looking towards the field.

From behind, it was then when I heard a parent of a player, disgusted by the play, yell out, "Come on man, you gotta knock that down!" Knowing the parent, I ignored him, baffled that he would say something like that. A couple of minutes later, now on the field watching the clock tick down, the parent continued with the same comments. He wasn't directly saying them to me, but you could tell I was his target by the tone of his voice and by how loud he was speaking. "If we had just knocked that pass down we would be advancing..." I stopped ignoring him and looked directly at him, almost daring him to repeat it. I looked away, which caused another comment from him. The game ended with us losing, and you could tell that the loss was bothering this adult more than it was bothering the team. "We gotta be accountable for our mistakes," he said, looking down and shaking his head. "Things have to change."

I stood up, boiling inside at this nobody who was berating me for a 7v7 mistake, and started walking towards my teammates, who were near the parent. Part of me wanted to punch him right in the face since I was twice his size and could probably knock him out after everything he said, but instead I stayed quiet.

Coach Trifone praised our efforts, only pointing to the positives and not the negatives. He talked to me after too and told me how great I was during the two-day stretch, and that he was proud of all the hard work I had put in for the team. I thanked him but was still bothered by the parent making those comments towards me. On the drive home, that was all I was thinking about. I kept replaying the moment in my head and kept thinking of things I could have said to him.

"You try covering him."

"I don't see you out here busting your ass."

Or, which at the moment I was beating myself up for not saying this... "Go fuck yourself."

It just stayed on my mind, because it was the first time I had experienced something like that. Some 50-year-old dad who I had known since fourth-grade, was telling me that I just lost the game for my team. I was 17, and he was doing that to me. It bothered me so much and eventually caused me to blame myself over and over again for the moment. It honestly ruined what was a fun and enjoyable weekend for me, because I was pissed at myself for not doing better and for not standing up for myself.

The confrontation and comments stayed with me for a couple of days, which had its good and bad effects. On the bad side, I was letting negativity fill my body on what was a meaningless game really, but on the good side, I was using that negativity and anger to fuel myself through weight lifting and training during the rest of July. It pushed me to my limits, as anger and motivation flowed through me to get to August preseason, determined to prove that parent wrong and to prove to myself that I was worthy of being a football player. It seemed like it was never going to stop, but all of a sudden, that angry, negative motivation came to a screeching halt when myself and the team received some heavy news.

Timmy Graham throws to his father while junior Brian Peters practices with a wide receiver (June 5th, 2015)

Hudson Hamill talks with Coach Forget in-between games at the Grip it & Rip it tournament (July 10th, 2015)

CHAPTER FIFTEEN

Jim Mulhearn

By late July, Jim Mulhearn was nearing his final days on Earth. Knowing full well that any day could be his last, Sam Giorgio and I decided to make our way to Roton Point to see our friend on the afternoon of July 30th. We arrived at Roton and made our way up to the lawn overlooking the ocean, where Jim sat looking towards the water. When he turned and saw us coming, a massive smile broke out on his face, and he began laughing. From the last time I had seen him during spring practice, you could once again see the damage ALS was doing to him. Over the course of a year when I first met him after doing the ALS Ice Bucket Challenge, you could see how one of the worst diseases known to humanity had ravaged through his body.

The sight of him laughing made me incredibly emotional, seeing once again this man being beyond positive while staring down the face of death. Jim had been one of the few people I had cried in front of, but I knew that on this day, I had to keep everything the way he liked it; purely positive. Sam and I stood with him for nearly half an hour, talking about whatever came up. Jim had gotten to the point where talking had become extremely difficult for him, but he used all his strength to converse with us that day. We exchanged memories from the previous season, laughing about moments on the field and off the field. Nothing mattered during that time in my mind, because I was enjoying the time around one of the best influences I had met in my life. I overuse the word positive when describing Jim, but that's because that is the best way to describe the man. He was predicted to be weeks away from death, but here he was chatting it up with us at his favorite spot at Roton Point, enjoying the day as if it was his last. It was incredible, especially in the mind of a 17-year-old kid.

When the time came for us to leave, we were prepared to say our goodbyes when we decided to get together and take a photo. Jim posed for the picture with his thumb up, but then stopped my mother from taking the photo, citing that he did not want his glasses on for the photo. Laughing, we helped get his glasses off and took a photograph. We then shook his hand and said our goodbyes, with Giorgio and I seeking his advice for the season ahead. I went up to him before I left and like I did every time I saw him, I thanked him. Smiling, he looked at me but struggled to speak.

I smiled back at him and shook his hand, telling him, "I'll see you later Jim." He gave me a thumbs up, and I walked away.

Nine days later on the night of August 8th, 2015, Jim Mulhearn passed away at the age of 68. He died while in hospice care with his wife at his side.

 I was sitting downstairs in my house that night, watching baseball when my mom came down and told me the news. Never wanting to cry in front of my mother, I said nothing. About 15 minutes later, I told her that I was going to a friends house to hang out for a little bit and that I wouldn't be out long. I drove around town that night, not stopping at my friend's house, but ended up outside the Darien High School football field. For a good while, I looked out onto the dark field, and once again, put to rest the myth that football players don't cry.

The news affected everyone on that team, especially Hudson Hamill who was extremely close to Jim. "He had such an impact, it was some real-life stuff," says Hamill about Mulhearn. "Growing up in Darien, especially when people say that Darien is a bubble, we never really had anyone like Jim. But just seeing how caring he was around us, even while suffering from this terrible disease, yet his number one thought was Blue Wave football." Hudson remembers seeing Mulhearn days before death and recalls from the moment the conversation Jim had with him. "The last time I saw him, he told me, 'I'll be watching from the press box in the sky.' He told me that we were going to go undefeated and that we were going to win a state championship." After that special moment with Mulhearn, Hudson made it his priority to live out Jim's dream for the team, and dedicated every touchdown, every interception, every play to his beloved mentor.

Timmy Graham took the death of Jim just as hard as Hudson and the rest of the senior class. Graham remembers Mulhearn, saying, "He was so motivating, and was such a major key to our success, not just on the field, but in life." In a town with expectations mounting on the shoulders of children everywhere, Mulhearn was exactly what Graham described him as. He wasn't just an on-field motivator; his off-field role with the team was what he was known for. He shaped us, he molded us; he let us know it was okay to be ourselves and most importantly, to chase happiness.

The loss was tough for us players, but Coach Trifone took the loss of one of his best friends the hardest. Following his death, Trifone, like many of us, remembers one of his biggest regrets. "I didn't feel like I did enough for him," says Trifone, remembering his friend. "But I was just so impressed by this man; he was so motivating to me. I never envisioned what was going to happen... And at the end of the day, he was doing more for us than we were doing for him."

On his deathbed, Trifone sat next to Mulhearn and gifted him a Blue Wave football helmet. He told Jim that for the 2015 season, the team would be wearing a special "JM" decal on the back of their helmets in remembrance of him. Jim, who always knew what to say, gathered enough strength to speak. He looked into Trifone's eyes and said to him five words; "You ain't seen nothing yet."

PART IV

The 2015 Season

'From the very beginning I told the kids we're going to run the table, go undefeated and win FCIACs and states. Those were my words. It was part of my bucket list."

- Jim Mulhearn, nine days before the Blue Wave's 2014 State Championship loss

CHAPTER SIXTEEN

The Dream

Win Rocky Win

He was invisible to most. Nothing against him but Rock Stewart, who was getting ready for his third varsity season, was not your everyday football player from Darien. In fact, he wasn't like your ordinary teenager from Darien. What really separated Stewart from the rest of his teammates and classmates though was simple:

"I didn't drink," Stewart says.

It isn't too shocking too some. However, in a town like Darien which is infamous for its underage drinking scene, Stewart was essentially playing with social-suicide by not attending any parties during the season or even during the offseason. Even I succumbed to the pressure of it all, getting a beer or two in so that I could fit in with the rest of the culture. To Stewart though, he saw no benefits in the idea of alcohol consumption. His first reason was that he signed commitment, something a lot of players did not take as seriously as he did. He also played three other sports, so he didn't have time for parties. His main reasoning though to not drink wasn't just the non-drive he had for it but because of something that happened before the start of the 2015 preseason, something that changed his outlook on life forever.

"The main reason was going into senior year, I had three tumors removed from my body," he says. "That was honestly a big reason for me not to drink."

The operation gave Stewart a broader outlook on things as well, creating an opportunity for him to start enjoying the little things and not dwell in the past. For example, Stewart never relived the 2014 state title loss since his newfound mentality gave him something else to focus on. "I always was thinking about the next game," Stewart recalls. "I always was focused on what was next and not what was behind me." Stewart was also in the same boat as Sam Giorgio and me; all three of us were on the junior varsity squad as juniors while the rest of our teammates played or rotated at the varsity level at some point during the season. He, like us, spent the majority of his varsity time on the scout team, which was not something he was used to after the years he spent at the youth level.

Stewart entered the Darien Junior Football League late, joining our team going into our seventh-grade season. Stewart was never really a football fanatic since his dad played soccer at Duke (winning a national championship while there) and had no knowledge of American football. "My dad couldn't tell you what an 'In' route is," Stewart says with a laugh. This, however, was something a young Rock Stewart took notice of when picking his sports as a kid. Stewart was aware of some parents pushing their children to play certain sports, even at a young age, so he decided to pick sports that were not in his family. At first, he settled on lacrosse and basketball (which he played on both varsity teams his junior year), then decided to play football starting in the seventh-grade because of one reason and one reason only:

"I played football for one day a year. The reason I chose football over soccer is because I wanted to play in the Turkey Bowl," he says. "I thought it was *the* coolest thing."

The dream didn't stop there for Stewart. "I told myself all four years that I was eventually going to score a touchdown in the Turkey Bowl," he continues. "It was really selfish, but that's how I got myself through everything."

Stewart was a staple in the youth team offense when he first started playing football, becoming Timmy Graham's favorite target during the eighth-grade season. By his sophomore year though, Stewart was stuck behind Christian Trifone on the depth chart, making him almost useless. Stewart found personal purpose on the scout team during the 2013 and 2014 seasons, although he was once again rendered invisible by those around him, something that didn't go unnoticed by the wide receiver. "I was the guy everyone forgot about when we were out on the field," Stewart remembers. "It showed when people came back from previous years to visit during practice; they never talked to me, they would always talk to the other guys."

This wasn't the only thing that Stewart saw as difficult. Stewart was always astonished by the helmet stickers that Coach Trifone would hand out to varsity players after games, but Stewart began to develop a problem with the system. "I remember thinking as a sophomore, 'Damn, those stars on the helmets are so cool,'" he says. "I would think, 'Man, I work my butt off every single day at practice and the team wouldn't be here if it weren't for that, so why don't I get stickers while the other guys did?'"

That was something that stuck with Rock Stewart, which made him create his own rule of giving away half of his stickers to younger guys after every game during his senior year. Even after everything Stewart had gone through: his uphill battle to gain a spot on the team, him coping with invisibility, not being noticed by the stars of the team, and of course his operation before the season… Nothing was going to stop him from achieving that childhood dream he dreamt that fateful morning when he watched the Turkey Bowl for the first time.

He was going to score in front of the Thanksgiving morning crowd. It wasn't a matter of *if*; It was a complete matter of *when*.

Unfinished Business

After months of grinding in the weight room, playing 7v7 and through summer camps, the 2015 preseason was finally upon us. The culmination of nearly ten years of playing football in Darien was coming together, and the excitement surrounding the team was through the roof. As seniors, we were ready to chase the dream, to fulfill our destiny, to complete the prophecy set upon us. Arriving in Coach Trifone's classroom for the first meeting before Hell Week, I took my rightful spot in the front of the room, two years after standing in the back corner, watching guys like Silas Wyper, Alex Gunn and Nick Lombardo listen to Trifone speak.

Standing in front of the team, Trifone was all business. He spoke directly to the senior class, reminding us of all the years of hard work and dedication. It all built up to this, and the goal was simple; go undefeated, win a state title. The elusive title had dodged us since 1996, and this was the year to do it. It had to happen, or else everything we had worked for would amount to nothing. It was a hard truth, but it was *the* truth. We knew that if we didn't go out and win state, then nothing mattered. We would have failed not only ourselves but also the two teams that helped pave the way for us leading into the season.

Unlike 2013, but slightly similar to 2014, we were ranked high in the state of Connecticut preseason polls. Sitting at #3, we were behind #2 New Canaan and #1 Southington.[1] Both teams were on our radars, obviously because of the Turkey Bowl but also because Southington was our main competition in Class LL. Both teams were anchored by their quarterback, with Michael Collins returning and Southington being led by Jasen Rose, who had thrown 47 touchdown passes during his junior season in 2014. Both quarterbacks were highly touted and praised by the media, with newspapers and websites debating back and forth about who was the best quarterback in Connecticut. Then there was Timmy Graham, who wasn't even being considered in those conversations. Having committed to Bryant University to play football, Graham's news was overshadowed by Collins' commitment to the University of Pennsylvania and Rose's countdown to commitment with offers from UConn, Syracuse, Wake Forest and Wisconsin.[2]

It bothered Graham, but it didn't consume him because he saw the issue from both sides. He had struggled with turnovers during his junior season, so he knew he didn't belong in that conversation. The more important thing to Graham was the state rankings, which again, he didn't seem to have a problem with. "Of course we wanted to be the #1 team in the state going in, but we didn't deserve to be the #1 team in the state," says Graham. "New Canaan had beat us in the state title game and Southington was on a two-year winning streak. Still, we used it as motivation."

The motivation was going towards a single goal that was on Graham's mind throughout August. He didn't care about anything else, he had committed earlier in the summer, so there was only one thing going through his head. "Going into my senior year, my mindset was I was going to do everything I could to win the state championship for the town of Darien. 1996 was the last one, and I wanted us to be the guys to win it, I wanted to be known as the kid that won that state championship that Darien had been waiting on for such a long time."

Mark Evanchick agreed with that claim, something he saw eye to eye on with Timmy. There was still the idea of wanting to have fun, but Evanchick saw the bigger picture in his mind as something else. It wasn't about the sack record; it was all about the title chase. "Don't get me wrong, it was all still fun," says Evanchick about the lead up into the preseason. "But later on it morphed into, 'I want to win a state title for this town, I don't want to get out of here without a ring on my finger.'"

As we sat in Trifone's room listening to him speak, the thoughts of state championship glory overtook us. We could be the kings of the town, the kids who broke a 19-year drought, the ones to do the impossible. In the mind of a 17-year-old, that possibility was mind-bending. We wanted that glory, we wanted that stardom, but inside as well, we wanted it for Jim. He was one of the main factors in going all out that season, and we couldn't fail on his dying wish. Trifone confirmed those ambitions, instilling us with the goal to "Win for Jim." Along with that, in regards to the previous year's losses in the state title game, Trifone had rubber wristbands made for all players that had a two-word phrase printed on them: Unfinished Business.

We took the field for the first time as a team on that hot August day, ready to embark for one final time on the journey we had grown to love, the ride known as Hell Week. After two years, Hell Week had become somewhat of a fun, sick tradition for us. We liked to joke around with the sophomores about how terrible it was, and how you would never be the same after running with Carlozzi on the first day.

We must have been slightly cocky, because the heat manhandled us, creating an environment that I had never come close to during the first two Hell Week sessions of my high school football career. Along with that, Coach Forget decided to reintroduce the infamous hip flip drill to us linebackers. For 25 yards, we had to stay in a low position on a straight line while flipping our legs over the other to simulate turning into coverage while downfield. Giorgio still remembers the pains of hip flips vividly, saying that "It's the most brutal burning sensation you ever feel in your legs, combined with the ridicule of feeling remarkably un-athletic as Coach Forget yells at you to do them 'right.'"

On the offensive side of the ball, Timmy Graham was staying relatively stationary through the first few drills and team sessions during Hell Week. He was given a pass on conditioning as well, due to a calf strain he had sustained in the lead up to the season. Playing it safe, Trifone sat out his star quarterback, unwilling to lose him in what he and Timmy felt was an insignificant part of practice for him. "I mean, I wasn't what you would consider a mobile quarterback," Timmy says with a quick grin. "So I don't think missing conditioning effected me that much." Unfortunately, the rest of us were not as lucky as Timmy. We once again suffered under the wrath of Carlozzi, wondering why we even taunted the underclassmen when we could not even get through the sprints ourselves.

By the end of it, we were all exhausted on the field but circled as a team to stretch ourselves out before going inside and calling it a day. We were all laughs and smiles in the stretching circle though, playfully insulting each other through sometimes wildly inappropriate sing-alongs, and enjoying the team moment together. It was an excellent ending to a great day of practice, something we all needed, especially with all that had happened in August. We were becoming a team once again, the pain of the 2014 state title loss no longer visible on the outside. A good first day was exactly what the doctor ordered; we knew that we could only go up from that point moving forward.

The SWAT Team

Some point during the 2013 season, the No Fly Zone was born under the direction of defensive backs coach Andy Grant. The idea was simple and silly. Wherever the Darien defense went was declared a "No Fly Zone" by the defensive backs, alluding to the notion that quarterbacks would have an incredible amount of trouble throwing against our defense. The group, which consisted of the core four of Hudson Hamill and Tyler Grant on one side along with Bobby and Christian Trifone on the other, started to run with the idea of the No Fly Zone by the beginning of 2015.

It got to the point of complete absurdity by August; whenever a helicopter or plane would fly over our field during practice, Coach Grant would stop in the middle of a drill and point out the intruding flying object to the four primary members. The reaction varied, but it was always something new. Sometimes, Hamill would drop to the ground and simulate using his leg as a cannon firing at the plane. Other times, Hamill and the other defensive backs would all take a knee and prop a fake bazooka onto their shoulders while once again firing towards the plane. My personal favorite was when they would reach into their pockets (which didn't exist because they were wearing football pants), pull out a "rock" and slingshot the rock towards the plane in the sky.

The No Fly Zone also had their squad signal, bashing their arms together to form an "X" and raising it high into the air for all to see. "That actually developed in 2014 with Timmy Lochtefeld," says Hudson Hamill about the group signal. "He would put it up and say something along the lines of, 'Shut that shit down,' or something. So then every time we made a play going forward, the No Fly Zone would throw up the

'X.'" Through the preseason, the No Fly Zone became a staple at Darien, something that was so frequent that they started to call it the "NFZ" simply.

Sam Giorgio, Mark Schmidt and I were not included in the No Fly Zone because we were linebackers, even though we dropped into coverage on nearly every play. Upset at this, one day during Hell Week we decided it was time to form our own on-field club. Playing off the football stereotype that linebackers can't catch, and because Sam Giorgio had quite possibly the worst hands on the entire football team, we decided to call ourselves the SWAT Team. The name, like the No Fly Zone, was simple and stupid when you took a step back and looked at it. We knew how ridiculous the name and idea was, but we took off with it, only really to have it so we could mock the No Fly Zone behind their backs whenever we had the chance.

Just like the No Fly Zone too, we decided to come up with our squad signal. At first, the three of us chose to smash our forearms together in a hammer swinging motion. That lasted for about an hour when Giorgio and I decided to make ours a little more provocative and offensive towards the No Fly Zone. We took the "X" aspect of the defensive backs and decided to put a twist on it. Instead of raising our "X" into the air, we would bring it down and cross the "X" right at our crotch with a thrusting motion with our hips (We admitted later that we had stolen the gesture from a 90s wrestling group in the WWF). The taunt was dirty, really inappropriate, but wildly hilarious to Sam, Schmidt, and I. For the remainder of the week, the three of us would run around after every play and throw down the crotch chop towards the defensive backs and other players on the team while giving a quick but loud "SWAT TEAM" after each time we did it.

All week long, we continued on our way of mocking the No Fly Zone at any chance we were given. Even Coach Forget joined in on it, labeling the defensive backs as the "DIA," also known as the Darien International Airport. Meanwhile, Sam and I continued our crotch pointing shenanigans, something Giorgio still loves to this day. "It was honestly the perfect relief, because of how serious and stressful practice was sometimes," says Giorgio. "But then after swatting a ball down, we would look and give each other the crotch chop. That was all I needed to keep going." By the end of the week, the SWAT Team had made its on-field debut against Trinity Catholic in a controlled scrimmage that we were having against the team. In one of the more memorable moments of the season, I was playing outside linebacker alongside Sam and Schmidt when all of a sudden I had an opportunity to intercept the ball. I had a clear path to the end zone, but when I caught the ball, I held onto it for about half a second and then slammed it to the ground. I turned to Giorgio, who was looking at me like I had just killed a man and threw the crotch chop right at him.

Not everyone got the reference. After I came off the field, Coach Trifone looked at me confused and asked why I didn't take the ball into the end zone. Defending my decision, I shrugged and told him, "Coach, I read swat." Once again puzzled, he walked away baffled by my actions on the field. Had it been in a regular season game, there was a good chance I would have taken that ball to the house. But in a scrimmage? Someone had to defend the week-old legacy of the SWAT Team.

Final Preparations

By late August the team was functioning highly at all levels. After Hell Week, we had eased into our regular practice schedule with the start of school looming around the corner. The excitement built towards our opening game, which felt like it was years away with how our schedule worked out in the spring. Instead of opening on the 12th or 14th of September as we had in the previous years, we were beginning on the 18th because our bye week was assigned for the first week of the season. So, while all the other FCIAC teams got to play on Friday the 11th, we got to sit at home and patiently wait for our turn to play.

It didn't seem to halt our progress on the practice field, especially for me since I was making my final case to become the starter at outside linebacker on opening night. The outlook didn't look good from my perspective though because Finlay Collins had performed above expectations in the scrimmages and practices through August. He was a natural fit at the position, something I was not after years of playing lineman and an attempt at playing wide receiver.

Along with that, Coach Forget was refusing to name a starter leading up to the end of preseason. He kept his rotation mentality and stayed true to it, although I began to notice that Finlay was getting the first set of the rotation, which I took as a hint of what Forget was planning. It was an uphill battle for me from the start, but even with the possible chance of me losing the battle, I still kept hope that I would be on the field for opening night at Boyle Stadium against Stamford. That was my dream, that was my goal, and I wasn't going to let anything stop me from achieving it.

The preseason officially came to an end on the morning of August 31st when we had our final practice an hour and a half before the first day of school. Trifone, who knew as a teacher that tiring out his players before school wasn't the best idea, kept the practice light for us. We walked through the offense and defense, did some basic agility drills and then called it a day before being dismissed for school at 7:30 am. There was a slight problem in that because school started at 7:40 am, and I had wanted to rush home to take a shower, so I didn't come off as disgusting to all my other classmates during the first day of my senior year. Always a quick thinker and not wanting to be late to my first class, I ran into the locker room, changed out of my football clothes and jumped in the old showers in the locker room, using hand soap from the sinks to clean myself... It was a success, at least in my mind.

Right off the bat during my first class, I walked in to find Spencer Stovall and Timmy Graham sitting in the back corner talking. The course was Law & Government, taught by one of the biggest football fans and supporters in the school, and with three football players in the same room together, it was a personal jackpot for all sides. If we needed to come in late the day after a game or after a lengthy film session? It was no problem, only if we gave the teacher a heads up and weren't more than 10 minutes tardy.

Like sophomore and junior year, the time I spent in class wasn't about what we were learning or what the teacher was lecturing on, but it was a constant football daydream. It wasn't like I was ignoring the teacher or the work, because I did the work and always participated right in the beginning to get class credit, but my main priority was thinking about anything related to the team or related to the game in general. I tried to keep that mentality throughout the day, but when I reached the later periods of the day or was sitting on a padded chair in the Tech Ed offices getting in a well-deserved nap, I was in a dream. It was as if I was 12 years old again, dreaming about being a superstar on the fields of Darien High School.

A personal favorite of mine was daydreaming about playing in the Turkey Bowl, which was the #1 bucket list item for me going into senior year. I imagined myself running out in front of the 10,000 fans and taking in the entire atmosphere. I dreamt of being on the field with only 30 seconds left, the game tied and New Canaan driving down the field. The crowd was nervous; momentum was on their side when out of nowhere, I intercept it and take it back 80 yards for a touchdown. The crowd would erupt, I would celebrate with my teammates, the game would be ours. I would then be woken up by a slap from reality when my teacher called on me for staring at the ceiling for three straight minutes, but I didn't care. The dream that had stuck with me since I was an eight-year-old kid was so close that nothing else was on my mind. My senior year was here; that's all that mattered.

Coach Trifone addresses the team before practice one morning
(August 22ⁿᵈ, 2015)

The self-proclaimed "SWAT Team"; Myself, Sam Giorgio, and
Mark Schmidt (August 26ᵗʰ, 2015)

Timmy Graham sits on the bench during a preseason scrimmage against Trinity Catholic (September 11th, 2015)

The 2015 Darien High School football seniors (August 28th, 2015)

CHAPTER SEVENTEEN

Are We Out of the Woods Yet?

Stamford Week

Sam Giorgio sat through his AP English Language and Composition class Thursday afternoon, but the lessons on Truman Capote's revolutionary nonfiction novel *In Cold Blood* went right through his ears. His foot bounced on and off the floor, his pencil tapped rapidly against the wooden desk in the second-floor English room. He didn't give a damn about the idea of Capote creating a sympathetic character out of a convicted murderer because, in a little over 24 hours, Giorgio would be making his varsity debut, something he had been thinking about since the third-grade. It drove Giorgio nuts that day, the nerves were taking over, and he had no control over it. Feeling almost sick to his stomach, he got up and left class for good and began to head downstairs towards the Technology Education department. "It's funny," says Giorgio. "I would go into the Tech Ed office and put up film onto the projector. Throughout the day, I would get Schmidt and guys down there, and we would watch film together. That week, I probably spent 25% of my school day watching film on Stamford."

Giorgio's nerves only got worse the next day. Wearing a

button-down shirt, Giorgio would excuse himself from class throughout the day to run down to the Tech Ed office, lock the door, and start watching film. "I was terrified," he says, laughing. "I had never started in a varsity game, and we are opening at Boyle Stadium, not to mention." The journey had nearly reached its completion. Giorgio was a varsity starter, his dream had come true, and he felt like throwing up.

Nervous breakdowns weren't only something Giorgio was experiencing, but something I was struggling with throughout the entire week. Friday for me, like Sam, was a complete mess. I couldn't think about equations or the breakdown of a neuron but instead only could think about the lights shining brightly at Boyle later that day. The position battle with Finlay Collins was over, and I knew in my mind that Collins would be the one out there to start the game, not me. It didn't consume me because I knew I would be out on the field for kickoffs and a bunch of other special teams, along with rotating in at linebacker in situations that I was needed. I was excited, I was pumped up, but I also was shaking uncontrollably under my desk, darting my eyes to the clock at any chance I got.

While Giorgio and I struggled to keep our focus, guys like Timmy Graham and Hudson Hamill were cooler than cool in school that day. Graham walked into each of his classes wearing his Blue Wave Football polo shirt with his Beats headphones over his ears. He would sit down, moccasins on his feet and glance forward, thinking about his reads and the offensive game-plan that had been set-up during the prior weeks. He didn't just know the offense; he knew the Stamford defense. After weeks of preparation, Graham knew inside and out the Stamford tendencies all the way from the way their coverages to how their outside linebacker stepped inside during an RPO (run/pass option). Those were the lessons and knowledge Graham cared about that week, not the readings on the basis of American government that his teacher was lecturing on. His priorities were set from September to December, and those priorities laid strictly within the Darien High School football team. He had a senior season to worry about, and he knew along with everyone else that a first impression meant everything in the competitive FCIAC and Class LL bracket. It started with Stamford.

Hudson Hamill was all smiles, laughing with friends and teammates down the hall while making plenty of noise about the upcoming game at any chance he got. The brash, loud mouth style of Hudson did not fit his looks, but he didn't care. He was going to talk however he wanted to talk because Hamill knew once game time had arrived he would be locked in and ready to go. Like Graham, but on defense, Hudson and his legion of defensive backs knew exactly what to expect from the Stamford offense. He wasn't concerned about the size of their star running back, because he knew that Mark Evanchick and the guys up front would take care of that from the start. All he was thinking about were his zones and the coverages he would be calling out all night long; with those, he wasn't even close to worried. Coach Grant had taught Hamill and the secondary every single route and tendency that the Stamford offense had shown during the 2014 season and the 2015 preseason. There was nothing to stress out about, Hamill had been here before and done exceptionally well under the circumstances. All he had to do now was step out onto the field and execute, and he knew that. "You only get nervous when you're unprepared," says Hamill about his pregame confidence. "I learned that from Silas Wyper. If you are really prepared for a game, there is no reason to be nervous."

When the final bell of the day rang at 2:20 pm, the same feeling that had drilled into me two years earlier as a sophomore walking to the locker room before Hillhouse hit me again. A heart-pounding thrill took over my body as I walked down towards the locker room. Red Gatorade in hand, I entered the locker room to the sound of blaring music all around me. Timmy Graham had arrived early, sitting in front of his locker preparing his travel bag hours in advance, not wanting to have to worry about any of that stuff in the minutes before leaving on the bus. I opened my locker to the site of my white away jersey, #44 glowing in the light while I read across the back, "BARTHOLD." I carefully put my school backpack away in the back and grabbed my football bag, always trying to keep everything as neat and organized as possible. During practice, my locker was a mess. The day of a game, it had to be extremely neat.

The bus was scheduled to leave at around 4:45 pm, so a lot of players went home to get something to eat or had something dropped off. Not wanting to leave, I had my mother drop off a favorite of mine; a bacon, egg, and cheese on a roll with a hash brown in it from Mama Carmela's Deli that she had picked up earlier. Then with Giorgio and Schmidt, I went into the empty school cafeteria and sat with them, anxiously waiting until it was time to leave.

A little before 3:30 pm, I got up and left the cafeteria to head over to the training room. I had loosely followed this ritual during my junior year, but I decided that during my senior year I would get my wrists and right ankle taped precisely three hours before kickoff. I had experimented with different timetables during my junior year and had decided that three hours was the perfect time to get my wrists and ankle comfortable before the game officially started. Retreating to the locker room, I would then wait until 4:30 pm when we were summoned to Coach Trifone's classroom for a final defensive meeting.

Following the meeting, we were then escorted to the bus waiting outside of Darien High School. Before the bus left,

Coach Trifone stood up and began to hand out pieces of paper to every varsity player on the bus. They weren't just ordinary pieces of paper; they were letters that Coach T had written personally to the team, something he had been doing for years. The notes were a massive highlight for every player who felt a personal connection with the words Trifone wrote in each sentence. Looking down at the page, I read each word carefully during the entire 20-minute ride to Boyle Stadium.

In the letter, Trifone wrote with passion, writing, "Do not waste a second... play hard and put out on every play like it (is) the last one of your high school career." He continued, citing a speech done by New Orleans Saints head coach Sean Payton, where Payton speaks about football players being the most fortunate athletes in the world of sports. Following a few sentences telling the team to cherish the moment, Trifone ended with:

"Earlier this week I talked (about) the qualities of a championship team. There are three of those you can begin to display tonight.

1. Be Relentless

2. Overcome obstacles & just make up for it on the next snap

3. Have an Edge."

After reading Trifone's letter over and over, we pulled into the lot at Boyle Stadium. For ten years, we had dreamed about our senior year. Now, it was finally here.

Friday Night Lights

It was almost like slow motion poetry while walking out onto the field at Boyle with my shoulder pads in hand and my backpack on. I looked around, taking in the beautiful stadium that had served as the home for the 2014 Turkey Bowl/FCIAC Championship. This time around, it was a warm September evening, and our opponent was different.

The stadium would not be holding 10,000 screaming maniacs, but the atmosphere and aura around Boyle were still there. While some players went immediately into the locker room, I stood around on the field along with a couple of other seniors, taking in every inch of the stadium. I was trying to enjoy the moment, knowing that opening night was not something I would experience again under the lights of one of Connecticut's oldest high school football stadiums.

I finally went into the locker room underneath the home stands that we had used during the Turkey Bowl and began to prepare for the game. I sat down in the far corner of the locker room, something I always preferred to do and started a pregame ritual that many consider "odd" in a sense.

After learning that standard pump-up music got me too excited and eventually led to me being exhausted before a practice or 7v7 session had even started, I turned to a somewhat different approach in the eyes of many. Being an open-minded individual, I considered many different methods to the idea of what I should listen to before a game. I continued my search when out of nowhere a couple of days before Stamford, I hit the musical jackpot.

Always a massive and proud Taylor Swift, I turned to Swift's pop album *1989*. I was listening to it on the way to class one day when I realized how perfect the songs were for my pregame needs. Not too intense, the songs delivered what I needed; an upbeat, happy sounding tune that got me up and moving but not to the point where I was bashing my head against the wall and exhausting myself before kickoff. So sitting in the locker room while Timmy Graham blasted French Montana on his phone and Mark Evanchick lived through the words of Bad Meets Evil, I lip-synced along to the words of "Out of the Woods" by Taylor Swift without any of my teammates knowing.

It worked wonders for me because, by the time I was out

on the field for stretching, I was ready to go while also being focused on the task at hand. I was beyond excited on the field, jumping up and down and throwing high fives at any chance I got. I rolled through the linebacker pregame routine with Giorgio and Schmidt while Sam and I gave one final crotch chop towards each other before going into the locker room. Still not having heard from Coach Forget about the plan for defense, I sat alone once again in the corner, eagerly awaiting a decision. It was then when Forget came up to me and gave it to me straight:

"Fin is going to start, stay near me though."

I nodded and slapped hands with him, plugging my headphones back in and refocusing myself. I expected the decision but still knew I had a chance of playing, so I didn't sweat over it. I threw my shoulder pads on, pulled my jersey over the top of it all and strapped up. We were called to gather around Coach T with the seniors up front, where he delivered the pregame sermon. Afterward, following a quick team prayer led by Pastor Greg Doll, we began to head for the exit, eager to finally get the season started.

Up front, we walked out of the locker room to the site of the relatively large Stamford crowd. The noise was coming from a closer source though, and upon arriving onto the field and looking back towards the away crowd, we saw a massive sea of Darien supporters cheering us on. Kids of all ages dressed in Blue Wave everything screamed, yelling for Timmy Graham and Mark Evanchick to acknowledge them. On the other side of our stands was a huge mass of students forming the student section, having made the trek from Darien to Stamford for the opening game of the Darien football season.

The captains went out for the coin toss, with us winning and deferring to the second half. As if the dream wasn't already alive, I was now getting the chance to run down the field for the opening kickoff of my senior season. Still understanding that I had a job to do and I could think about my dreams later, I jogged onto the field and took my place in the kickoff lineup. Even then, my thoughts continued to race back and forth through my head. The student section broke out into a loud "OOOOOOOOOHHHH" chant in the build to the kick, which made my heart pound even more. Then, just like that, junior kicker Riley Stewart (the younger brother of Rock Stewart) booted the ball downfield, and I was off to the races. Stamford's return man caught the ball and began to accelerate, but was met by a sea of seven defenders led by sophomore stud Max Grant, the younger brother of Shelby Grant. With the pile growing and the return man not going down, I came full speed alongside Schmidt and jumped into the mound, falling to the ground while the whistle was blown. Just like that, the season was officially underway.

In front of the Darien faithful under the comforting lights of Boyle Stadium, we demolished the Black Knights of Stamford on their home field. Mark Evanchick wowed the crowd for the third consecutive opener, tearing down the Stamford offensive line and collecting sack after sack. Not to be outdone, but Mark Schmidt made it seem like he never left, forcing a fumble and flying all around the field on defense and special teams. It was the start of something extraordinary for Schmidt, especially when halfway through the game the Darien football Twitter account tweeted the famous words, "#SchmidtHappens."

Opposite of the returning Schmidt was the debut of Sam Giorgio. The nerves died down quickly for Sammy G, who earned his way to three tackles throughout the day and creating an extreme sense of confidence in himself. "Once that first play was over, I was so locked in," says Giorgio of the moment. "Nothing was a distraction." By the second quarter after patiently waiting, Forget gave Collins a break and threw me into the game, allowing me to achieve the long sought-after goal of being a varsity player. I didn't put up Evanchick numbers but walked away with a tackle under my belt during the first half on an off-tackle play.

On the offensive side of the ball, an under-appreciated Timmy Graham put all media doubts to rest, going 18/20 with 261 yards and 4 TDs. Graham was unstoppable, surgically picking apart the helpless Stamford defense as he found Colin Minicus for three of his touchdowns. By the time the first half was over, Graham was already done with all of his work and was ready to cool down and let the junior varsity guys take care of the rest. Walking into the locker room when the second quarter ended, we led Stamford by a score of 47-0. The locker room mood wasn't as you would expect, only because we almost had a sense of knowing that this was going to happen. We were laughing and recalling moments from the first half, but it wasn't surprising. "We knew how good we were," says Timmy Graham. "So it wasn't a surprise for a lot of us."

We went out for the second half, where Trifone kept the varsity starters in for about one drive on each side of the ball. Then, he called it a day for us and began to sub in the juniors and sophomores of the junior varsity team. After 24 minutes, our playing time was over but our night was only beginning. Sticking with a tradition that Mark Evanchick had popularized during our junior year, the starters and guys who were done for the day would put on a sideline hat to signify that their work was done. Being prepared for the moment, I grabbed my white hat from underneath the bench and put it on, joining in with the rest of the seniors. We laughed and joked with each other while cheering on the junior varsity guys, but by the end of the third, I began to hear a consistent group of voices yelling and yelling in my direction, "#44! #44! Over here!" I turned and saw a bunch of

DJFL players up in the stands, also yelling towards guys like Mark Evanchick and Timmy Graham, hoping to get any acknowledgment from us. We laughed and walked over to them, seeing the pure joy in their faces when they realized we were coming to speak to them.

Hudson Hamill remembers the moment too and goes back the reasoning behind talking to the younger fans who idolized us from the stands. "I used to think, 'damn, those high schoolers are really cool' when I was a kid," says Hamill. "So obviously, I felt like we needed to give back." Timmy Graham goes along with that statement, especially with being one of the most well-known players on the team due to his status as the starting quarterback. "Talking with those little kids when we were up, it was just awesome," he says. "It's a huge part of being an athlete because everyone is watching you. You want to be a good role model to those kids and want to give back to the community in any way you can."

For the majority of the fourth quarter, we stood and conversed with the kids of the DJFL, talking to them about football and giving them tips on how to be better players, on and off the field. I loved every minute of it, getting the superstar treatment that I had been chasing ever since watching Brian Kosnik play back in 2008 and considering him the God of all Gods. For nearly the five minutes while we talked to the kids, I stood on the sideline playing catch with one of them from the stands. You could see the absolute shock and awe in the face of the kid, getting to play catch with a real Darien High School player. The game was nearing its conclusion though, forcing us to move back closer to the field. We gave out as many high fives as we could and shuffled back towards the coaches and the teammates, reading the scoreboard in the process: Darien 47 Stamford 12. The word had spread; Darien meant business.

Rock Stewart consults John Carlozzi in the locker room (September 18th, 2015)

Schmidt, Giorgio & I make our entrance at Boyle (September 18th, 2015)

CHAPTER EIGHTEEN

The Birds

Football First

As the upperclassmen had taught us from the 2013 and 2014 teams, there was no time to gloat in a victory. Mark Evanchick was always on top of that, valuing the team's success rather than his own, even though he was now only 14 sacks away from the Connecticut sack record. The media hounded him with questions regarding the record, and as always, Evanchick politely directed his answers around his teammates, not himself. He didn't give a crap about that record, because that's not what mattered to him. His primary goal was pursuing the elusive state title, and it started with himself and the team staying laser-focused, even after blowout wins. "You've got to look at it in the sense of, 'our games are numbered,' so you have to make the most of them," Evanchick says. "Even if they were blowouts, you couldn't slip up once, because if you lose one game, our seeding is changed in the state playoffs."

Evanchick was right, one loss and we were dead in the water, fighting off elimination for the rest of the season. The next two games were the most dangerous stretch of the season until we reached November, meaning the focus had to be at an all-time high. We would be traveling to Greenwich on Saturday afternoon and would follow that up with our homecoming game against St. Joes (after another bye week). If we could fight through and win both those games, our status for the state playoffs was a near lock. A weak string of games would anchor our October schedule, and then we would wrap up the season with games against Staples High School and New Canaan.

The focus was on Greenwich though, a gritty and tough team led by new head coach John Marinelli, who was the former offensive coordinator at New Canaan under his father, Lou. John Marinelli was only 29 years old taking the head coaching gig at one of the most prestigious high school programs in the state, but he was suited for the job. His fast-paced offense had given opponents fits over the years at New Canaan, and that was not going to change once he got to Greenwich. Although Greenwich wasn't supposed to contend in 2015, there was still worry in the eyes of Trifone, who knew that Marinelli would be putting everything he had into this game to seize a career win in only his second head coaching game.

The week leading up to Greenwich was brutal. Trifone had us locked in from the minute we stepped out of class and onto the field, continuously reminding us of what Marinelli and his potent offense had done to us in previous years. For me, I wasn't worried about defending receivers or anything like that because I knew Finlay Collins would be the primary defender all game long, due to his ability to drop into coverage better than me. I instead was focused on a larger issue, a physically bigger issue... Greenwich All-State tight end Scooter Harrington, who had verbally committed to Boston College earlier in the year.[1]

The Monday before the game, I stood on the field lining up for a walkthrough of our punt team when coach Erik Maul, the special team's coordinator who I had known for years, came up to me and notified me that Harrington would be lining up against me all game. I paused and looked at Maul, surprised at what he had just said. "Really?" I asked him.

"Yes. You think you can handle that Barthold?" he responded firmly.

"I think so, yea."

"Well, you're going to have to do a lot better than 'I think so' because I can find someone else."

I then reassured Maul that I could handle the 6'6 245-pound Harrington, even though in my mind I had little to no faith. I was 6'3 195-pounds at this point in the season, significantly larger than I was last season and even compared to the spring, but I was no match for the All-State Division I prospect who could bench press and squat two of me. Still, there was part of me that was accepting the challenge, not wanting to let my coaches down while also proving to them that I could do whatever they needed me to do. I saw the positives in it as well; if I could block an All-State D-I prospect, then their faith in me would sky-rocket.

That week, I went along with some of my teammates and tried to get as much film in as I could before Saturday afternoon. By this time as well, I had learned that my AP English Language & Composition teacher was not taking attendance, so my 17-year-old mind took advantage of that and skipped the class all week, electing to go down to the Tech Ed offices with Sam Giorgio and break down anything I could find on Harrington. I kept trying to find a way to block his attacks, but there was nothing I could see. His speed, his strength, and his agility were insane, causing me to nearly lose hope and tell Maul that someone else should take on the challenge. Then by the grace of God, It was Giorgio who pointed out something I had missed entirely somehow while watching film in the Tech Ed offices.

"He stops Brit. Look," Giorgio said, pointing out to a play where Harrington was stopped on a punt. "Don't wait on him, just attack him low and he'll stop." Astonished, I saw it, and couldn't believed I missed it all week. Harrington, who played both ways on offensive and defensive would rest on a punt if he didn't get by his man within the first couple of seconds. Most of the guys trying to block Harrington would wait and let him get the first move in, but if I went after him low enough and aggressive enough, he would conserve his energy for a different play. Elated and relieved, I hugged Giorgio and ran off to my next class, finally having a strategy to use the day of the game.

Pain & Suffering

After finishing our pregame stretches in Greenwich Saturday afternoon, we gathered quietly in different corners of the significantly larger locker room than we had during the previous week. Timmy Graham sat on a bench with a football in his hands, twirling it back and forth while looking straight forward. His history at Greenwich wasn't phenomenal, having thrown only one touchdown pass and struggled to connect with his receivers during the 2014 season. After such a strong showing against Stamford, Timmy knew he had to stay consistent and continue down that path to create plays and momentum for his team. There was no pressure to do well in Timmy's head, only because he expected to do well in his mind. Timmy refused to fail himself; he refused to fail his teammates; he refused to fail his town. If he played well, his teammates played well. All he had to do was take the snap and run the play, and everything else would take care of itself.

Meanwhile, Sam Giorgio laid on the ground as John Carlozzi heavily tapped both of his ankles after Sam had felt some pain in them during the Stamford game. It wasn't a significant pain, yet it was enough to cause discomfort. He didn't need to see a doctor only because pain was part of the game, something he had always known. After Carlozzi had finished, Giorgio got up and headed over to the bathrooms to put on his eye black, officially making himself ready for battle.

Eventually, the call was made for us to leave the locker room. With extreme focus, we marched two by two down the road that led to Cardinal Stadium. It was a quiet five-minute walk through a wooded area that cleared slowly to reveal a packed and rabid Greenwich fanbase. On the other side in the smaller grandstands, the Darien faithful had traveled heavy once again and were flanked by another massive student section. We reached the gate to enter the stadium, where a group of Greenwich youth football players, maybe in fifth-grade, stood watching us. Always living by the mentality of being a good sport around children, I extended my hand out for one kid who was looking for a high five. Right before slapping his hand, he pulled it back and started booing with the rest of his teammates while their adult coaches encouraged them to continue going. I walked on with Mark Schmidt at my side, where he looked at me and said, "Shit man, that's kind of fucked up."

We arrived on the sideline to a standing ovation from our crowd, the adrenaline rushing once again when I saw the people cheering and screaming for their beloved Blue Wave. The Greenwich student section and our student section began exchanging colorful chants towards each other while we stretched, adding to the big fight atmosphere. I returned to the sideline, still extremely focused, when I looked into our student section and saw the most incredible sign that put anything Greenwich chanted to rest. In reference to our FCIAC Championship victory, something Greenwich hadn't tasted since 2007, along with our dominance as a hockey program over Greenwich the prior season; a student held up the words:

"KISS MY RING."

My serious expression broke at that moment as I laughed and threw a thumbs up towards the student holding the sign. I turned my attention back to the field, where our captains were standing getting ready for the coin toss. I bounced up and down, eagerly awaiting the game to begin, ready for the war that was ahead.

From that opening kick though, the game was a complete ass-kicking. Timmy Graham had a minimal role in the game because Shelby Grant broke loose on multiple occasions against the Cardinal defense, resulting in 7.6 yards per carry. The offense was nearly unstoppable, causing me to breathe easy until late in the first quarter when we were forced to punt deep in our own territory. I trotted onto the field, trying to remain composed before lining up against Harrington. I got in my position, looking down the entire time. When the whistle blew, I looked up and saw Harrington towering over me. Our junior punter Dillon Jones called for the snap, and Harrington raced right by me. Realizing my mistake, I stepped to my right to slow his progress and finally collapsing to the ground to cut him at his legs. Jones got the punt off half a second before Harrington arrived, causing me to breathe a sigh of relief while jogging off the field.

By the second quarter, Greenwich was being smothered by our defense, which was once again being led by Mark Evanchick. There was no solution for the powerhouse defensive end, causing Greenwich to run away from wherever Evanchick lined up, which made it quite easy for our defense to find out where the ball was going on each play. Coach Forget would blitz hard to whatever side Evanchick wasn't on, causing mass destruction at the line of scrimmage and making it extremely hard for Greenwich to get anywhere.

On one of those plays, Forget called for Sam Giorgio to blitz right up the middle. Giorgio, who loved a good old fashion "A-Gap" blitz, blew through the Greenwich line and had a free shot at their quarterback. The quarterback, seeing Giorgio, rolled to his left which caused Giorgio to cut quickly in the other direction. "I cut, and something didn't feel right," says Giorgio about the moment. A sharp pain ran through both his ankles, forcing Giorgio to slow down in his pursuit of the quarterback. Evanchick came out of nowhere though and grabbed the quarterback from behind, forcing a fumble that was recovered by Tyler Grant. Giorgio came off the field after the play, refusing to show any pain in his body language, telling Carlozzi and other trainers that he was fine after the play when he clearly wasn't. "It hurt like hell, but I didn't care."

Unfortunately, Giorgio wasn't the only linebacker to get hurt that quarter. Running down on one of the kickoffs following a Shelby Grant touchdown, Mark Schmidt sprinted towards the return man when all of a sudden he heard something pop in his leg. An intense pain ripped through Schmidt's right leg, causing him to go down and realize that something was wrong. Schmidt got up, like Giorgio, and didn't mention it, deciding that it was probably something mild and that he could manage it. "I wanted to play the rest of the game, my mentality was 'fuck it,'" says Schmidt. The pain lingered with Schmidt the rest of the game, causing him to limp on and off the field while masking the injury from coaches and trainers who approached him. It would wait until after the game, Schmidt told himself. Then, he would see what was wrong.

Injuries weren't just happening on our side but were also plaguing Greenwich as well. I was standing on the sideline, slightly annoyed with the fact that I had only been on the field for a couple of punts when Coach Trifone called me over and told me I was needed for a kickoff. Looking at me before sending me out on the field, he said to me, "Show me something good. Give me something Brit!" I nodded and ran out, pissing myself off before the play. On the kick, I raced down the field, using anything I could find in my mind to motivate me. The Cardinal return man broke down towards our sideline, dodging our defenders and creating a vast amount of space as he came closer and closer. Being the last line of defense and forcing him close to the sideline, I went against everything I was taught on how to tackle and strictly went for damage on this play. Hitting him at his shoulders, I slammed him to the ground with all my weight and all his momentum colliding at once. I heard a scream from underneath me as I rolled from the tackle. I ignored it and didn't even look at the player, opting to go straight to the sideline where I sat down, happy with my work.

When the game ended, we had blown out Greenwich by a score of 58-21. Shelby Grant finished with 186 yards and five touchdowns, while Mark Evanchick totaled 11 tackles to go along with 5.5 sacks. Timmy Graham had himself another solid outing even though Grant was the star, throwing for 252 yards and a touchdown with no turnovers. It was a massive win, moving us to 2-0 going into our bye week. We celebrated before going into the handshake line, where I saw the Greenwich return man in a sling over his left arm. Walking off the field, Giorgio, Schmidt and I looked at each other. I smirked a little and then followed up with one word…

"Oops."

Like Stamford, we didn't celebrate too much, knowing that we were good enough to blow a team like Greenwich out. Still, we enjoyed that night on the bus ride home and went out in pockets, avoiding any major parties that would cause a scene and possibly get us in trouble. Before leaving the Darien locker room after arriving back home, Hudson Hamill stood in front of the team and reiterated the statement of not doing anything stupid and doing anything that could get the team in trouble. We all agreed and left with smiles on our faces, ready to enjoy the next couple of days off before returning to the field for our bye week practices.

Hudson Hamill shows Alison Mulhearn (Jim Mulhearn's daughter)
the initials "JM" which he wrote on his wrists for every game
(September 26th, 2015)

A Darien student holds up a sign during the Greenwich game
(September 26th, 2015)

CHAPTER NINETEEN

It's a Physical Game

After taking Sunday off entirely, the team returned to Darien High School on Monday to get a light lift in and break down the film from the Greenwich game. Mark Schmidt was still recovering from his injury against the Cardinals, but was realizing that things were not getting any better when his leg was swelling up to nearly twice its original size. It was excruciating for him to walk during the school day, which finally led him to question if his leg was actually alright. Looking back, Schmidt sees the issue of his decision making at the time. "I probably should have gone to a doctor right away, but I didn't," he says. Instead, he consulted the advice of coaches and other players who agreed that the swelling was because of a knot that was in Schmidt's leg. The only way to solve the problem in our eyes was to roll his leg out fiercely with a muscle roller, hoping to remove the knot and let Schmidt return to practice.

Gathering in the weight room, Schmidt laid down onto the floor while Mark Evanchick, the strongest person on the team, pressed the muscle roller down onto Schmidt's right leg. Cutting into his injured leg, Schmidt pulled back and stopped Evanchick from continuing. The coaches, still believing it to be a sturdy knot, decided to give it another try but with a different plan this time. "They had like four guys holding me down," says Schmidt. "I had a guy on each one of my arms and another on my injured leg while Evanchick rolled it out."

Outside, the sounds of Schmidt's sheer pain could be heard from across away. While he was being tortured in one room, I sat with a group of teammates in the team weight room where Bobby Trifone was getting ready to do a bench press set with the song "Locked Out of Heaven" by Bruno Mars sarcastically playing. When we heard the cries of pain from across the hall, we turned the music down and went over to see what was going on. "I just remember screaming," Schmidt recalls. "I was on the ground screaming, 'FUCK FUCK FUCK' because it felt like something was tearing in my leg." After going back and forth for nearly a minute on Schmidt's leg, Evanchick stopped, allowing Schmidt to clutch what was left of his damaged limb. The coaches, after watching the sequence of events, decided that what Schmidt needed was a couple of days off.

While Schmidt recovered from his ordeal, Sam Giorgio was also following up on his injury at his doctor's office after school. While being examined, Giorgio was expecting maybe a mild sprain or something that he could play through. When the doctor came in after the examination, it was the news Giorgio was not ready for. "The doctor told me that I had micro-fractures in both of my ankles," he says. "I looked at him and said, 'yea, that's probably not good.'"

The doctor recommended a surgery that would place pieces into the ankles to support them better with all the heavy lifting and physical exertion that Giorgio put out on a daily basis. Asking for a different option, Giorgio was told he could rest for about two months, which would allow the ankles to heal naturally without surgery. Refusing to accept either option simply because it would ruin his senior season, Giorgio opted for a different approach: "Physical therapy and a bunch of Advil," says Giorgio. "That was it." Giorgio then started attending physical therapy on a regular basis in a process Sam laughs at now. "I would get a doctor's note and leave school if I had a free or a joke class and then, go to physical therapy from 1:30 to about 2:30 pm almost every single day." Giorgio would then speed back and return just in time for practice.

The bye week could not have come at a better time for the team as we recovered from nagging injuries across the board. The week was set up to be full of light practices with little to no contact, given that we had plenty of time to prepare for St. Joe's in the next 14 days.

By Tuesday, the 29th of September, we were back on the field. We were again planning a light practice with only shoulder pads and helmets with limited contact to avoid anything from happening during the bye week. It was a gloomy late September day, and the team was extremely laid back during stretching and walkthrough drills. We broke into position groups where we as the linebackers began to do an exercise that we had done dozens of times leading up to this point, where a running back runs towards two linebackers who will meet him in a gang tackle.

The drill went fine for the first couple of reps, and after going the first time, I lined up again in my linebacker stance. Forget reminded us to take it easy and stay at about 50%, which I nodded to confirm the reminder. I put my mouth guard in, and the whistle blew, causing me to react and move forward. The linebacker opposite of me came down extremely hard, going nearly twice as fast as I was. I went down to wrap up the running back when all of a sudden I didn't feel but instead heard a massive crack coming from my helmet.

The next thing I remember was lying on the ground with my eye closed, exhaling a long and weak, "ffuucckk." I tried opening my eyes but my brain wasn't letting me, so I continued to breathe slowly on the ground. There was no pain in my head or anything, just an incredible sense of weakness in every single part of my body. I went out of consciousness for a couple of minutes, yet when I came back to it, I heard Coach Forget talking to me, saying, "Take it easy Brit, we got the trainer coming." I knew it was a concussion but was thinking it was a mild one, maybe causing me to be out for the week which was fine because of the bye week. Kate, the on-site team trainer when Carlozzi wasn't around, arrived and began asking me questions.

I knew the answers to the fundamental questions; where we were, what day it was, but had to think for a moment to tell her that it was Tuesday. I got it right though, once again making me believe that the concussion wasn't severe at all. Kate then asked me to open my eyes, to which I responded, "I can't, the sun's too bright."

There was a pause, followed by Coach Forget saying, "Brit, the sun's not out."

I swore again. I knew that wasn't a good sign, so I immediately began to think of the worse case scenario. I was going to be out for a month, forcing me to miss the bulk of my senior season, something I had worked so hard for during the past decade. I came close to crying while lying on the ground, but Coach Forget stood by, continuing to let me know that everything was going to be alright.

A Shattered Dream

It was the first time during my decade-long football career that I had sustained a diagnosed concussion. There were plenty of times through youth football and high school as

After I got home from practice, there were less negative thoughts flowing through my mind. Watching my friends practice was a motivating factor since while watching, I began to miss football more and more. It was emotional but a real motivating factor. It forced my mind to start to think about finding a way back, even though it seemed impossible. Entering my bedroom, I laid down on my bed with my hands over my head, trying to figure out what I could do to get back as soon as I could. Getting up, I went over to my desk in my dark room to look at my physical calendar, since I wasn't able to use a phone as part of the treatment for my concussion. I counted carefully on the calendar, where I had all the games listed for the 2015 season. I counted eight weeks from the day, trying to figure out what the earliest date could be for my return if everything went smoothly during my recovery. It ended up being Tuesday, November 24, only a couple of days before the 2015 Turkey Bowl.

The Turkey Bowl. Goosebumps ran over my entire body. If I could get back for the Turkey Bowl, that was all that mattered. That was *the* game, the biggest of them all. I knew that entering high school, playing in the Turkey Bowl was one of my main goals, one of my only true goals. Still, my cluttered and barely functioning brain knew that realistically, there was a minimal chance I would be playing in the biggest game of the year only two days removed from returning after a major concussion.

Still, I kept on thinking. I knew that if I showed rapid improvement, even if I wasn't feeling rapidly better, I could revisit a doctor and get cleared earlier than the eight-week mark. Sitting in my room, I made six weeks my end goal of returning to the football field. That way, I would return in early November for a meaningless game against Fairfield Warde where I could reintroduce my body to football and prepare myself three weeks ahead of time before the Turkey

Bowl. In my mind, it was a fool-proof plan that was going to work. Nothing was going to stop me, not after everything I had put myself through to get to this senior season. I wanted to be out there with my teammates, my brothers... my family.

I was coming back, no matter what.

Blind Sided

While I began my quest to push myself to impossible limits to return to the field, my teammates began preparation for our homecoming game against St. Joe's. The Cadet's were coming off two straight wins against Brien McMahon and Danbury High School, making the game an early-season showdown between two undefeated FCIAC teams. The game was huge for us because, with a win, we would be on the fast track to an FCIAC title berth due to our relatively soft schedule leading up to our late November showdown against Staples High School.

By the second practice, after I came back to watch, Coach Trifone came up to me on the field where I was sitting in my folding chair facing forwards. First asking me how I felt, he then proceeded to ask me if I wanted to do something a little more productive since I was still a member and senior on the team. Letting him know that I would be happy to do anything for the team, he then led me over to the end zone with the other coaches and handed me a big stack of play cards. "You're going to help run the scout offense," Trifone said with a smile. Having always been somewhat fascinated with the art of coaching, I accepted immediately, once again feeling like I was back on the team contributing. The "job" was huge to me. Instead of sulking on the sideline, I was back on the field laughing with my teammates and enjoying the moments while also half distracting myself from the sadness that had surrounded me following the injury. I also began to notice an extreme positive throughout it all too; I got to show up to practice every day in sweatpants and slippers, while also not having to run after practice during conditioning.

However, It was a different story when I returned to the classroom that week. I was warned by my doctor to take it easy the first few days back, and I had no problem with that since I had already been a lazy student during my senior year. The first class that I went to was my math class, where we began the school day with a simple exercise to refresh our memories from the previous lessons. My teacher was aware of my concussion, so he gave me a more straightforward problem set and told me to take as long as I needed. I thanked him and looked down to the paper, where the numbers mashed all together in my head. I had no idea what I was looking at, had no idea what number was on the page, and was beginning to feel my head almost burst from both sides like it was being pressed on. I looked up to my teacher and pointed to the door hoping to be excused. I took the rest of the period off, slightly scared from the experience.

The next day things were a little better in my math class, where I was able to decipher the numbers slowly but still took nearly three minutes to complete a problem (before the concussion, it took me probably close to a minute). Thinking that I was making progress, I continued with my day which led to my final class, Neurology. Sitting in my chair, my teacher turned on the projector to present the lesson for the days. It was fine for me until she turned off the lights, causing a massive burning sensation and screeching pain in my head from the projector, which forced me to get up and leave without warning. I went straight to the bathroom and stared into the mirror, tears forming once again in my eyes. Feeling nauseous, I looked up and said one phrase…

"Why is this happening to me?"

Life continued to move forward afterward, not pausing for

me and my limitations. In fact, life continued to move forward for the team as well, with St. Joe's coming to town after what had seemed like an incredibly long two weeks. On a sunny mid-October afternoon, we stormed out in front of our crowd for the home opener, wearing our black jerseys with white pants. The crowd cheered loudly for us, causing me to smile but also feel a sense of sadness by missing the home opener for my senior year. There I was dressed in khakis and Timberlands with my #44 jersey on, feeling a massive itch to be hitting someone out on the actual field.

As I battled emotional pain of missing out, Mark Schmidt continued to hound Coach Forget, telling him that he was good to go and that his leg was fine. Schmidt knew he was lying, but in all fairness, his leg did feel a little better after all the Advil that he took pregame to numb the pain down a little bit. After going through warm-ups and showing the coaches that he was fine, the decision to let Schmidt play was made, all to the excitement of the player himself.

Unlike in 2014 after scoring 17 points in the first half, the Cadet's offense disappeared in the 2015 contest. The stout defense led by Mark Evanchick pounded the opponent at every single turn, causing mass frustration on the St. Joe's sideline. Evanchick was unstoppable, collecting 3.5 sacks which put him only five sacks away from the all-time Connecticut sack record. Timmy Graham was on fire against the Cadet defense, throwing for 254 yards and a touchdown that led to a score of 21-0 Darien near the end of the first half. Still, Graham got the ball once again with only a couple of minutes to go. He drove quickly down the field and was at around the 25-yard line when he dropped back to pass. Looking deep, Graham brought his arm back to throw when out of nowhere a St. Joe's defender cracked Timmy from his blind side, nearly breaking the quarterback in half and causing a fumble in the process. Always a quick thinker,

Hudson Hamill saw the ball pop out and grabbed it, darting towards the end zone for a crazy 22-yard touchdown.

The celebration was short lived as Graham laid on the ground in an incredible amount of pain from the hit. Looking back, Graham still remembers the extreme agony he was in afterward. "That was the most pain I have ever been in," he says. "It felt like someone had stuck a knife in me and dragged it down my back." Graham was immediately rushed to the training room at halftime, where Carlozzi went to work to find out what had happened to the star quarterback. Coach Trifone, knowing his team was up 28-0, stood outside the locker room thinking about what to do about the quarterback situation. He had junior Brian Peters at his disposal; although he knew one more touchdown would put the game in the bag, so he went into the training room and asked Timmy for a favor. "I remember Trifone came into the training room," Graham says. "He looked at me and said, 'I won't force you, but I need one drive out of you.'" Graham nodded, fighting through the discomfort as he stood up and headed out for the second half.

"It was tough, only because I really couldn't turn my body when I threw," says Graham. The offense got the ball to start the second half, where Graham gingerly made his way out onto the field. He took the snap and went to drop back, feeling the stabbing pain in his back as he did so. Unable to turn his body, Graham dumped a quick pass to Shelby Grant, who broke through the St. Joe's defense for a 64-yard touchdown scamper, effectively putting the game to rest along with Graham's day. Limping off the field, Graham took off his shoulder pads and helmets, immediately going to Carlozzi for more treatment on his physically destroyed back.

Thankfully, the injury turned out to be nothing major. Graham had bruised his oblique but wasn't expected to miss any time because of the injury. It was great news following the 49-7 drubbing of St. Joe's, something that made almost every player on the team let out a big sigh of relief. Injuries were the last thing the team needed after everything that had happened at Greenwich, especially considering that Graham was the motor of the entire offense. On the defensive side of the ball, things were a little less optimistic on the injury report. Mark Schmidt, who had totaled five tackles in the game, continued to feel extreme pain after the game. In fact, he was unable to stand at all in the locker room following the victory. After Giorgio and I helped him, Schmidt finally caved and decided to visit a doctor during the team's off day on Sunday.

Arriving at the doctor's office, Schmidt was hoping to receive news similar to Graham, guessing that it maybe was just a massive bruise that could be healed with proper treatment. The doctor though saw something completely different. The doctor found that during the Greenwich game, Schmidt had partially torn his right quad. Surprised and shocked, Schmidt told the doctor that he had played after the injury against Greenwich and St. Joe's, who responded with the same surprise and shock that Schmidt was emitting.

Afterward, Schmidt saw the situation in a more serious light. "Yea, I definitely made a mistake playing on it," he says. "It was dumb. In the moment though, my mentality was to play through it, because that was football." The damage Schmidt had done to his quad was significant, especially after Mark Evanchick had slowly torn it more while rolling out his leg in front of the coaching staff. It didn't help either when Schmidt pushed through the pain and played against St. Joe's. Now, with the weaker part of the schedule coming up, Schmidt was advised to take a month off from playing to heal, which officially put him on the injury report with me, leaving Sam Giorgio (who was fighting his ankle injury) as the only senior linebacker left standing after only three games.

Still, the team was 3-0 heading into a stretch of very winnable games, making us seniors extraordinarily pleased but also very focused on not messing up during that stretch. On the field, we needed to stay sharp. Off the field, we needed to remain out of the big party scene and away from anything that could get us in trouble. Although the scheduled games were easy, the season was about to become a mental and emotional test for all those involved in the decade-long quest for state glory.

A group of DJFL players and fans gather on top of the Darien High School cafeteria while watching Darien play St. Joe's (October 10th, 2015)

Tyler Grant & Shelby Grant walk out together before a late October game (October 30th, 2015)

CHAPTER TWENTY

A Mental Test

It's a Trap!

The night before our Friday night showdown with Brien McMahon High School, Mark Evanchick sat quietly at home briefly going over the film notes that Coach Forget had sent out the Monday after St. Joe's. Evanchick had memorized everything earlier in the week but was going over everything one last time, just to make sure he knew it all. Unsurprisingly, he passed the test. Even against an opponent like McMahon, Evanchick wasn't going to slip up on his rigorous mental preparation for the game. He never went out the night before a game, not only to stay out of trouble but more or less to get as much rest as possible before a Friday night showdown.

Friday nights were always extremely special to Evanchick, mainly because of the lack of stadium lights at Darien High School. He relished in the opportunity to play on Friday's, strictly because of the feeling he got. "It's really the atmosphere and the build-up," Evanchick says. "Usually you're used to waking up on a Saturday and going straight to the field. But with Friday nights, it builds throughout the day. It's prolonging; the anticipation builds, it makes it that much cooler." With it being his senior year as well, Evanchick

316

started to enjoy the little things more and more. Strong or weak opponent, it didn't phase Mark. Humble as ever, he understood that every play could be his last, that a freak injury could occur, causing him to have to end his playing career prematurely. It wasn't negative thinking, but more of a realistic reflection. He knew the dangers of the game but also recognized that the positives outweighed the negatives, causing him to continue to do what he loved while enjoying every single minute of it.

Evanchick was also no stranger to the pressures of being a high school athlete. It seemed like out of everyone on the team, Evanchick had the most pressure weighing down on him during the 2015 season. It didn't bother him, once again ignoring the outside influence of the state sack record and the state title predictions that were all over Twitter and other news websites. The media was blocked out in his mind, because their opinions or predictions didn't matter, even if they were in support of us. "Yea, the media definitely hyped our team up pretty big," he says on the situation. "We didn't need to pay attention to that though. We had the belief in ourselves that we could do it and nobody was going to stand in our way until we got that state title."

McMahon wasn't a dangerous opponent. Coming into the game, they were 1-3 with losses to both Stamford and St. Joe's, teams that we had no trouble with earlier in our schedule. Trifone didn't care though, reiterating all through the week that his former team could pose as a threat to the always looming "trap game," or game that we were massively favored to win in. Trifone was in no mood after such a great start to fall victim to the brutalities of a trap game, so the focus remained extremely high during preparation that week.

On the sidelines, while the team prepped for McMahon, I was slightly less upset because Schmidt had joined me in the injured reserve festivities. During practice, Schmidt and I would assist in anything that was needed during scout drills but then would run around like a bunch of 12-year-olds playing catch the rest of the time. We tested our ability to make one-handed catches and would make the grabs harder than they had to be, much to the dismay of our teammates who were running with Carlozzi until near death. When Friday night came at Brien McMahon High School, Schmidt and I continued our childish actions pregame when there was nothing for us to do. Not wanting to watch the team stretch and warm-up, we instead grabbed a football and tired ourselves out with circus shots and pure acts of stupidity; torn quad, concussion and all. "Oh it was awesome," says Schmidt on it all. "The team is stretching and locked in while we are taking basketball shots with a football into hoops we are making with our arms, it was just us having fun."

After our fun and games, Schmidt and I watched in our sweatpants, slippers and jerseys on the sideline as our teammates decimated Brien McMahon by a score of 42-10. Timmy Graham threw for a total of 195 yards to go with four touchdown passes and no turnovers, spreading the ball out to a total of seven receivers. Minicus and Hamill combined for 98 yards and three touchdowns, adding to their already impressive numbers while nearing the halfway mark of the regular season. Defensively, sophomore Nick Green, who started in place of Schmidt, debuted with substantial numbers, collecting a mass of tackles during the stretch of the game. Sam Giorgio, who was still banged up and feeling the effects of his ankle injuries, continued to impress while stuffing up the middle and forcing McMahon to run outside where they met Mark Evanchick. Like the previous games during the season, the starters were out midway through the third quarter, giving way for junior varsity players to get game experience while also providing the varsity guys any extra rest that their bodies needed, Giorgio included.

The following weekend, we returned to our home field for a game against Danbury High School, who was coming into the game with a winless record on the season. The game wasn't even considered a trap game but more or less a guaranteed victory. You could call it arrogance or cockiness, yet we felt it was just confidence in our abilities. Even though the game was pitting the #3 team in the state[1] against a winless team, the crowd was expected to be significantly larger than at previous games, because a win against Danbury would give Coach Trifone his 200th career victory. On game day, as Schmidt and I played catch, fans shuffled into the stands at Darien High School with signs reading "#200" in support of Trifone, cheering at the sight of the coach when he came out of the tunnel for the first time. Not wanting to give the team the idea that this game was a guaranteed win, even though we all knew it was, Trifone did not acknowledge the signs or cheers.

Trifone was able to breathe pretty easy going into halftime holding a 42-0 lead against Danbury, especially since Shelby Grant was averaging a ridiculous 17.6 yards per carry to go along with two touchdowns. During the second half as the game drew closer to an end, chants from the crowd began to break out in tribute of the head coach while a smile broke out on his face. With only seconds remaining, both Bobby and Christian Trifone went up to their father and hugged him, congratulating him on the incredible achievement. When the final horn sounded, we had prevailed 49-6 and began to celebrate our beloved coach. On the field, a video tribute played on the scoreboard where former players ranging from Brien McMahon to Darien High School shared favorite memories of Coach Trifone while also congratulating him on the milestone achievement.

Speaking to the media after the game, Trifone was near

tears but was quick to turn the attention away from his achievement to the reason why he reached the milestone. "You can not reach milestones like this without (first) great athletes," he said. "I've been blessed my entire career with absolutely incredible athletes, phenomenal staff and third, a family that understands what your passion is and (understands) why you aren't home for four months."[2]

The celebration continued afterward with a cake being presented and the team gathering around. I stood there happy for my coach but bothered by one thing... My head was pounding from everything that had happened that day. From the yelling and screaming I did during the game, it was clear that my mind wasn't ready for the exertion I put it through during the day. My teammates were going to McDonald's following the game, but I declined the invitation, instead opting to go home and rest my still damaged head. I didn't want to raise any concerns from my parents, knowing that I was so close to being cleared and that the slightest bump would change that, so I told them I was tired and in need of a nap. With my head caving in from both sides, I went up to my bedroom and closed my eyes, praying that the pain would go away forever.

Halfway There

The Danbury game marked the halfway point of our season, putting us at 5-0 and atop the FCIAC alongside New Canaan. The Friday night following the Danbury game, we were scheduled to travel to Wilton High School for what was our final Friday night lights game of the season. The day of the game, we didn't follow the usual tradition of dressing in button-down shirts and ties for school. Instead, we decided that each position group would dress-up for Halloween since the holiday was the following day. The Halloween tradition was picked up from the 2013 seniors when Alex Gunn and the offensive linemen dressed up as police officers while the quarterbacks and receivers dressed up as convicts. We decided to expand on the idea, which resulted in Sam, Schmidt and I gathering up in Giorgio's upstairs movie room to create our costume for school the next day.

Since we were linebackers, and in football terminology, we were the guys who played in "the box," the three of us decided to paste together cardboard boxes to wear around which were labeled, "Coach Forget's Box." The costumes, which had football context along with an incredibly inappropriate context, were vulgar enough to get us possibly removed from school that day. We took our chances and showed up to school wearing our ridiculous costumes. Not to be outdone, Timmy Graham showed up with his receivers in a full Big Bird costume, with Shelby Grant dressed up as Elmo and Hudson Hamill as the Cookie Monster. Confident in our abilities on the field for the night game, we enjoyed the entire school day in our ridiculous costumes.

When the school day ended, the idea of the Wilton game being our final Friday night game was present in the locker room and became a centerpiece of our minds during the drive up Fujitani Field that evening. In his pregame letter, Trifone wrote:

"Seniors, this is the last game you will ever play together under Friday night lights... I tell you every day, you have to play with passion every day and on every play. If you are truly a champion, you will dismantle them in every phase of tonight's game and LND, "Leave No Doubt" who the best team in the FCIAC is...

Vince Lombardi once said: 'It is impossible to be a champion occasionally! You have to put your best foot forward every day... every play.'

* * *

Play like a Championship Team Tonight!!!

Sincerely,
    T"

Reading the letter, I became upset, realizing that I only had one Friday night opportunity during my senior year, and that was against Stamford earlier in the season. His words of telling the team to play with passion struck me hard too, knowing that I was missing game after game with my teammates and losing the chance to play at every corner. I continued to try to stay optimistic after reading the letter, understanding that I was possibly only weeks away from being cleared, which would allow me to play with an unwavering amount of passion once I returned.

While Schmidt and I were out again for the week, Sam Giorgio sat with his pads by his side riding on the bus to Wilton. He wasn't going to need them, however, since he talked with Coach Forget hours before the game. The defensive coordinator told Sammy to take the night off. It was a weak opponent, a meaningless game, and Forget needed his inside linebacker at full health for the tail end of the regular season. Giorgio didn't relent, knowing that he needed to rest his rapidly deteriorating ankles so he could make it the rest of the way. He was playing through extreme pain day in and day out, so the idea of a night off where he wasn't putting intense pressure on his ankles was a welcomed thought.

There on that night before Halloween, the SWAT Team sat on the sidelines watching our teammates warm-up, chuckling at the fact that we all had ended up injured at precisely the same time. We were supposed to be the "Three Musketeers," playing all three linebacker positions and being the seniors leading the way. For all three of us though, the only thing that mattered was that we were healthy and playing in the Turkey

Bowl in a little less than four weeks. I was distraught and still battling waves of sadness over the fact that I had missed such a big bulk of my senior season but kept looking towards the bigger goal like Giorgio and Schmidt: The Turkey Bowl. That was the only regular season game that mattered and was honestly the only reason I was fighting so hard to come back. That night in Wilton, that's all we talked about. "I just want to play in the Turkey Bowl. That is all that matters right now."

Walking out for the game, the atmosphere was less than ideal for a Friday game. Coming out of Wilton's tunnel, we saw that our fans had arrived in full force while the Wilton fans didn't show up at all. Their stands were empty, only except for their band, who made up the majority of their fanbase, which made it seem a little sadder for the struggling program. As Giorgio, Schmidt and I laid back on the sideline, the team went on a rampage against the Wilton Warriors. Timmy Graham, who was putting all those Friday night doubts to rest, torched the Wilton defense. By halftime, Graham was putting up video game numbers under the lights at Fujitani Field. Right off the bat, he connected with fellow senior Rock Stewart for a 52-yard gain, signaling to Wilton that he was here to play. He completed 16 out of his 17 passes for 330 yards and five touchdowns, two of those went to Minicus, who had 113 receiving yards by the end of the second quarter. Graham didn't step on the field during the second half; instead, watching from the sideline as the junior varsity guys took over and finished off a 48-7 victory over Wilton.

The day after the Wilton victory, I visited my doctor for a follow-up on my concussion and neck injury to see how much improvement I had made. The neck was still extremely bothersome for me, but I brushed it off as being okay, lying to the doctor with the hopes that he would clear me. The concussion symptoms had gotten better since I was no longer getting constant headaches or having trouble looking at problem sets in school. Even though I was still experiencing headaches here and there, I decided not to bring them up. The doctor went through all the motions, carefully examining me and testing my abilities. After finishing up, the doctor looked at me and prepared to give me the verdict.

"Well, I'd say you're good to go."

An extreme feeling of overwhelming ecstasy took over my body as I broke out a huge smile in front of the doctor. It was a fantastic feat for me since I had fought hard and achieved the goal I had set. After giving me the news, I shook his hand and thanked him with my massive grin still on my face, already thinking about putting my shoulder pads and helmet on for Monday's practice. I rushed home and gathered all of the football stuff that I had put away in my closet, eagerly waiting for the opportunity to go to Darien High School to put all of it back into its rightful place inside of my locker.

Not everything was joyous that day for Darien football. At around the same time, Mark Schmidt went to visit his doctor to see if he had made any progress in the month that he had taken off for his partially torn quad. Inside the white walls, Schmidt sat quietly waiting for his doctor to come in and check out his leg. Schmidt was still in an incredible amount of pain when he exerted pressure on his right leg, although he didn't seem to mind it. He knew he could play through it since he had done so against both Greenwich and St. Joe's earlier in the season. Even if he thought he could play, Schmidt understood that the decision came down to the doctor, who had the power to either clear him or shut him down depending on what he saw during the examination.

When the doctor walked in, Schmidt perked up to look his best. He wanted to nail the first impression and make it seem like all was good, even though it wasn't. The doctor put Schmidt through a series of tests, trying to get a good understanding of how the quad had healed during the time off. The final analysis was the game breaker; Schmidt had to extend his right leg all the way out to a straight position, which would allow the doctor to see if the quad had made any progress. Schmidt gripped the sides of the examination bench and pushed with everything he had, but failed. The pain was too much as he let out a deep breath, looking at the doctor for some leniency. The doctor though, needing to do his job, looked at Schmidt and gave him the grim news.

With everything he had seen, the doctor made the call to shut him down for the rest of the year.

Schmidt refused to believe it, asking the doctor again what was wrong with his leg, saying that he felt fine even though he wasn't. The doctor explained it to Schmidt again, telling him that his quad had not heal as expected during his month off but instead became more damaged over time. Desperately looking for any silver-lining, Schmidt begged the doctor to clear him. The doctor, who was looking out for Schmidt and his long-term health, refused to do so. Not wanting to decimate the already heartbroken linebacker, the doctor told Schmidt that he would consider clearing him for the state title game in December if Darien made it.

Getting into his car, Mark sat alone in his thoughts. He drove home in silence, thinking about everything the doctor had told him during the visit. Anger filled his body on the drive home, but he remained collected since Schmidt had never been an overly emotional guy. He then got home and skipped by his parents who asked him how the appointment went. Finally, the emotions overtook Mark, who limped into his bedroom and began to cry. The child inside of him was crushed, his lifelong addiction to football now a pile of dust. It consumed him, the idea of letting his team and his town down along with knowing that the state title dream was now out of his hands. It was up to the rest of the team to continue that pursuit, something Schmidt was no longer a part of.

Cherish It

The morning of Saturday, November 7th was quite gloomy. Clouds had covered the sky to create a dark shadow over the field at Darien High School. I sat alone in the grandstands three hours before kickoff with my blue #44 jersey on while listening to M83's *Hurry Up, We're Dreaming* album. I watched a DJFL practice on the field, seeing the young players run wildly around the turf in their blue and white jerseys mimicking the actions of stars like Timmy Graham and Mark Evanchick. When I stepped onto the field to do my pre-pregame warmups (consisting of basic sprints and stretching on the field before the team officially comes out), I gave high fives out to any player that came up to me after their practice, as they wore the blue and white with extreme pride.

I took everything in during the lead up to the Warde game that morning. Everything from watching the DJFL practices to enjoying John Carlozzi taping my wrists and ankle, only because I knew what it felt like to have something I love ripped away from me in a matter of seconds. After my concussion, I had a new sense of the game, knowing that there was a possibility of me getting injured once again and this time forcing me out for good. I no longer cared that I was not the starting star outside linebacker. I was more worried about enjoying being a football player in general. Besides, Finlay Collins was having a breakout year defensively which made me incredibly proud, knowing that during the summer I had been a part of some of his development on the field at 7v7 camps and CCSU. There was no jealousy in it, since I knew I would be playing special teams and on defense occasionally. Instead, there was once again that sense of enjoyment and need to savor every moment of every minute. I had already lost six weeks of my senior year. In my mind, I wasn't going to miss another opportunity to live out and enjoy my dream.

The Warde game was another easy win for our team. Timmy Graham had a quick day, throwing 13 total passes for ten completions to go along with four touchdowns; two of which went to Rock Stewart. Mark Evanchick stayed efficient on defense, collecting eight tackles with 1.5 sacks, bringing him only half a sack away from the state record. I was playing by the second quarter when Forget decided to give Collins some rest before the big game the following week against Staples. I felt pretty rusty in the game since I hadn't been doing any contact drills during practice and was still getting back into the groove of hitting. I had also lost over ten pounds during my time off because I wasn't cleared to lift weights, so the power that I utilized earlier in the season was nowhere near what it used to be. I still played well for my standards, totaling three tackles on the day in what ended up to be a 56-19 win over the Fairfield Warde Mustangs, putting us at 7-0 on the season.

The victory was once again celebrated, although a little less than our previous blowout victories. There was a somber feeling within the senior class, knowing that the next week would be our final game played at Darien High School on Senior Day. There was the always present dream of running out of the tunnel and being honored individually, something we all dreamed about back in 2005 as third-graders; but there was also the fact that after next week, we would never play a football game again on the fields we grew up around for a decade of our lives. For the next week, it wasn't about Staples or playing for a berth in the FCIAC Championship. It was about living out our childhood dreams on our field of dreams for one final game.

CHAPTER TWENTY-ONE

The Beginning of the End

Senior Day

The night following the Fairfield Warde game, Sam Giorgio decided he was going out on a drive with a couple of his friends. Trying to stay away for any parties, Giorgio had made it part of his postgame routine to drive around Darien at night for hours at a time. Maybe he had picked up the need to drive around from the sermons he listened to from Springsteen, or perhaps it was because of the peaceful nature the drives through the backstreets of Darien during nightfall gave him. There was something in the night that eased Giorgio after a physically draining game, almost as if he was driving off the sharp pain in his ankles or the bruises that covered his shoulders. Giorgio didn't just like the drives around with his friends but loved them, since it was an escape from the troubles of the game he worshipped.

In the midst of his drive, Giorgio heard the music he was playing stop because of a call that was coming through to his phone. It was from his mother, which puzzled him, since she usually would let him be alone during the weekend nights after a football game. He answered his phone and asked his mom what was up. "She paused and then started talking,"

Giorgio says. "And then she told me that my grandfather had passed away."

It stunned Giorgio, who had been extremely close with his grandfather ever since he was a child. "My big thing with my grandfather was that he was the whole reason I played football," Sam says about him. "He loved the game, and he was thrilled to find out that I was a starting football player my senior year because he never had one." The news devastated Giorgio, who had wanted his grandfather to watch the rest of his season to play out, to let him live his dream through his grandson and see him succeed in ways that he always wanted out of Sam and his brother.

While thinking about his grandfather, Giorgio also began to experience a feeling that a lot of the seniors, including myself, were starting to feel around that time. "His death reminded me that this was it," Giorgio says. "This was my senior year. And it hurt because these guys were my brothers, I loved them. Yet it was coming to an end."

As Sam grieved the loss of his grandfather, Mark Schmidt sat inside another doctor's office refusing to give up on the season just yet. After his first doctor had informed him that his season was almost entirely over, Schmidt began to attend rigorous physical therapy sessions to try to gain an advantage so that he could convince doctors that he was okay to play. That day, the doctor put Schmidt through the same series of tests that the previous doctor had, with this time Schmidt pushing himself as hard as he could to pass. It came down to the final test which he had failed previously, where Schmidt had to extend his right leg completely straight. Schmidt gripped the sides of the examination table hard, pushing with everything he had inside to get his leg to straighten out while trying not to show any emotion on his face. Even with the excruciating pain that was running through his right quad, Schmidt managed to straighten out his leg in front of the doctor. Seeing that the determined linebacker had passed the test, the doctor gave Schmidt the thumbs up and cleared him.

Ecstatic, Schmidt immediately rushed to practice following the appointment to give notice to the coaches. He went up to Coach Forget and notified him of his return, which caused a response from the defensive coordinator that surprised Schmidt. "You know Mark; Nick Green has been playing pretty well. Take another week off and rest," Forget told him. Schmidt, who wasn't having any of what Forget was telling him, had his own response.

"I said to him, 'Coach, I'm 100%. You have to let me play,'" Schmidt remembers of the conversation. "Obviously that was bullshit because I was still in a lot of pain, but I was cleared, so I was going to play." Forget, seeing the fire in the eyes of the senior, decided to give Schmidt the start on Saturday. Schmidt broke out into a smile and thanked his coach, rushing after towards the locker room to get ready for practice.

Schmidt coming back was a massive deal, not only because he was playing again but also because it was Senior Day, which was capped off with a big-time game against Staples to determine who would face New Canaan for the FCIAC Championship. If we won, it would be a repeat of 2014 where the Turkey Bowl would be moved to Boyle Stadium and double as the FCIAC Championship game. If we lost, we would play New Canaan at Darien High School, although that was never an option in our minds. We knew we were going to beat Staples which is what made the build-up to Senior Day that much bigger; we understood it would be our last game played at Darien High School. I had been watching high school football, playing youth football and then finally playing for Darien High School on the stadium field for almost all of my life. All in all, that field was holy to me.

I arrived at Darien High School at around 9:30 am for the 1

pm game against Staples. I sat inside the locker room for about half an hour which is when I went into the training room to see if anyone was in there to tape my wrists and ankle. Kate was there, so she taped me up as I sat in silence. Afterward, I went out through the tunnel to the empty stadium where I slowly walked onto the turf field. I turned my music off and listened to the silence around the stadium, only hearing the sound of a whistle from an early morning DJFL practice being held in the end zone near the parking lot. For almost another half an hour, I slowly walked back and forth around the field, soaking in all the memories that I had made during my countless games on the stadium. I went to the end zones, waving the DJFL players and coaches farther down to which they obliged, where I remembered getting my first Coach Trifone speech way back in the fourth grade. I went to the middle of the field, where we had sat together as a team in eighth-grade following our monumental championship victory.

During our pregame stretches, I continued to soak in the moments on the field while watching Timmy Graham do the same. He sat on the bench with a football in hand, looking around the stadium and at the fans who were slowly entering. Hudson Hamill, who was usually one of the loudest players on the field during warmups, stood quietly while taking it all in. He saw his name flash across the video board and remembered how he dreamed of a day like this. It was here now, and it was time to enjoy it.

We gathered in the locker room before the game officially began. Coach Trifone had posted the letters on each locker hours before the game, which resulted in all of us seniors sitting by our lockers and reading the words Trifone had written to us over and over again. Sam Giorgio sat next to me silently while Hudson Hamill bounced up and down to the music that was playing over the speakers. Then there was

Mark Schmidt, who had been through a rollercoaster ride in his attempts to get back. The five-minute warning came, and calmness continued to flow through Schmidt. He opened his locker one final time before the game and grabbed a bottle of Advil. Opening it, Schmidt took a handful and threw them down into his body, doing whatever he could to ease the pain that was ripping through his right leg. He then proceeded to walk through the entrance to the track locker room, where he sat in silence alone, waiting for the final call to come.

Since it was Senior Day, Trifone sent out the underclassmen first because tradition was that seniors would be announced individually. It was a surreal moment, sitting alone in the locker room with my fellow teammates. I looked around and thought about the incredible statistic that defined our grade: 50 eighth-graders had played on the 2011 co-championship team. Now, only 14 of those players would be walking out on Senior Day. We laughed and joke while sitting alone in the locker room together, with Spencer Stovall leading the way into making the situation light and more laid back. We then got a knock on the door to notify us that was time to go, so we all got up in alphabetical order and headed for the tunnel.

With my last name starting with a "B," I was going to be the first one to be introduced. We turned the corner to the tunnel where everyone paused, giving way for me to walk through the Darien High School tunnel and slam my hand against the "Punched In" sign one final time. I stood still underneath the sign, awaiting my cue to run out where the underclassmen had formed a high five line to extend the tunnel all the way onto the turf. I then heard the words I had fantasized in my mind since I was a child, hearing the stadium announcer belt out, "#44…" I closed my eyes. I gently put my hands up onto the sign together and then spread them wide to reveal the words "Punched In." I began to walk forward with my heart pounding, taking each step as if it were my last. Then, all of a sudden…

"BBRRIITTTTOONN BBAARRTTHHOOLLDD!"

The adrenaline rushed through, forcing me to sprint at full speed into the bright sunlight that came down onto the field. I heard the cheers of the crowd, feeling every emotion at once take over my body. I hit the field where Coach Trifone was waiting to shake my hand and give me a hug, where he also said, "Proud of you, Brit." I looked at him and somehow through it all managed to thank him. I then proceeded to line up next to my longtime head coach, ready to watch the rest of my teammates come out for the festivities.

While the rest of my teammates felt a warm reception from the crowd, Mark Evanchick got the biggest roar from the stadium when his name was announced. The living legend was ready for a big day, needing only half a sack to secure the Connecticut record for sacks in a high school football career. Media members from all over the state showed up in full force to hopefully watch the record held by NFL star Dwight Freeney be broken, putting all the pressure on the 17-year-old Evanchick to deliver to the fans.

It didn't take Evanchick long once the game started as he manhandled the Staples offensive line early. He wasn't able to find the quarterback, however, as Staples was a run-heavy option team that rarely put the ball in the air. Staples also held Timmy Graham and the offense at bay which shocked the Blue Wave faithful after having seen such dominant performances from the air-raid of Darien. At the end of the first quarter, we led by a score of 6-0, which was only the second time all year that we did not lead by double digits after the first 12 minutes.

In the second quarter, Graham found Colin Minicus in the end zone, pushing the lead to 12-0. Almost immediately afterward, Christian Trifone blocked a Staples punt, forcing a safety and putting the score at 14-0. We traded possessions back and forth with the Wreckers of Staples as both teams played stifling defense. Then, with under a minute to play in the quarter, Staples junior quarterback Andrew Speed started to drive down the field in hopes of getting on the board before halftime. Speed dropped back to pass near the 50-yard line when Evanchick beat the Staples left tackle to the outside. Evanchick cut quickly back inside, and before Speed could react, Evanchick pulled him to the ground for his 62nd and a half sack of his career, breaking Freeney's record.

The crowd erupted at the sight of Evanchick sacking Speed. The sideline jumped in sync, with John Carlozzi holding up his fist in celebration. Evanchick, humble as ever, was swarmed by his teammates as the crowd rose to their feet to applaud the record-holding defensive end. Evanchick didn't bask in the moment; he chose instead to head straight to the sideline where his father was waiting to hug him. Burying himself into his father's arms, the crowd stood and cheered at the sight of the legendary football player conquering the record that had overshadowed him all season long.

I Can't Hear You…

Even after Evanchick's once in a lifetime moment, there was still an entire half of football to be played, especially since we only held a 14-0 lead going into the third quarter. Trifone went quickly from smiles to game-mode after retreating to the locker room where he ripped into the offense for what was the worst half we had played all year. Penalty after penalty along with three fumbles destroyed the offense during the first two quarters, which in turn forced Trifone to call out Timmy Graham and the other seniors to step up and play. Graham answered the call, hitting Shelby Grant in the third quarter for a quick six points, creating a three-possession lead.

On the defensive side of the ball, Mark Schmidt was having the comeback of his life. On his still extremely damaged right leg, Schmidt collected a sack to go along with ten tackles on the day. It was incredible, almost as if there was nothing wrong with him. He moved quick and crisp, reading each play and flying to the ball with ease. Opposite of him, an incredibly motivated Sam Giorgio played his heart out, putting together his best performance up to that point with ten tackles of his own while the memory of his grandfather ran through him.

Early in the fourth quarter, the offense was stopped short of the first down marker deep in our territory. Trifone elected to punt, sending me out with the rest of the special teams unit to try to fight our way out of our own end zone. Dillon Jones sent the ball flying past the 50-yard line, giving the defense plenty of room to work with against a Staples team that was desperate for points. The defense stuffed Staples on the first play, creating a second and long situation which Sam Giorgio remembers vividly. "They were running their stupid triple option, and I was engaged with one of their guards," Giorgio remembers. "I went to get off the block, but a guy came from the left side. He went straight at me, going helmet to helmet to the side of my head."

Giorgio hit the ground and felt slightly dazed but still got up after seeing the Staples running back get tackled. "Then all of a sudden, I was getting set for the next play," Giorgio recalls. "But what's weird was I didn't hear the whistle." Giorgio then looked over to Schmidt, who was relaying the defensive play call from the sideline. Schmidt, yelling the play at the top of his lungs, looked at Giorgio, who was staring at him confused.

"I looked at him and was trying to give him the play," Schmidt remembers of the situation. "But he wasn't responding." Schmidt dashed over to Giorgio and grabbed him, yelling at him to see what was going on. Giorgio, still confused, grabbed Schmidt back and yelled:

"I CAN'T FUCKING HEAR YOU!"

Schmidt looked at his friend shocked. He turned and looked forward, seeing the Staples offense getting ready to snap the ball. Schmidt then gave Giorgio the play call through hand signals and continued with the drive. After a few plays, Staples was forced to punt which allowed for Giorgio and Schmidt to come off the field. While walking off, Schmidt continued to try to communicate with his fellow linebacker. "I remember Schmidt kept trying to talk to me, but all I could see were his lips moving. I kept telling him, 'Mark, I can't hear you,'" says Giorgio.

After reaching the sideline, I went to talk to Schmidt who was still going back and forth with Giorgio. I asked them what was going on and Schmidt replied with his eyes wide, "Dude, he can't hear."

Giorgio then ripped his helmet off, after which he started to feel the effects of the hit he had taken. "My head was pounding. Every side was throbbing all over," Giorgio says. "It took about three minutes, but I finally started to get my hearing back." Giorgio played the injury off as minor during the moment, telling Carlozzi that he had gotten his bell rung but that he was okay. A couple of plays later, Giorgio was back in on defense, not willing to leave the field on which he had grown up on. "It was pride," Giorgio says about going back in. "I had made it that far, and considering how much we went through during 2014 and the offseason, there was nothing that was going to stop me from playing." Even in a slightly dazed state of mind, Giorgio and the rest of the defense held well, leading the way to a 27-0 victory over Staples, clinching us a spot in the FCIAC Championship game against New Canaan on Thanksgiving morning.

Following the win, there was a consistent mood among the

seniors as we stood on the field. "That was it," Hudson Hamill remembers about the moments after the win. "We had played on that field for a decade, and that was it." I stood on the field with my shoulder pads on, grasping a football that I had picked up after the game. There were plenty of practices to be held with the Turkey Bowl and state playoffs coming up, but the sadness was still there. Slowly, we began to leave the field with a smile on our faces, remembering all the good that had occurred on the field behind us. The laughs, the wins, the losses, the fights, and the family bonding. I walked off the at Darien High School for the final time on a game day and headed straight to my parents, who greeted me with a hug. I thanked them and moved towards the locker room, ready to celebrate with my teammates our FCIAC Championship berth.

As the rest of us slowly made our way into the locker room following the game, a beaten and battered Sam Giorgio stayed on the field. He was proud after having put out 100% effort on Senior Day, even through physical and emotional pain. He didn't smile afterward. He walked over to Coach Maul, who had something that Giorgio had given him before the game started. Giorgio then looked at Maul and asked for it back, wanting to look at what he had given him one final time on his home turf. Maul reached into his pocket and pulled out the prayer card that had been given out at the wake of Sam's grandfather. Giorgio took it and proceeded to walk off the field, grasping the card while heading towards the locker room. The day was won, the goal achieved. Now, it was time for the real test of the season, the game of all games...

The Turkey Bowl.

CHAPTER TWENTY-TWO

The Battle at Boyle

"We Were Barely 17..."

Mark Evanchick sat alongside myself and the rest of the seniors as we gathered at Noroton Presbyterian Church in Darien. It had become an annual tradition the night before the Turkey Bowl to join together as a team at Noroton, where we along with our parents celebrated with a pregame dinner. Coach Trifone stood and spoke about the season, giving gratitude to the parents and supporters who had come out to every single game leading up to the Turkey Bowl. He then proceeded to talk about the players, especially us seniors, who he had grown so close to during the past ten years. Evanchick listened quietly, although he wasn't listening to the words Trifone was speaking. He instead was lost in his thoughts, mentally preparing himself for what would be his fourth Turkey Bowl played in, something that had not happened in decades at Darien High School.

Suddenly, the thought was interrupted by a loud round of applause after Trifone had asked for the senior class to stand up. Evanchick along with the rest of us did so, waving to the parents and mouthing the words "Thank you" over and over again to the loud clapping. We were all dressed in polos, having been ordered to do so by Trifone who wanted us to look professional and like adults around the true adults that were in attendance. In essence, we were all still 17-year-old kids, yet there was a need to act mature, especially around our parents. The crowd of adults continued clapping with smiles covering their faces, the sheer joy and sense of pride coming out of their bodies with every clap. After a minute, we then sat down and continued to eat our meal.

Most of us, like Evanchick, spent the time pondering about the upcoming game. Mark though was different in his thoughts, since for him it was about realizing something that he had not thought about for quite some time. "Being at the church, knowing that it would be my last Turkey Bowl meal ever, that was a real 'holy shit' moment for me," Evanchick says. "I couldn't believe it had already been four years; it honestly flew by." That was all the star defensive end could think about that night at the church, even after trying to change his thought process back to the game that would be occurring the next morning. It stuck with him, flying around his head at any turn during the evening.

There were guys like Sam Giorgio, Mark Schmidt, Rock Stewart and I who were not thinking about our fourth Turkey Bowl, but were instead thinking about our *first* Turkey Bowl. Yes, we had been on the sidelines during the 2013 and 2014 games, but this year was different since we all had a chance to go in and play in front of our hometown. The childhood dream was within our reach, which was something we all talked about hours before the dinner at Noroton Presbyterian Church.

Before we shuffled over to the church for our meal, the team met in Coach Trifone's classroom for the annual Link Meeting which was held the night before the Turkey Bowl. It was mostly a chance for the seniors to stand in front of the team and say whatever was on their mind and was one of the most special moments of each year. Never being someone who liked talking in front of big groups, even if they were my teammates, I strayed away from speaking at great lengths during the previous year. This year though, I told myself over and over again that I needed to talk. After building up enough courage, I stood up and headed to the front of the classroom, where I faced and looked out to my teammates but more specifically, my senior brothers in the front row.

Not having planned anything, I started to talk without any direction or goal. I spoke from the heart, recounting to my teammates about my struggles socially and mentally through middle school and high school. I paused and looked down, then looked back at my teammates and told them that through all my pains, football was always an escape for me. Through bouts of depression, through episodes of mental breakdowns; football was always there for me. I paused again and told my teammates that I wanted to keep it short but had one more thing to say.

I told the story of my childhood dream after watching Brian Kosnik and Matty Wheelock run out onto the field during the 2008 season and how after that moment, all I ever wanted in my life was to be a Blue Wave football player. I thanked Coach Trifone for giving me the opportunity to live that dream, yet there was still one more goal I needed to achieve, and that was to play in the Turkey Bowl. I looked at the coaches and my senior teammates and with passion, reiterated the statement. "I don't care if it's one play. If I play in the Turkey Bowl, then my dream is complete."

I ended with that and started walking back to my seat. It was then when Timmy Graham, who had been by my side as my quarterback through DJFL and had been an incredible but soft-spoken teammate through high school, hit me on the arm and said, "I got you, Britton." I nodded and returned to my seat, sweating bullets but also proud that I had spoken.

Back at the church, our pregame dinner was starting to wrap-up with Coach Trifone telling the parents that us players had to get to bed early. We were to arrive at Darien High School by 6:30 am, so every single minute of sleep would help that night. Getting up, we thanked the parents who had helped organize and run the event and shook hands with the fathers who showered guys like Timmy Graham with the repetitive phrase, "Go get 'em tomorrow." It was nearing 8 pm, so initially, I thought about heading straight home and going to bed. While leaving the church though, Sam Giorgio and Schmidt pulled me aside and asked if I wanted to hang out for an hour or so before we all headed off to sleep.

That night, Sam, Schmidt and I along with Marcus Pagliarulo (who was living happily after leaving the team) drove through the streets of Darien while Giorgio blasted "Paradise By the Dashboard Light" performed by Meat Loaf. As we made into the night, we discussed various topics to take our minds off of the Turkey Bowl. What was supposed to be an hour turned out to be a few hours, reaching nearly 10:30 pm the night before the biggest game of our lives. Unfazed and still wanting to have a little fun, we pulled into the private neighborhood of Noroton Bay which overlooked Long Island Sound. Ready to call it a night, I nearly told them to drive me home, Sam asked if we wanted to do one more thing before we went to bed. Taking the bait, I asked him what exactly he had planned.

It turned out one of our friends was across the street at Weed Beach in his car with his girlfriend, coincidentally living out the lyrics of "Paradise By the Dashboard Light." Naturally, Schmidt and I were in, so we drove to the beach and turned off the car lights to go undetected. We sat there for a minute, waiting for another friend to show up in his car so we could create an even bigger spectacle of the situation.

When he arrived, we drove slowly in the dark up to the parked vehicle, creeping up to nearly five feet away as the couple sat in the backseat. We called our friend in the other car, counting down from ten. When we hit zero, we blasted our bright lights into the car and started honking to the sheer terror of the couple.

Our friend in the car, who was rightfully pissed off, covered himself and stormed out, heading straight for us. He then slammed his fists onto the hood of the car and headed for the driver door. Laughing uncontrollably but also slightly terrified of the rage inside our friend, we went to drive away but nearly crashed into the other getaway car. As Sam tried to regain control of the vehicle, Schmidt screamed "GO GO GO!" while we swerved and eventually sped off into the night, proud of completing our mission. It was 11 pm, and we were wide awake, laughing to the point of tears about how great the prank was. As we collected ourselves, Sam paused and looked at both Schmidt and I. His smile went away with a quick realization:

"Holy fuck, the Turkey Bowl is tomorrow."

Tale of the Tape

It was the crack of dawn, almost an hour before the team was supposed to report to Darien High School on the morning of Thanksgiving Day. Alone, John Carlozzi stood in his gym getting in a final workout before heading over to the high school to tend to the needs of the players. Before leaving his gym, Carlozzi dropped to his knees and began to do push-ups, going all the way to the point of his muscles giving out on him. Carlozzi was dressed in the same attire from the previous year, after spending almost half an hour going around his house asking his wife where she put his lucky socks from the 2014 Turkey Bowl. "I am a very superstitious guy," Carlozzi says with a laugh. "The hours and preparation before that game were overwhelming."

After hitting an insane amount of push-ups on his first attempt, Carlozzi stopped and caught his breath. He thought about the number that he had reached, letting it sink into his mind. "I told myself, 'Okay, that number is New Canaan's score. Now it's time for Darien's score,'" Carlozzi says. "I then pushed myself to do one more than the previous number. After that, I was good to go."

Timmy Graham was one of the first people to arrive at Darien High School, having been up for a while in the build-up for the game later that morning. Like he had done since he was a kid, Graham had picked up his clothes that he laid out on the ground the night before and carefully placed them into his bag, always double checking to make sure he didn't forget anything. His mentality was simple; get everything not related to the game out of the way first. That way he could focus solely on his opponent during the hours leading up to kickoff.

Calm and collected, Graham sat down at his locker. He turned the music up on his headphones, indicating to those around him that he was in no mood to talk. No distractions were necessary at this time because Graham knew how focused he had to be for this game. It wasn't any other game to him. It was instead something bigger. This game was *his* legacy, and failure was not an option.

Like in 2014, the FCIAC Championship/Turkey Bowl was expected to draw close to 10,000 fans at Boyle Stadium. To make it even more prominent, the state of Connecticut would be watching since the game pitted the #2 team in the state, Darien, against the #3 team in the state, New Canaan.[1] In the weeks leading up to the game, members of the media went back in forth on comparing the two teams at every level. The most critical and most covered comparison was the quarterback position, pitting Timmy Graham against New

Canaan's Michael Collins.

Collins was once again arguably one of the best quarterbacks in the state, passing for 2,395 yards to go along with 46 touchdowns and only five interceptions. Collins had made headlines leading up to the game too, after throwing for nine touchdown passes against Trumbull High School just weeks before Thanksgiving. With all the attention on the outstanding play of Collins, Timmy Graham was relegated to a lesser role, although he was putting up better numbers compared to his junior season. After throwing 24 touchdowns against 14 interceptions in 13 games, Graham had thrown 26 touchdowns with only one interception through eight games in 2015.

Even with the improvement, all eyes were on Collins, who was being dubbed as "one of the two best quarterbacks in the state."[2] Unfortunately, Timmy Graham wasn't the other one being considered. "You know, you hear it," Graham says about the media doubts and not getting recognition. "But it doesn't matter, what matters is who wins on Thanksgiving morning."

Arriving a little after Graham, I sat down next to my locker with a Gatorade and a plain bagel that I had grabbed on the way out of my house. On my phone I was playing "Rocky Mountain High" by John Denver, hoping to utilize the song as something to keep me calm in the hours before the game. I stood up from the bench in front of my locker after noticing the coaches coming in and posting the alumni letters on the wall. Every year though, I only focused on one letter out of the dozens posted on the wall. It was my brother's letter, which he had written in the fall of 2012 after graduating and heading off to college. I read the whole thing over and over again, and with it being my senior year, I grabbed it from the wall and walked it over to my locker. There was one line that I read like poetry and took extremely seriously because it meant the world, especially coming from my brother. In one sentence, he motivated me like nothing had motivated me before:

"I am forever in debt to the game of football."

I took the words in again then proceeded to get up and return the letter, pasting it back onto the wall. I then sat back down with Giorgio and Schmidt near our lockers, staying silent as we waited for the biggest game of our lives. Schmidt's head bounced up and down as "Vibration" by Alex Wiley poured through his headphones. I watched as guys like Spencer Stovall stood alongside the other lineman, coaching them on specific schemes that they would be using throughout the game. Hudson Hamill looked carefully through the scouting book, trying to pass the time anyway he could. Colin Minicus, with his iconic one eyeblack strip, paced through the locker room impatiently waiting for the buses to arrive.

As I sat waiting, I went through the message that Coach Trifone had given us the night before when he handed out the team letter along with the New Canaan scouting report. It was one of Trifone's signature messages and phrases, "Hold the Rope." In one of his greatest lines, Trifone wrote, "Who could you trust to 'Hold the Rope?' When you can look at every member of your team and say to yourself that you would trust anyone to hold the rope, you are destined to win!"

I looked at my teammates and my senior classmates, all of which I had played with since I was around eight years old. Here we were, hours before the biggest game of the season, all connected as one team with a common goal in mind. There were no egos, no selfishness, no individualism. We were holding the rope together as a group, having the backs of each other through anything that came at us.

I smiled. New Canaan didn't stand a chance.

* * *

Game On

At Boyle, the team sat tightly together in the locker room underneath the away stands since the FCIAC decided it was no longer a good idea to have us walk through the hostile New Canaan crowd. The locker room was not even a locker room but instead a glorified storage closet with benches lining the walls. Nobody seemed to care since all focus was on the Rams of New Canaan, who were stationed across the field. Earlier before heading into the locker room, myself and the other seniors stayed out on the turf where we were honored during pregame. Even while walking out with our parents holding our arms, you could see the intense focus in the eyes of guys like Timmy Graham and Mark Evanchick. Immediately afterward, we jogged back to the locker room where the final countdown to the Turkey Bowl was underway.

In my black pants and black #44 jersey, I stood up in the corner. It was still a constant circle of thought for me, thinking about playing in a game that was bigger than the Super Bowl growing up. It was only a couple of minutes away which in turn, created massive nerves within my body. I nearly zoned out entirely until I noticed that Coach Trifone was calling the seniors forward for the pregame prayer. I shuffled forward and joined my teammates by locking arms and prayed the words of the Lord's Prayer. With that, my heart pounded harder and harder as we got up and headed for the door that led to the screaming Darien fans awaiting their beloved Blue Wave.

The scene was electric at Boyle as we ran out onto the field. On the warm November morning, the two towns packed in and around the stadium pushing the crowd numbers to 10,000 once again. The roar of the crowd shook me, although I tried to stay relatively collected knowing that I couldn't get too excited before the game. We stood on the sideline, taking in the incredible atmosphere. Timmy Graham grabbed a football and quickly began throwing, while Sam Giorgio and other players got together and did some final pregame stretching as the crowd chanted: "BLUE WAVE FOOTBALL!"

While the rest of the team went out on their tangents for final preparations, Mark Schmidt looked at me with a football in hand and screamed, "Britton... LET'S GO!" Keeping up with the tradition that we had done before every game since McMahon, Schmidt and I ran slightly onto the field and began to do our circus catch routine, minutes before the biggest game of the year in front of 10,000 people. "That was amazing," Schmidt remembers of the routine on Thanksgiving morning. "You know what? It kept us calm, especially in a moment like that. We didn't need to be coked up, so we played catch and took basketball shots instead."

After our pregame routine, Schmidt and I slapped hands and made our way back to the sideline. In the midsts of both student sections hurling insulting chants at each other, I found Giorgio and signaled to him that it was time. We looked at each other and crotch chopped towards the New Canaan sideline, indicating that the SWAT Team had arrived at Boyle. New Canaan then won the toss and deferred their decision to the second half, giving Timmy Graham and the offense the ball first. In our own territory, Graham tried feeling out the New Canaan defense but did so to no avail. Unable to get anywhere during the first drive, Trifone sent the punt unit out to hopefully pin New Canaan into their territory.

When Trifone called out the punt team, the adrenaline in my body took over. In my mind, I repeated over and over again, "This is it, this is it." Jogging onto the field, I saw the cameras of the network that was streaming the game and saw the hundreds of fans packed in the end zone after being unable to secure a seat in the stands. Forgetting that I was on the field to do a job and play football, I stood in awe from the perspective on the field of the absurd amount of people watching us play. It was then when I heard the announcer at the stadium over the speakers say, "Darien to punt." Standing there, I realized something. I was about to play in the fricken Turkey Bowl.

My heart continued to pound as I got set into my stance next to junior long snapper Brian Keating. All week, we discussed how we would defend the possibility of a New Canaan blitz. I would take the man who was lined up on me, and if they blitzed, Keating would grab the guy coming between us. Sure enough, New Canaan showed blitz up the middle which I called out from my stance. I then turned my attention to the man lined up in front of me, worrying about stopping him and then releasing to run down the field. Sophomore personal protector Sean O'Malley gave the count quickly, setting the wheels forward for Keating to snap the ball back. I engaged my man furiously, staying low and winning the battle right from the start. Keating released immediately, however, forcing junior Cord Fox to attempt to chip the blitzing backer. He shoved him aside, where Sean O'Malley went to pick him up. The linebacker quickly dodged the block and dove into our punter, knocking the ball to the ground to the roar of the New Canaan sideline.

I stood, dumbfounded by what happened. Sean O'Malley was visibly frustrated and yelled, "WHAT WAS THAT???" A massive argument ensued, trying to solve what had just happened. Running onto the sideline, we were met by Coach Maul who furiously explained that Keating released too early. Slightly relieved, although pissed at the fact that New Canaan now had the ball at the 15-yard line because of a miscommunication, I slammed my helmet onto the bench and buried my face into my hands.

It didn't take Michael Collins and the offense long to find the end zone from such a short distance. After only a couple of plays, Collins dove in from the 5-yard line to give New Canaan a 7-0 lead just minutes into the game. Timmy Graham watched from the sideline, but did not panic, knowing that New Canaan had done the same thing the previous year. Being behind wasn't an issue at all, so Graham wouldn't let it get anywhere near his head. Stepping out onto the field only minutes after New Canaan had scored, Graham drove down the field and hit Hudson Hamill on a 29-yard bullet that resulted in a touchdown. After the pass, Graham stoically moved back to the sideline, avoiding any celebrations. He sat down on the bench with Coach Ross, discussing strategy for the following drive.

New Canaan went back on offense, and during the weeks leading up to the game, the Rams made it their priority to slow down Mark Evanchick in any possible way. Early in the game, they double-teamed the defensive end, causing Evanchick to become a non-factor in the pass rushing game. The defense held its own under the direction of Bobby and Christian Trifone along with the rest of the No Fly Zone, causing New Canaan to punt on consecutive drives.

The two offenses stalled out during the remainder of the first quarter, keeping the score at a low 7-7 entering the second. Timmy Graham kept his composure early in the second; after only a minute of play, he found Colin Minicus on a 39-yard deep ball that gave us the lead. After stopping New Canaan once again, Graham returned to the field to hopefully orchestrate a big drive that provided us with a two-possession lead. After a couple of near competitions, Trifone called out the punt team once again.

It appeared that the game would go into halftime with us leading 14-7 but Collins, who had struggled through the first 20 minutes, finally found his groove and threw an 18-yard touchdown pass with a little under two minutes to go, tying the game at 14. We entered the locker room at halftime where Trifone told the team he was content with the effort, although not entirely pleased. We were outplaying the Rams by a considerable margin, yet we were tied after two quarters. Not wanting to cause any panic or point any fingers, Trifone then dismissed us players to our respective position coaches, allowing for any halftime adjustments to be made.

New Canaan got the ball to start the second half but was unable to move the ball anywhere thanks to the play of a one-legged Mark Schmidt at the second level and the Trifone twins' pass coverage. It also seemed like New Canaan made major adjustments in their locker room at halftime since Graham and the offense became stuck and forced us to punt on consecutive drives during the third quarter. Avoiding frustration, Graham returned to the sideline after each drive and quickly went to the film, which was being uploaded after each play to the iPads that we had on the sideline. Graham watched the film from the drives closely and then realized a gap in the New Canaan coverage during the previous drives. He notified the coaches of what he saw, forcing them to rethink the plan for the next trip.

Graham got the ball back with a little over four minutes to go in the third quarter. He drove quickly down the field by connecting on short passes to Hamill and Shelby Grant out of the backfield. After reaching the New Canaan 28-yard line, Graham executed the plan that he had devised during his time on the sideline. On the left side, Colin Minicus lined up as the wide receiver while Rock Stewart, who was having a career-best game, became set as the slot receiver. On the snap, Minicus darted on a five-yard in route as Stewart crossed him and drove up the field with a wheel route. The New Canaan defense became disoriented, allowing Stewart to break free down the sideline. Graham saw the opening and stepped up in the pocket, launching the ball in Stewart's direction for a 28-yard touchdown pass to put us up 21-14. Our sideline erupted in sync with the crowd, roaring in approval of the beautiful throw by Graham that gave us the lead with only minutes left in the quarter. After being swarmed by the team, Graham once again retreated to the bench without showing any emotion, knowing that the game was nowhere close to being over.

The celebration was short lived. Collins and the Rams drove down the field in a matter of seconds on our defense. When New Canaan reached the red zone, however, the defense began to hold due to the play of Sam Giorgio clogging up the middle to stop any attempted runs. After three consecutive stops, the Rams faced fourth down on the 1-yard line. Instead of electing to send out the field goal unit, the Rams stayed on the field in hopes of tying the game at 21 before the quarter ended. With a quick snap, Collins handed the ball off to the New Canaan running back who dove into the end zone, tying the game at 21.

Heading into the fourth quarter, Coach Trifone gathered the team and asked the seniors to come forward. When we did, he looked at us and said, "The last 12 minutes of the Turkey Bowl… Your last Turkey Bowl!"

Both defenses continued to play exceptionally well during the fourth quarter, creating a stalemate during the first four minutes. New Canaan found an edge, however, as Collins connected on a couple of passes that got the Rams in our territory. The defense then held its own, creating a situation where New Canaan either could go for it or attempt a 46-yard field goal with all-state kicker Peter Swindell. The Rams elected to kick the field goal, hoping to gain the lead with eight minutes remaining. Swindell missed the kick to the joy of the Darien crowd, giving us the ball back with a chance to take the lead.[3]

A motivated Timmy Graham stepped out on the field, needing to drive nearly 80 yards down the field to get a chance at scoring. Before getting the play call, Graham took a step back and took a deep breath in. He looked back a couple of years and realized that Silas Wyper, his mentor in 2013, had been in an almost identical situation during his senior year. Taking what he had learned from Wyper, Graham stayed poised throughout. With the sense of calmness overtaking him, the quarterback started the drive off with a bang by hitting Hamill for a 38-yard gain. The next play, Graham dropped back to pass to contain the momentum but was sacked by the Ram defense, resulting in an 8-yard loss. Not willing to let the Rams feel any confidence, Graham responded with a 42-yard dart to Colin Minicus. Now in the red zone, Graham quickly went to work by rolling out to his right where he saw Hudson Hamill sprinting towards the corner of the end zone. Graham threw the ball up, forcing the much smaller Hamill to leap over the defender and grab the ball. As Hamill hit the ground, the New Canaan defender ferociously moved his hands in an "incomplete" motion. The referee ran forwards and raised his hands into the air to the frustration of the defender but the joy of our sideline. It was 28-21 with four minutes left.

The defense came back out on the field, needing one final big stop to clinch the FCIAC title. On the first play of the drive, Sam Giorgio, who was still suffering from the effects of the Staples game, got set after receiving the play call from the sideline. Everyone knew the Rams would be throwing the ball, so Giorgio immediately dropped into his coverage zone when the ball was snapped. Reading the eyes of Collins, he moved towards the receiver that was being targeted. When Collins released the ball, Giorgio lifted his arm to deflect the pass but was instead slammed into by the New Canaan receiver. Collapsing on the ground, Sam grasped his left shoulder. He went to move it after the play but to no avail, which is when he realized he had dislocated his shoulder.

"I was in so much pain," Giorgio remembers about the hit. "And I remember going to the sideline and desperately looking for Carlozzi. I then saw Tim Lochtefeld, who was visiting for the Turkey Bowl. I remember he looked at me and yelled, 'You better get back in the fucking game, Giorgio!'" Staggering through the sideline unwillingly to even miss a single play, Giorgio found Carlozzi and gave him the simple order, "Put it back." Carlozzi went to work on Giorgio but play continued on the field as Collins and the Rams tried to find a way to tie the ball game. With a little over two minutes remaining, New Canaan faced a fourth and 10 situation on their own side of the field. Collins dropped back to pass when Mark Evanchick, who had been a non-factor all day, ripped through the New Canaan line and brought Collins to the ground, causing a massive explosion of sound in the Darien crowd. Evanchick bounced to his feet and saluted the crowd, fired up after the game-changing sack.

It appeared as if the game was over. I stood on the sideline with the defense celebrating, thinking that the game was in the bag. The New Canaan defense had other plans, however, and forced Graham and the offense into three straight dead plays. While celebrating with my teammates, I heard Trifone scream, "PUNT TEAM!" Surprised, I jogged onto the field and looked around, realizing there was still over a minute left to play and that Collins would be getting the ball back.

Needing to drive down the field 70 yards to tie the game with no timeouts remaining, Collins went to work. He dropped back to pass immediately and connected with receiver Kyle Smith, who broke free up the middle. Sophomore Nick Green, who had come in to replace Giorgio, caught Smith from behind and forced a fumble which Christian Trifone dove on, giving us the ball with under a minute to go.

A massive celebration ensued afterward as I jumped on Mark Schmidt and screamed and yelled in victory. For the second year in a row, the Turkey Bowl had come down to a thrilling conclusion that in the end resulted in us winning the FCIAC Championship. As soon as the clock struck zero, I grabbed our team 12th man flag that we had in memory of Jim Mulhearn and stood on the field, waving it back and forth while excitement overtook me. Parents stormed the field overjoyed, hugging each other and running out to find their children. Sheer joy was surrounding the Darien sideline, while heartbreak and devastation poured over the New Canaan side.

Through the mess of adults and players celebrating on the field, there was Timmy Graham, who had remained emotionless throughout the game. Postgame, Graham felt relieved and overjoyed after proving his doubters wrong once again. He had put on the best performance of his career, going 34/47 for 462 yards with four touchdown passes. On the opposite side of the field, Michael Collins had gone 19/40 with 205 yards and a touchdown. Graham took notice of it, and after being counted out by the media time after time again, he finally spoke without a filter postgame. "I remember right after the game talking with the media," Graham says, " I remember saying, 'You can talk (about Collins) all you want, but we won the game. Now that's what you're going to talk about. We won the game.'"

In the minutes and hours after the game, there was nothing to worry about. We went home with our families still feeling the ecstasy of the win while also handling the bruises all over our bodies from the war we had been through. There was food waiting for us, NFL football on TV, and the excitement and fun of being a 17-year-old on Thanksgiving. We were all smiles, happy to be around our loved ones and happy to not have to worry about football for the rest of the day. Playoff preparation could wait until Friday because Thursday was ours; the spoils of another sweet victory over our hated rivals was ours.

CHAPTER TWENTY-THREE

Our Last Days as Children

Darien & Goliath

Like the previous two years, we were back at Darien High School the morning after Thanksgiving to start preparing for the state playoffs. Unlike the previous years, however, we were no longer in the Class L bracket but instead the Class LL bracket, which meant we'd be playing bigger schools that were mostly unknown to us. At #2 in the state of Connecticut, we faced a heavy bracket in Class LL after the drawing occurred Thanksgiving Day. Following the New Canaan win, the Class LL seedings took shape:

#1 Shelton (10-0) vs. #8 West Haven (7-3)
    #2 Darien (9-0) vs. #7 Staples (7-2)
    #3 Southington (10-0) vs. #6 Conard (8-2)
    #4 Newtown (9-1) vs. #5 Glastonbury (8-1)[1]

Out of the eight teams in Class LL, four of them were placed in the state of Connecticut Top 10 Poll: Southington at #1, Darien at #2, Shelton at #4 and Glastonbury at #7. Simply put, the bracket was stacked, and all roads seemed to lead to Southington, who was riding a 30-game winning streak dating back to 2013 coming into the state playoffs along with being the two-time defending Class-LL State Champions.[2]

Coach Trifone refused to allow us to look ahead to Southington since he did not want us to overlook Staples in the state quarterfinals. He reminded us that we only had four days to prepare for Staples, since the playoffs started the Tuesday night after Thanksgiving. Not wanting to disappoint him, we listened to our head coach but also secretly kept an eye out for Southington, knowing full well that we were going to blow Staples out of the water in route to a showdown between #1 and #2 in the state of Connecticut.

Our confidence showed its full colors on Tuesday, December 1st. We stomped on Staples, winning 41-7 behind Timmy Graham's four touchdown passes and Mark Schmidt's 11 tackles and an interception. Immediately following the Staples victory though, our attention shifted straight to Southington, who had utterly decimated Conard by a score of 48-6.

The motor behind Southington, Division I recruit Jasen Rose, had an incredible game. The 6'4 225-pound quarterback rolled through Conard, rushing for 188 yards with an astounding 26.9 yards per carry, complimented by four rushing touchdowns. It wasn't a one-time performance either since the senior quarterback had been filling up stat sheets the entire year. Coming into the state semifinals, Rose had thrown for 2,417 yards, 39 touchdowns, and only five interceptions. On the ground, the 225-pound tank barreled for 14 touchdowns, proving he was a threat in the air and running too.

From what we saw on film, Southington was an extraordinarily talented and scary football team, unlike anything we had ever seen. I remember during the initial film session with the other defensive players, we watched Rose effortlessly put on a clinic against teams. We sat in silence watching him play when all of a sudden one player quietly said, "They're like New Canaan on steroids." Mark Schmidt remembers the film sessions and build-up to the game as well, realizing something that he didn't think about at all during any other games. "They seemed 3x bigger than everyone else," Schmidt remembers. "That was the first time I said, 'holy shit, this game might be the last time I play football.'"

It was a hard but possible truth, one that a lot of us accepted. In the days leading up to the Monday night game, we enjoyed the practices and team time more than usual, knowing that this game, unlike Staples, had the chance of really being our last football game ever. When that feeling hit, it hurt because it wasn't something I was thinking about or a lot of my teammates wanted to think about. We weren't accepting defeat, that's the last thing we wanted to do, although we were preparing ourselves for what could happen on December 7th. On the practice field, the stress was evident when Hudson Hamill and Andrew Clarke got into a fight, one that had to be broken up and resulted in both players running laps upon laps. "It was our competitiveness but also our frustration about the game," Hamill says. "We both wanted to win so badly, but our frustrations came out on each other."

The stress wasn't just during practice but also during the school day as well. It got to the point that I, along with some teammates, started to zone out completely in school. Southington haunted us in every class, something Timmy Graham remembers, saying, "It was very hard to focus in school when you knew you had Southington, the best team in the state, on a Monday night."

Luckily, the stress was put on hold the Thursday before the Southington game when Sam Giorgio, Mark Schmidt, Tyler Grant and I were invited to speak on behalf of the Darien

High School football team at the fifth/sixth-grade DJFL end of the year banquet. Honored and thankful for the opportunity to take our minds off Southington for at least an hour, we graciously accepted and attended the dinner. Walking in with our Darien football clothes on, the kids pointed us out the minute we showed up. Smiles broke out as eyes widened on the faces of the kids who were mesmerized by the sight of us high school football players at such a close distance.

We were ushered up onto the stage and given a microphone, where we were asked to talk about why DJFL was so crucial in making us the football players we were today. Speaking from the heart, all four of us talked and laughed through memories of the times we spent as kids together running around at Darien High School playing the sport we loved. After about 20 minutes, we then opened up to questions from the players, which caused a riot as the kids lined up for a chance to ask us anything about our football careers. Questions spanned from what positions we played in DJFL to what our favorite high school game was, although one question stood out from the rest.

A young fifth-grader took the microphone and nervously began to ask his question in front of us. He looked up and asked the million dollar question: "Why do you guys play football?"

I smiled at the question and then looked around at the parents in attendance, realizing I had a chance to send a positive message to a town that was full of competitiveness in everything you did. I took the microphone and directed my response right back to the kid, saying, "Well, why do you play football?"

"Because it's fun," he responded, which garnered a few playful laughs from the parents.

"That makes two of us," I said to him with a smile. "That's

the only reason I play. Because it is fun."

After we finished answering questions, the four of us left to a round of applause while parents shook our hands and wished us the best of luck against Southington. We thanked them and left, heading separately towards our cars and into the night.

When I reached my car, I sat quietly for a second, reflecting on the banquet I had just been at. I thought about it for a while, pondering them that I had just sent to the Darien High School Class of 2022 & 2023. I was happy with what I delivered, but suddenly, a feeling of overwhelming sadness began to take over. It was at that moment that I had the realization that a lot of my teammates were having… football was ending. I had not thought about it ever since I came back from my concussion but for some reason, talking with to those kids and seeing them look at us like we were superstars, it hit me that I maybe only had days left. It hit me like a ton of bricks, forcing me to stop my car engine and sit, waiting patiently for the tears to stop coming from my eyes.

Evanchick vs. Southington

As if having the #1 and #2 teams in the state playing in the playoffs wasn't enough, more drama was added in the days leading up to the Monday night showdown. On the night of December 3rd, Mark Evanchick was named the Gatorade Player of the Year in the state of Connecticut, a massive honor for him.[3] Evanchick humbly accepted the award but ignored any press about it, instead choosing to stay concentrated on the game ahead and stay focused on what the team was working on as a whole.

The decision to crown Evanchick as the Gatorade Player of the Year didn't go unnoticed and without controversy, as Southington blew up over the ordeal since they believed that Rose was the one who deserved the award over anybody else.

Immediately after the announcement, Twitter exploded with attacks against Evanchick. After the initial tweet announcing the award from GameTimeCT editor Sean Patrick Bowley, it was a non-stop assault on Evanchick and the rest of the team.

"Good luck taking @JayRose1010 down like that. I think he'll prove next week he's the true CTPOY (Connecticut Player of the Year)"

"@SPBowley @CPTVSports ever heard of Jasen Rose? The QB for Southington….."

"@SHS_Knight_Krew @SPBowley @CPTVSports Rose will put that kid on his ass."

Initially, the tweets mostly came from students but eventually turned into adults attacking the 17-year-old Evanchick as well.

"@BWaveSuperFans @SHS_Knight_Krew @SPBowley lol you won't be saying that when Jay trucks this loser 3 times."

"Hahahahahahahahahahahahaha what a joke."

"Class act @JayRose1010 at least you're playing football in college #notlacrosse."

At the beginning of it all, Evanchick continued to do what he always did, which was ignore the media and let his play on the field do the talking. He didn't even read any of the tweets, only having heard about them through other teammates who tried showing them to him. Eventually, Evanchick was unable to ignore the press any longer after he listened to what Rose had to say during an interview. "This is a team sport," Rose said. "We're looking to get the win, Gatorade Player of the Year doesn't really mean that much. If we get the win and he gets the Gatorade Player of the Year, I'd rather take the win."[4] Later that evening as well, Rose went out on Twitter, retweeting a tweet from Sean Patrick Boley that stated:

"<Turns on the HYPE machine>
ROSE VS. EVANCHICK!

ROSE VS. EVANCHICK!
ROSE VS. EVANCHICK!
#Cthsfb"[5]

A couple of days before the game as well, the Southington offensive line joined in on the fun, telling the media that Evanchick "is fast and he's good with his hands, but its nothing that can't be dealt with."[6]

Unlike Southington, Evanchick stayed quiet on social media and through interview requests, but he began to read the tweets and articles as a means of motivation. And then, out of nowhere, steam began to bellow out of the star defensive end.

"I read every single comment on Twitter, GameTimeCT; I read everything," Evanchick remembers. "It just infuriated me. I've never had a fire lit under me as I had for that game. There's no game I wanted to win more than that one."

Timmy Graham reiterated the same sentiments as Evanchick since he was once again being counted out as a lesser quarterback compared to Rose. "Honestly, the whole media coverage with high school athletes is awful," Graham says. "But it was motivation. I wanted to beat them so bad, they talked so much shit, and we didn't talk any to them in the lead-up. But they kept posting all this stuff on social media, so that was my motivation."

The team needed all the motivation we could get, especially against such a talented and confident Southington team. On Monday, nobody on the team even thought about a single thing going on in our classes, instead, putting all our attention into the Southington game. Sam Giorgio, Mark Schmidt and I skipped a couple of classes to meet in the Tech Ed offices where we did any final film breakdown we could before the game later that evening. Before we knew it, the final bell had rung at Darien High School, and we were on our way to the locker room to prepare for our journey back to

Boyle Stadium for the neutral site state semifinal game.

It was a cold December evening when we arrived about an hour before kickoff. Mark Schmidt was locked in during the entire bus ride, going through his coverages and scheme fits in his head to make sure he knew them from memory. He stayed super focused on his opponent and felt relatively good getting off the bus. The focus died the minute Schmidt looked over to the Southington sideline, where he saw Jay Rose, in full pads, looking out towards us. Seeing Rose for the first time in person, Schmidt remembers saying to himself, "Holy shit, that's a big boy."

Hudson Hamill had a different approach than quietness, which didn't surprise anyone. While making his way onto the field off the bus, Hamill jawed with the Southington players. "It was pure confidence," Hamill says, who, unlike the majority of us, didn't think for a moment about the possibility of us losing. "I could talk all the shit I wanted because I knew the team could back it up. They thought they were going to walk all over us, but I wanted to make a point from the start that we weren't going to take their shit."

Following the civilized chat with the Southington players, we then walked into the locker room which we had used for the Turkey Bowl only weeks earlier. Something was different though, and we noticed immediately. On the white walls of the locker room were all the tweets directed at Mark Evanchick and the rest of the team, with the most vulgar of them being highlighted in yellow for everyone to see. You could see the fire in Evanchick's eyes as he looked at each and everyone, and you could see the fear in the rest of our eyes while we moved away and gave Mark as much space as he needed. John Carlozzi remembers it as well, saying, "Evanchick just kept pacing back and forth, all I could remember thinking was, 'Why would you piss this guy off?' You've never seen that before, it was downright scary. I had never seen Mark do that."

Evanchick's pacing was eventually halted by Coach Trifone, who entered the locker room to address the team before the game. We as a team were expected a classic Trifone speech since it was such a monumental game, but instead got something completely different. Staying quiet, Trifone looked at us seniors and said, "I don't know how many of you know this, but today is Jim Mulhearn's birthday." Trifone paused as tears began to form at his eyes. He composed himself and then continued. "His daughter is in the stands tonight watching. I ask one thing of you guys tonight, don't win for me, don't win for yourselves... Win for Jim, because he's watching."

We came out onto the field to the roar of our faithful crowd, who packed into Boyle alongside the student section. Southington didn't disappoint either, bringing their fans in full force along with their student section to counter ours. I looked around at both crowds, inspired by the lights shining down on us. There was a big fight atmosphere at Boyle, and I loved every second of it. The night dreams came crashing back to reality rather quickly though when Southington rushed out of their locker room to a thunderous reaction from their fans. The film didn't do them justice; they looked 2x bigger in person than on video. As fear took over in my body during my pregame catch routine with Schmidt, Mark Evanchick stood still and locked his eyes on Rose, not letting him out of his sight.

We won the coin toss and deferred our decision to the second half, meaning Evanchick and the defense would get a shot at Rose to start the game. Nerves, however, still played a key factor during the final seconds before the game began. As the kickoff team lined up to start the game, Christian Trifone stood with his eyes closed, slowly breathing and thinking about the moment. "I didn't even know what was coming,"

Christian says. "I closed my eyes again while running down and said to myself, 'Hey, I don't know how this one's going to go. They look great on tape; they got a lot of athletes, they got a lot of size. This one is up in the air.'"

Southington took the field and right off the bat began to drive against the defense. A couple of plays in, Southington fumbled the football, giving us the ball in a quick turn of events. Timmy Graham rushed onto the field, understanding that he needed to take full advantage of the situation and started to organize the offense. It only took Graham a few plays, and following a designed screen pass to Rock Stewart, the score was 7-0. The crowd cheered in approval over the quick score while the sideline went nuts, not knowing how many more chances we would get to score that easily against a team like Southington.

Rose and the offense retook the field down by a touchdown, hoping to answer Stewart's touchdown. On second down, Southington ran a designed jet sweep to the outside where Bobby Trifone was waiting. Trifone put his head right on the ball, forcing another fumble that was recovered by Finlay Collins all the way down to the 11-yard line. Graham once again trotted out and quickly went to work, finding Shelby Grant on a quick flare route for a 3-yard touchdown.

The fans in attendance on our side lost their minds after the play, celebrating the fact that we had a two-touchdown lead against the #1 team in the state midway through the first quarter. While the fans celebrated, Coach Trifone pulled the team aside and told us to stay composed, reminding us of who we were playing and how talented they were. Understanding the need not to get ahead of ourselves, we stayed focused and continued with the game.

The defense continued to play well against Rose and Southington, especially Mark Schmidt, who came into the

Myself, Sam Giorgio, Tyler Grant and Mark Schmidt taking questions at the DJFL dinner (December 3rd, 2015)

Peggy Barthold, Pete Graham, and Cathy Giorgio before the start of the Southington game (December 7th, 2015)

Mark Evanchick at Boyle Stadium during the state semifinals game against Southington (December 7th, 2015)

CHAPTER TWENTY-FOUR

Finish

A Lasting Memory

There was a lot of thinking that went on the morning after Southington. I sat in my car in the Darien High School parking lot, where I parked my car facing straight into the football stadium. I was already late for my first class, so I stayed in my car and looked out onto the turf. The previous week in the build-up for Southington, the thoughts I had were constructed around the idea that my football career could be over if we lost that game. Now, after beating Southington and claiming a spot in the state title game, I had an official end date for my football playing days. It wasn't a fun thing to think about, although it was a riveting process in my mind. I could ignore it, but the idea of it being the end caused me to think about it a lot as I tried to figure out how it had gone by so quickly. It only felt like a year since I was snapping balls to Timmy in DJFL and just a couple of months since I had watched Silas Wyper battle North Haven up at Vanacore Field. Now all of a sudden, I had four more days of practice and one more game to play, and that would be it. I quickly got out of my car following that thought and headed inside, doing my best to put those thoughts aside for another time.

Unsurprisingly, the thoughts didn't go away once I walked into my Law & Government class and sat next to Spencer Stovall and Timmy Graham. They too were lost deep in their thoughts about high school football, which showed when the three of us turned in our project later that day about what our own country would look like if we had complete control (An island of 250 people, a pure democracy, relied heavily on agriculture; the other students weren't impressed). It wasn't easy to ignore those thoughts since we walked by the stadium on the way to almost every class and saw our teammates in every single one of those classes.

It was tough on Sam Giorgio as well. He sat utterly unaware of what was being taught in his advanced Calculus class, looking back on everything that had occurred during the previous seasons. From the hellacious time spent on the sophomore scout team, the disrespect he felt on the junior varsity squad, all the way to the hard work he put in with Carlozzi to compete for a starting job. Then there were the injuries, the physical therapy and the hidden concussions that he buried to do what he set out to do; which was to achieve his childhood dream. That was it really for Giorgio. It was gratifying to him to know that he had reached his goal, but like everyone else, he didn't want it to end. The season flew by; it didn't feel like they had played 11 games already. But he knew he had to face reality at some point and that at 2:20 pm, the daydreaming and sad thoughts would have to stop. There was still one game left, one that had to be won no matter what.

When we were slaughtering Southington on Monday night, Shelton High School was battling Newtown High School in a tight game that went all the way down to the final minutes. In the end, Shelton was able to fight off a vicious comeback by Newtown, giving them a 35-28 victory and a

destiny." After speaking those words, Trifone began to walk off the field while ordering the sophomores and juniors to follow him to the tunnel.

It grew eerily quiet as they left, leaving only us seniors on the field. We stood in a circle and looked around at each other. Bobby Trifone broke the silence with one single but effective word: "Damn." We laughed and then began to share our memories of football at Darien, from the bad all the way to the great.

Always being someone who was afraid to speak, I decided though that this was the right time to make a useful contribution. "50 of us played on that eighth-grade championship team," I said. We looked around at each other, noting the 14 that remained from that team.

Timmy Graham looked at me, then signaled for the group to come in closer. "Let's finish what we started boys. I love you guys." We then started our slow walk to the tunnel, where Coach Trifone, who was fighting back the tears, and the rest of the team lined up and began to clap as we walked off the field at Darien High School for the last time. When we reached the locker room, I took off my practice gear and gently put it into my bag, trying not to think about everything that was going on. We, seniors, had gotten through the last practice. Now, it was time to do what was bestowed upon us way back in DJFL… It was time to fulfill our destiny.

The 12th Day of the 12th Month

The drive up to New Britain for state title game was a long, peaceful ride. On the coach bus we rode on, we sat with our music playing, thinking about the upcoming game against the Shelton High School Gaels. The thoughts of it being our last high school football game had passed, only because our true determination was in winning the town of Darien its first football title since 1996. Most of that pressure was on the shoulders of Timmy Graham, who sat with his straggly red beard on the bus thinking about his reads and check-downs that had been installed during the last week. It was indeed a calm setting on the bus, with no sense of urgency or anxiousness present. In fact, Mark Schmidt wasn't anywhere close to stressed out about the state title or the fact that it was his last game; he was passed out on the shoulder of Andrew Stueber during the entire bus ride up to New Britain. When we came about 15 minutes outside of the site of the game, Coach Trifone stood up and started passing out the pregame letter to the team. I took the note and began to read…

"Dear Blue Wave:

Of course, this will be the final letter of the year… which makes it the hardest one to write as no matter what happens, today we will hug and say goodbye to our seniors for the final time. Needless to say, our seniors have no raised the bar to an even higher level, and we are grateful to each and every one of them for that. I will miss spending my afternoons with all of you. I will miss the camaraderie in the classroom watching film, pasta dinners, and even the bus rides. But most of all, I will miss perhaps the toughest (group) that I have ever had the pleasure to coach!

Remember your roots that got you here… the skinny, lanky DJFL players that struggle in the first couple of years. Then in 6th grade, we began our journey with destiny as we played deep into the playoffs both in 6th and 7th grade. As you all know, the final foundation was laid in 8th grade when both teams won the championship against New Canaan teams who had NEVER lost a game… until then.

Now, after ten years, you are at the very edge of everything you have ever talked about… and more. You have 48 minutes of high school football left, and then a lifetime to talk about it!

PLAY HARD, SEIZE THE DAY, PLAY TOGETHER, WIN

TOGETHER!!!
  Sincerely,
  Coach T"

I didn't try to think about Coach Trifone's message a lot after we arrived and went into the locker room. I didn't try to think about it while Carlozzi taped my wrists and ankle for the last time, I didn't even try to think about it when I pulled #44 over my shoulder pads for the final time. When we prayed the Lord's Prayer, it didn't cross me or affect me in any way. The reason was simple. I didn't want to think about it, that's all it came down to. I wanted to go out and win a football game, that was it. Even as I tried to remain focused on the game, Coach Trifone came forward after the prayer and delivered his final pregame speech to us. "Last week, we celebrated our 12th man's birthday," he said to us. "Now today, on the 12th day of the 12th month, you have the opportunity to win your 12th game for your 12th man." A hush fell over us. Trifone then got up and headed for the exit. Looking up at the sky, Hudson Hamill raised his arm up with the initials "JM" written on his wrist tape. Our 12th man was watching, and it was time fulfill the chosen one prophecy but also, fulfill his dying wish.

Running onto the field for the game, we stayed together as a team while Shelton ran wild and excited all over the field. Schmidt and I got together with a football while everyone else stretched, running to the end zone as I screamed, "LET'S GO!!!" For the last time, Schmidt and I showboated and did our pregame routine, ignoring the state title game that was minutes away and instead, letting the child inside of us out for a moment. After, Schmidt and I embraced in a hug and then headed back to the sideline to join our teammates. With the game nearing, the intensity surrounding the state title grew. During the end of the national anthem, Shelton raised their helmets and yelled in defiance, hoping to get any reaction out of our team. Not intimidated at all, we looked at their sideline and laughed. After everything we had gone through, we weren't going to bite. Instead, we did our talking on the field.

On the first play of the game, Christian Trifone picked off Shelton's quarterback and returned it for a 20-yard touchdown. Already off to a bad start, it turns out that Mark Evanchick hit their quarterback so hard that the player's collarbone broke, forcing him out of the game.[1] Timmy Graham then got the ball after another defensive stop, finding Hudson Hamill on a 3-yard touchdown pass after only four minutes. The bleeding didn't stop for the Gaels, especially when Bobby Trifone picked off the Shelton backup quarterback and returned it for a 48-yard touchdown. Heading into halftime, we led 18-0, which was not a surprise to any of us. The second half was more of the same dominance that we had displayed during the first two quarters. Shelby Grant scored twice during the quarter on short runs, putting the score at 39-0 heading into the final 12 minutes.

It was easy to ignore the fact that this was our last football game together because of the fun we were having while dominating Shelton, but the feeling finally overtook me when Coach Trifone looked at us on the sideline and said, "The last football quarter of your life! The last of your life! Seize it!" All of a sudden, the feeling of sadness was overwhelming as I stood there listening to my head coach. I immediately turned towards the stands and looked up to find my mother, who was still passionately cheering us on with her #44 cowbell. During that moment, I thought back to the days of my early football career and how during every game since I was eight years old, I would look up to find my mother in the stands cheering me on. It was at that moment I had the

the Class-LL State Championship trophy. The tears went away in an instant as me, and the rest of the seniors rushed around the prize and held it towards the sky. "It was honestly incredible," Sam Giorgio remembers about the quick change of emotions. "We were history makers, the first to do it since 1996. It's just incredible." The trophy, which was not as cool as the rings we were planning on getting, was still an eye-opening moment when I got to hold it for the first time. I held it with Giorgio and Schmidt as we posed for a photograph. It was an amazing feeling as we stood there, reading "CLASS-LL FOOTBALL STATE CHAMPIONS" on the trophy over and over again. It was pure ecstasy, something that also distracted us slowly from the initial sadness that we had felt immediately after the game. After posing with the trophy for group shots, we then gathered as a senior class and kneeled on the ground for another photograph. We realized someone was missing though, which is when Spencer Stovall called for John Carlozzi to jump into the photo. Carlozzi obliged, running in with us for the celebratory picture of our crowning achievement.

The party didn't stop after the on-field celebrations. When we arrived back in Darien on our bus, we were greeted by a police escort that led us through the town and back to Darien High School, where our parents and other fans waited. Stepping off the bus, showers of cheers came down upon us as we played to the excitement of the crowd. In the parking lot sat a firetruck with its lights on, which we of course (as 17-year-olds) climbed onto so we could continue the raging celebration of our state title victory. Rock Stewart stood screaming at the top of his lungs at the highest point of the firetruck, drawing loud cheers in the process. Sam Giorgio, with a smile on his face, looked to the rest of the teammates in a rare Giorgio moment, yelling, "Hey guys! WE FORGOT HOW TO LOSE!!!"

After about 15 minutes, we finally began to climb down while the parents started to shuffle out and started heading for The Goose, one of the local bars in town where the adults celebrated after each football victory. On that night though, The Goose was going to be on an entirely different level. Mark Schmidt, looking back on it, sees the humor in the moment. "Yea, I think some of the parents were more excited about the win than we were honestly."

As the parents left and headed to the bar, we were left at Darien High School, now forced to face the one thing every single one of us was dreading. With our pads and jerseys in hand, we walked slowly down to the gym where it was officially time to say goodbye to the game we so desperately loved. In 2013 and 2014, I didn't cry like other players because I was motivated and determined to get ready for the next season. In 2015 though, it was a different story. There was no next time; there was no road to redemption. There was only the sickening feeling of having to say goodbye to the only thing I loved in my life, and that was football.

I managed to hold it together through the majority of the sophomores and juniors who went down the line saying goodbye to the seniors, but that changed when it was time for us seniors to say goodbye to each other. Walking down the line towards my teammates for the past decade, I broke down completely when I reached Sam Giorgio. I looked at him. I saw us in eighth-grade when we were both undersized linemen just trying to make a name for ourselves. I saw us leading the junior varsity team in 2014, and finally saw the friend who had made me laugh countless times through our SWAT Team shenanigans.

Through short breathes and tears running down my face, I went through the rest of the line, saying goodbye to Mark Schmidt, Bobby and Christian Trifone, Colin Minicus, Hudson Hamill, Mark Evanchick along with the rest of the remaining seniors. I then reached Timmy Graham, who was fighting back a sea of tears during the goodbyes. I looked at my quarterback, who I would have died for during my DJFL days, and broke down once more. We rarely talked to each other, but the football connection was there in the gym that night. The memories of DJFL and working with Timmy overwhelmed me, along with the extremely selfless time he looked at me before the Turkey Bowl and promised to help me live out my dream. Through sobs, I hugged my captain and told him… "Thank you."

When we finished our goodbyes, we departed into the locker room where it was going around that the seniors along with some juniors would be invited to a celebration party at the house of one of the seniors. After months of avoiding parties and staying out of trouble, it was time in our minds to get all of our wild high school antics out after they had been building up for so long. I told my teammates that I was in and that I would see them there, but that I had one more thing to take care of before going over to the house.

After returning our gear to the equipment room, Sam Giorgio and I slowly walked out onto the dark stadium field on that cold December night. In my street clothes, I put my hands in my pockets and walked towards the 50-yard line with Sam, standing on the blue "D" that was at midfield. The sound of the night was soothing as I took a deep breath and looked towards the press box, which was dimly lit. I then looked towards Sam, who was staring into the distance towards the parking lot.

In the bitter cold, Giorgio stood with satisfaction in his eyes. With his #33 jersey in hand, he looked up towards the press box. Back in 2013, he set out to create a name for himself and to solidify the Giorgio name in Blue Wave history. Everyone laughed at him, counting him out from the beginning. Now, the doubters were officially wrong. The undersized kid who would never play football according to some stood proudly at midfield, now a Connecticut high school football state champion.

Nobody could take that from him, and he knew it. He smiled at me and started walking towards the parking lot.

I looked back towards the scoreboard once more. Ten years after meeting Coach Trifone for the first time, we had fulfilled the prophecy bestowed upon us. Catching up to Sam, I sarcastically remarked to him, "Hey Sam! Be perfect!" Giorgio, understanding the *Friday Night Lights* reference, laughed and jokingly responded:

"God damn it, Britton, shut your mouth."

We then got into our cars, laughing through our conversation and headed off into the shadowy night of Darien.

in the stands," says Wyper, now a Yale graduate. "I don't know if that's a feeling you were fortunate to have and should be glad to have had it; but something you shouldn't ever try to recapture because you might not be able to recapture it."

***

Hudson Hamill didn't stop the chase for perfection after football ended. He continued to dominate the athletic fields at Darien High School while helping lead the boy's lacrosse team to an undefeated season and a state title. After graduating, Hamill went on to play lacrosse at Washington & Lee University, where he was named to the Old Dominion All-Athletic Conference in 2018 during his sophomore year. He is currently in the Williams School where he is studying business and finance. Leaving the game of football was tough for Hamill, although he left Darien satisfied with everything he accomplished. "I think our three-year run is when the culture was fully developed," says Hamill. "To me, that's a pretty amazing accomplishment to look back on."

Rock Stewart followed in the same path as Hamill, helping the lacrosse team to its undefeated season in the spring. He went on to attend Williams College in Massachusetts, where he plays for the lacrosse team. Football didn't linger in his mind since he saw the ending as picture-perfect. "You know, maybe one more hit would be nice," Stewart says with a laugh. "But I'm okay with the way that it ended. I actually love the way it ended." The only thing that was hard for Stewart when the season was something that went beyond his football family. "The reason I cried when it was over was because it was the end of me playing with my brother," he says. "I loved playing with Riley. That was my favorite part of anything at Darien High School. It wasn't the state championships I won, not the FCIAC titles, not the All-American awards; but playing with my brother, that was my favorite thing."

In the fall of his freshman year, he was asked to join the football team at Williams but declined the offer. "Looking back, there is one day a year where I wish I had said 'yes,'" Stewart says on the decision. "That regret only happens during the Amherst-Williams football game. Every other day of the year, I am totally content with the fact that I said 'no.'" Stewart remains focused on his academics, and to this day doesn't drink alcohol. As a double major, Stewart plans to graduate with degrees in both Physics and Economics.

Colin Minicus joined Hamill and Stewart on the lacrosse team, which in turn gave him an opportunity to play the sport at Amherst College in the fall of 2016. Minicus accepted and has since gained an All-NEILA Honorable Mention on the team. Minicus still looks back on the 2015 season whenever football comes up and has considered joining the Amherst team on multiple occasions. Even through the contemplation, Minicus is satisfied with how everything ended. "To me, it is all about the build-up," says Minicus over the phone. "We lost two games our sophomore year, one game our junior year, and then zero games our senior year. Maybe we were the most successful and most awarded team in history, but we wouldn't have been able to do it without the two classes before us." Looking back, he misses it, but doesn't try to live in it. "As you get older, you slowly grow beyond it," he says. "I think right now, that's where I am."

Christian Trifone contemplated a career of college football following his life at Darien High School but instead opted to call it a wrap when he arrived on campus with his brother Bobby at Clemson University in the fall of 2016. Trifone felt it like a lot of other players, especially during that fall, when he realized football was no longer a part of his life. "It hit me pretty hard when I got to Clemson," says Trifone. "I missed training with the guys, I missed going to Mama Carmela's with the team, you know, all those small things." Like most, Christian refuses to try to go back in time to relive the superlative experience. "It's got to be tough to recapture that feeling," he says. "I don't think you could virtually redo all of that. It's a once in a lifetime thing."

Years later, Christian Trifone kept many lessons he learned on the football field with his teammates. "It's definitely a lot of pressure for sure," Christian says about high school football in Darien. "I think part of that leads to the bonding though. You don't bond by winning and not having to work hard. You bond in the trenches, you bond when things are tough. You've got to have each other's backs, and I think that's what football is all about." Trifone's incredible work ethic continued to show onwards after leaving Darien High School and into his years at Clemson; in the summer of 2018, Christian entered training in the United States Marine Corps Officer Candidates School.

Mark Schmidt was contacted by a couple of Division-III schools during the 2015 season but ruled out playing football again after the catastrophic damage of his quad was fully revealed after the season. Schmidt doesn't regret his decision to play through it, however. "It was a mistake probably," Schmidt says. "But really, I just wanted to play football. That's why I played through it." Looking back on some of the stupid things he did in high school, on and off the field, Schmidt laughs and says, "Oh yea, we as athletes definitely needed more supervision."

Schmidt would go on to attend Villanova University, where he is an admit to the School of Business. As a Wildcat, the always athletic Schmidt started playing tennis, a sport he never had played before, and eventually joined the club team at Villanova. Like Minicus, Schmidt still enjoys talking about

Blue Wave football from time to time. "You know, I think we were the greatest of all time," he says sitting back. "But realistically, what made us better than those before and after us is that we cared so much about winning. We sacrificed a lot of off-field activities, and it led to an incredible season." Like Minicus as well though, Schmidt doesn't try to relive it. "I loved every minute of it, every single second," Schmidt says. "But I knew there was life after football. So I moved on pretty quickly." Schmidt still is learning more and more about his high school career to this day, mostly when volunteering at local camps or practices during the summer months. "It's funny," he says. "I've had kids come up to me and say, 'Are you Mark Schmidt? Oh my God, you were my favorite player!' I never really thought of myself that way, so I guess it's pretty cool to have an impact on kids like that."

Sam Giorgio joined Mark Schmidt at Villanova, where the two were roommates during their freshman year in the city where, in a nice twist, Rocky Balboa hails from. When he isn't obsessing over Villanova basketball or playing for the Villanova Rugby team, Giorgio studies Biology with the hopes of one day working in the medical field.

For Giorgio, there was no urge to return to the fields of Darien High School, as he left satisfied after the 2015 state title game. "I loved my senior year, it was a dream come true," Giorgio says. "You know, life around the game was difficult for me. It was difficult for all of us I felt. Obviously, our football lives are different, but there are also components of our football lives that are so real. For all of us, Jim Mulhearn was such a big part of our lives, because we all wanted to do everything we could for him. Not only him, but you also have your brothers out on the field who are your closest friends since elementary school. I think really, you don't just *play* football. There's a community around it. And in the matter of missing it, I do, but it's not something I

people affect them externally," says Hamill on the controversial situation. "I think our class did a really good job of not listening to anything on the outside. In all fairness too, when you win so many games in a row, people aren't scared to talk shit to you cause they are expecting to lose. They're just trying to get in your head, and unfortunately, it worked (in 2017) on that group of guys. It's unfortunate too because it wasn't the entire class but now, they are all now labeled as thugs."

Timmy Graham watched on the sideline of Boyle as New Canaan rocked the 2017 Blue Wave. Looking at it, Graham shakes his head. "Peter got thrown into a terrible situation," he says. "It was very hard on my family with everything that happened to him. In the end, though, it was a learning experience for him."

Looking at it, there is no defending the actions of the three players on that night before Thanksgiving. Assault is assault, no matter what the situation. With all of them being former teammates and good friends, the issue hit me hard but also gave me a chance to look deeper into the matter now. There is a sense of high school athletics playing a role in the actions of the three players possibly, due to like what Rock Stewart said: "The feeling of being invincible." After winning for so long, maybe they felt like they no longer could get in trouble, that they could do whatever they wanted without consequences. There is also the chance that pressure played a role, and the confrontation was a built-up release that the players instinctively did. Perhaps it was once again the rivalry being pushed too far, or maybe, according to rumors surrounding the situation, parents are getting involved in ways that they've never been involved before.

Whatever the stance on the situation, the fallout from the incident was catastrophic to the town of Darien and the image of the townspeople and student-athletes. Article after article was posted about the incident, and fair or unfair, it was journalism under the free press. Darien students appeared to get sick of the negative coverage pretty quickly, which in turn created a dumpster-fire like situation, where apparently, players on the team along with a Darien High School class officer berated a journalist for his coverage of the events. According to the journalist, he received email after email from self-identified Darien students along with football players who attacked him for the way he covered the events surrounding the Turkey Bowl arrests. The journalist, who works in the reasonably poor city of Hartford, received emails, some racially charged towards the Hartford demographic, saying:

"You are an irrelevant man who knows nothing about Darien or what occurred. Please stay in Hartford you baboon, no one likes you."[7]

The stigma surrounding Darien only got worse, but the football team moved on in the midst of complete and utter chaos. In the state quarterfinals game, Jack Joyce was allowed to return to the team which was in desperate need of a quarterback. The two other players were still suspended indefinitely. Even in the middle of all the press and attention on the town, the Blue Wave played in front of a packed house of faithful Darien fans at Darien High School, eventually scoring a critical quarterfinal win followed by another win to place the team back in the state finals for the fifth consecutive year. In an FCIAC matchup, Trifone led the Blue Wave against the reinvigorated Greenwich Cardinals at Boyle Stadium. In a snowy mess with Greenwich students wearing shirts that read "Cardinals vs. Convicts," the Blue Wave prevailed 31-22, giving the town it's third straight football championship and #1 state ranking (#193 nationally) under a sea of controversy.

Guys like Hudson Hamill, Timmy Graham, and Mark

Evanchick look back on the situation with hopes of a bright outlook, but also note the partially damaged work of the 2015 class to change the culture of Darien being "bad guys." It was a hard pill to swallow, looking back on the sophomores we played with who had to be harshly labeled "criminals" as seniors, but in the end, Timmy Graham said it best. It was a learning experience.

In a town like Darien, learning experiences are hard to come by in the world of sports. The ideas of perfection and superiority are evident in every aspect of the town, from the recently broken lacrosse streak of 76 games to the now dominant football program that could barely win a game over a decade ago. Maybe now, from the actions of the 2017 football team, there is an awakening of the terrifying hidden aspects of high school sports that we seem to hide from. Maybe it is time to look at the real, pure reasons behind athletics, which Darien Athletic Foundation founder Mark Maybell put simply, but perfectly:

"For the love of sports."

For the love of sports. In Darien, under all the rubble of the storm of events during the previous years, it all comes back to the words Maybell said. For the kids in the youth programs, watching from the stands, there shouldn't stress or expectations on their shoulders. They shouldn't feel like they need to win a state championship or go undefeated because that's what is expected of them; they should go after what guys like Hudson Hamill went after, even when faced with expectations from others. They should chase their dreams, and only their dreams. They shouldn't cry after a losing because it will disappoint their parents; they should cry after a loss because of their passion and sheer love for the game. That's the beauty of football. The dreams, the passion… the love.

In the end, that mentality still lives in Darien, although it might be hard to really find. For some, through all the pressure, success and expectations, it appears as if the passion for fun and love has dissipated. It is still there, however, hidden in the town that strives for greatness. It is hidden underneath the rubble from the storm of events in 2017, waiting eagerly to rise up and reiterate to those in town what matters most; The ideals that lived in the lives of the 2015 seniors, amidst the pressure and expectations of the town… Passion. Love. And most importantly, dreams.

***

It's a warm September afternoon at the grounds of Darien High School in 2017, seven years after Hudson Hamill delivered his own prophecy, his own dream. The Blue Wave faithful stand cheering, while the stadium fills all the way around the fences surrounding the field. St. Joe's is in town, and in the middle of the second quarter, the heavily favored Blue Wave lead 7-3 against the Cadets. As the band plays and the crowd sings along to "Sweet Caroline," the sun beams down on top of the cafeteria, where the Darien High School class of 2023 stand watching. Wearing their DJFL jerseys, the group of 12-year-olds watching intensely as their heroes proudly wear the Darien helmet with the words "Blue Wave" plastered across their chest. There is no controversy in this group of seventh-grade players, no turmoil, no negativity; just a profound love for the game. They stare and watch, learning from the varsity guys as they dance through the St. Joe's defenders, playing with their bodies low as they use flawless technique.

One seventh-grader stands on the railing of the cafeteria roof, watching as the team drives closer and closer to the end zone. Just like that, the Blue Wave score and like the rest of his teammates standing by him, a smile breaks out on his face

Author's Note

I started to consider writing a sequel to *12* in December of 2019, right after Indiana had defeated Purdue to regain the Old Oaken Bucket. I wanted to continue to write about high school football and really, wanted to explore avenues outside of Connecticut. It took many iterations, many edits, many ideas... before I settled on just one. Originally, the idea was to follow two different high school seasons in the same year; One in Indiana and one in Virginia. Eventually though, through guidance from one of my very good friends and editor of *12*, I closed in on the Virginia story.

The story revolves around one of my closest friends and his senior season at Riverside High School in Northern Virginia. Riverside opened in 2015, his sophomore year. From there, they were given the challenge of building a program from the ground up in a county that had become a stronghold in Virginia football.

The story wrote itself for me, essentially. The first two seasons, the team had combined for two wins. Heading into his senior season, hope wasn't that high. Hence, *The Unbelievers*. I felt it was a different tone compared to *12*, as you weren't dealing with a team chasing perfection but instead, a team chasing an identity and a purpose. All in all, it was an interesting enough story for me to pursue, and that's exactly what I did.

About 100 pages into it though, I began to realize that it wasn't working out. Like I said earlier, the writing style and prose were some of the best I had ever done. I was clearly growing as a writer but in the end, I felt like I was forcing myself to write and wasn't doing it for the fun of it. I was forcing a *12* sequel to happen, I wasn't letting it happen. That, more or less, like I said, is writing. It's any profession, for that matter. You learn that pretty quickly. Sometimes, something feels right and you run with it, but down the road, you take a step back and realize that maybe the timing is wrong, or the passion really isn't there. When I decided to take a week off and evaluate things, I realized what I was really wanting to write was a passion project that I had been working on since May of 2019, a fiction novel titled *Growing Up*, revolving around adolescence in a fictionalized Darien, Connecticut. My attention shifted to that and just like that, *The Unbelievers* took a now permanent backseat.

I still think it's an incredible story. I still think that the 2017 Riverside story is fascinating, inspiring and heartbreaking. Really, those three adjectives define high school football and altogether, goes to prove that no matter how good a team is, no matter how bad a team is, all teams experience the same emotions on the field during their high school years.

So what I have done is included a few of the parts from the book, not all 100 pages. I have the Prologue, which sets the scene and then the first chapter, which provides Virginia football background. I then skip to the sixth chapter, which follows the first game of the season against Riverside's hated rival, Rock Ridge.

All in all, I hope you like this small preview. Enjoy.

The Unbelievers

Britton Barthold

Prologue

Tradition was a word that wouldn't be thrown around the Riverside High School football program for a long time, that much was known.

In sports, tradition has many underlying factors that go into defining it. Tradition is built around historic teams, ones that defy the odds and run the table, playing against the heavy favorites and capturing the hearts of those who watch. Tradition is built through championship seasons, rings on the fingers of the boys of fall who tirelessly work from July to December, simply for a piece of jewelry and their name etched in history forever.

In terms of tradition, high school football runs the nation. For some towns, it fuels the population for the entire autumn season. It trickles down from generation to generation, with the adults talking about where coaches may have it wrong, where certain players fit, to the kids at the lunch table and on the youth fields, emulating the teenage heroes that they admire every Friday night. It turns a simple game into a spectacle, a normal Friday night into a a town-wide showcase of a group of 17-year-old boys who only want one thing...

The glory of representing the name on the front, for those in the stands.

For those things to happen at a high level, on a weekly

basis, there must be tradition. There must be legendary teams, teams that even 20 years after, the townspeople can look back and recall the exact score of certain games, recall the exact moments that created the legend. There must be mythical players, the type of players who for years after still get recognized, the type of players who have kids walk up to them years later and say, "You were my favorite football player growing up."

Riverside High School didn't have that.

Dawson Drake knew that.

Sitting in his parked Jeep on the afternoon of August 25th, 2017... Dawson Drake knew that. He sat still for a moment, turning off the car as the music that was entirely too loud went silent, Dawson leaned back in the drivers seat and looked across the lot towards the stadium and the back of the home grandstands. The words "Riverside Rams" covered the fence in an ocean blue windscreen, the words in all capitals, bolded white. He looked up towards the press box, the same words plastered across it, this time in bright red. Next to each of them was a printed picture on the windscreen, zoomed in to reveal intense eyes of a Ram, the horns barely visible. The stadium was empty, but at its peak, it could hold north of 5,000, if the fans of Riverside wanted to do so. But, tradition was needed for such a rabid fanbase.

Riverside didn't have that. Dawson Drake knew that.

It was 4:15pm as Dawson looked down at his phone. He took the key out of the ignition, and opened the driver's door, stepping out while in one fluid motion, pulling his AirPods from his pocket and sticking them into his ears. Back to his phone he looked. It wasn't a question what song he would play. Within seconds, "Jump Out the Face" by Meek Mill started blaring into his ears, the volume at full blast. No questions asked. He looked briefly at the windscreens, then looked up to the press box.

Riverside Rams.

He turned towards the school, about a five minute walk from the stadium. Taking a deep breath he began the trek, alone in his thoughts, a place he always preferred to be, especially before a game like this. As he walked, the song nearing its end, the brick of Riverside High School came clearer in his line of sight. 10 minutes before he would have to be at the school. He had time.

With the song coming to an end, the music getting quieter, Dawson heard something behind him. The sound was initially faint but faster and faster it grew. He turned and looked, seeing a wave of buses roll into the Riverside parking lot. His face turned to stone. *Fuck 'em*, he thought.

In this moment, game day had officially come. All the hopes, dreams, worries and fears, all during the school day didn't matter. The buses had made it real.

Rock Ridge had arrived.

* * *

Inside at Riverside, Dawson looked into his locker, his matte blue helmet with the Riverside "R" on both sides of it. On the other side hanging were his white pants, not worn in a game situation since October of 2016 during their last home game, a 42-14 beatdown loss to Clarke County.

This wasn't Clarke County, though. This was Rock Ridge.

On the bottom of his locker sat his shoulder pads, a blue jersey, Nike. The #18 spread across the middle of the jersey, "Riverside" in small print right above it. On the top shelf sat his gloves, but he wouldn't be needing them, at least for a while.

He moved swiftly to the training room, where he quickly got his left wrist and thumb taped, his right wrist too, no thumb. Moving back to the locker room he went in front of the mirror and in one quick motion, spread a line of eye-black under each of his eyes.

At 5:15pm, it was time. It had been over 300 days since the Riverside Rams had played a football game, their last coming on October 28th against Freedom High School. They lost 51-14. Fully dressed, strapped and ready go, 65 of the Riverside Rams began to slowly make the five minute walk to the stadium as dusk began to settle over the field. It was quiet, the clicking of their cleats against the asphalt being the only sound as they walked two-by-two, with Dawson at the front of the pack. His chinstrap covered his mouth, his eyes locked forward on the words covering the backside of the home grandstands… the words only an hour before he stared intensely at, wondering if maybe this was the day that Rock Ridge would fall to Riverside.

When they arrived, the stadium sat empty. They packed into the Riverside team room, a large brick building equipped with whiteboards and benches for the Rams. Sitting in there, the silence only growing, the call was made for the team to start making its way out.

First, the specialists. Kickers, punters, returners, long snappers.

On the Rams side, students, some reeking of liquor, came pouring into the stands, screaming loud for Drake and the other specialists who had taken the field. Drake ignored it, instead focusing on the ball sitting in front of him. He'd lean down, look back to the punter, look back up and rocket it back to him.

Another booming kick. Another catch. Another roar from the intoxicated crowd.

One more booming kick. As it came down, a deafening sound came from the Riverside faithful… "FUCK YOU ROCK RIDGE!!!"

He snapped the ball. In the corner of his eye, he saw them.

They came out just like Riverside, the specialists first. He glanced at them for only half a second before turning back towards the kickers.

One final booming kick.

The crowd continued to pour in, with more parents beginning to make their presence felt on the Rams side. Alongside that, Rock Ridge's student section had shown up in great numbers, screaming back and forth with the Riverside students as administrators tried to control both sides. That didn't happen. This wasn't just some football game, and the administrators knew that. This was Rock Ridge and Riverside. This was the Phoenix against the Rams.

An hour before kick, the remainder of both teams came out, the sounds of the crowds cancelling themselves out as the Rock Ridge fanbase cheered wildly while Riverside answered louder. As the sun continued to set, both crowds roared in approval at the sight of the lights going on. The music was blaring, the crowds were rowdy and for the first time in a very long time, Riverside's stands were nearly full. For Drake, it signified one thing as goosebumps covered his entire body...

Friday Night Lights.

Twenty minutes to kick. At midfield, head coach Brian Day gave the signal, letting the Rams know that it was time to head in. The group came together, adrenaline pumping through every single one of their bodies as excitement and uncertainty overtook them. Knowing full well his role on the team as he entered his senior year, Dawson took note of the younger guys, the nerves running through their bodies. He slapped them on the helmet and looked them in the eyes. "Hey," he said, his hand still on their helmet. "Let's fucking go."

Moving towards the team room, Drake remained focused but took one more look back at the stands. The student section was full, but all he cared about was one face. He found it. Reassured, he went back into game mode.

This wasn't just any other game. This was Rock Ridge vs. Riverside. The battle to determine who was the big brother, who was the weaker one.

And no, this wasn't Texas high school football. This wasn't California high school football...

This was Commonwealth football. So for Dawson Drake as he sat in silence while the crowds continued to buzz, only one thing was for certain.

In 15 minutes, somebody was kicking somebody's ass.

NoVA (Chapter One)

If you ask almost any high school football player which state in America has the "best" high school football, there is a pretty good chance that they will go ahead and tout their own as the crown jewel of the gridiron. California, Florida, New Jersey, Texas... Those are the powerhouses, when you think of high school football. The shrines to America's Game, the cathedrals built in honor of the Boys of Fall who run out every Friday night, are what dominate these so called "state powerhouses."

Texas makes its claim. Places like Eagle Stadium, the $60 million stadium built for Allen High School in 2012, all for a team that ran through opposition at the highest level in Texas, winning three straight state titles from 2012-2014, becoming the first Texas team to do so in the states highest classification. Or, places like Ratliff Stadium built in 1982, 377 miles down the road from Allen, historically known for its role in the famed 1990 book *Friday Night Lights* about the 1988 Permian High School Panthers. Tourists travel from distant places, all just to get a glimpse at the field where Mike Winchell and the Panthers made a run for eternal glory.

Both are sanctuaries, stadiums that can hold north of 18,000 people on a Friday night, and both that tend to do so on a regular basis.

Many defenders of other states and the claim, though, point to Texas maybe historically as the "powerhouse." Schools like Bishop Gorman High School in Las Vegas, Nevada, with a program run more like a college program, scoffs at the idea of Texas being the ruler of the high school football world. The team dominated the middle part of the 2010s, claiming three straight national titles in the media from 2014 to 2016, never losing a game during the entire process and regularly scheduling Texas teams and decimating them. It seemed like the Gaels of Gorman had a possible claim, backed up by years of sheer dominance.

But yet, teams like Mater Dei High School in Santa Ana, California cry themselves to tears laughing when Bishop makes that claim, especially after snapping Bishop's 55-game win streak in 2017, followed by a 42-0 beat down of Bishop the following year. The competition was not even close, as Dei had slowly regained its national promise after becoming a school known for producing high level quarterbacks such as Matt Leinart, Colt Brennan and Matt Barkley, to name a few.

As you go down the list, the states become less and less significant. States like Ohio hold the history, with schools like Massillon Washington, who led by Pro Football Hall of Famer Paul Brown, hold the most claimed national titles for a single school with nine, ranging from 1935-1961. When Massillon Washington's run came to a close, Ohio continued its dominance with Moeller High School, which won five national titles from 1976-1982 and never returning close to that form, only again regaining titles at the state level in 2012 and 2013. Following that string of success, schools such as St. Ignatius and McKinley grabbed a few national titles in the 80s and 90s. The decline continued, with Ohio last claiming a national title in 2007, with their previous one before that coming in 1997. Ohio, although still a hot-bed for recruiting, has lost the allure of national dominance. Nostalgia is simply all that remains of a once rampant run of national titles for the Buckeye State.

Still, these states, such as Ohio remain in the conversation, may it be recruiting-prowess, history, or present dominance being the reason why. In 2019, High School Football America released a list of their Top 10 high school football states: Florida, California, Georgia, Texas, Ohio, Alabama, Pennsylvania, Louisiana, New Jersey and Tennessee. National titles, state titles, college recruits, all these attribute to these rankings. Some programs are recently dominant, some programs are historically the same way.

But what remains outside of those ten states are the 40 others within America, with all 40 playing the same exact game on the same exact field for the same exact reason, just like the perennial powerhouses. They wear the same equipment, follow the same rules, and play the same day. And just like a lot of other places, big or small, they believe in an American tradition, a past-time that rallies communities together in good ways and bad ways. No matter what happens that day, no matter what the troubles are, they seem to go away the minute the lights go on down where the grass always seems greener, even if it isn't. They come out in droves, willing to sacrifice a night's work just to see if maybe, just maybe, this is the year the boys of fall reach the impossible dream. No matter what your status, no matter who you are...

Across the country, the lights go on.

* * *

The Commonwealth of Virginia stands alone as a unique place within the United States of America, with his history in relation to the nation being what separates it from a lot of other states. It is home to the first permanent English colony

with that exodus came cost. Along with other reasons, more or less mostly due to a struggling football program altogether, Broad Run fell way behind their new foes, going 0-7 against Stone Bridge from 2001 to mid-2013 when after losing in the regular season, the Spartans defeated the Bulldogs 23-21 in the playoffs.

Even as Stone Bridge took over the Ashburn area in the 2000s, Broad Run did have its own string of success, going undefeated back to back seasons in 2008 and 2009 on their way to state titles. The team, after an early period of struggle in the early 2000s (going 34-45 from when Stone Bridge opened until 2008) had slowly regained momentum, but was still playing second fiddle to the younger but more talented brother, Stone Bridge.

"The Battle of the 'Burn" between Broad Run and Stone Bridge would eventually explode, becoming one of the highest attended sporting events in all of Loudoun County going forward. It was a spectacle unlike any other, a war between the two schools of Ashburn, the older brother in Broad Run and the baby brother who got all the love, Stone Bridge. It was a perfect storm, a perfect rivalry. The long running king of Ashburn, the historic school that had been there ever since the beginning, pitted against the new kid on the block, the fresh young blood that everyone wanted to be like. The story wrote itself practically, allowing for "The Battle" to quickly become one of the hottest rivalries in the entire state of Virginia.

Eventually, the crown of best within Ashburn wouldn't be relegated just to Broad Run and Stone Bridge, as Briar Woods would make its presence felt starting in 2005 when the school opened once again due to the rising population of the community. The school played its first varsity season in 2006, when Briar Woods ran off to a surprising 4-0 start to begin the program. The inaugural season would end with a 6-4 record, laying the foundation going forward under former Park View head coach Charlie Pierce.

The Falcons and Pierce would continue to build, finishing 6-4 once again in 2007 but reaching the playoffs for the first time, where they lost a heartbreaker to Millbrook by a score of 27-24. Quickly, Briar Woods was becoming known as a respectable program and in the third year, Pierce proved that the Falcons were going to stick around for a while. In 2008, Pierce led Briar Woods right back to the playoffs and after a down year in 2009, the Falcons would explode onto the scene in 2010. Led by freshman quarterback Trace McSorley after starting the season 2-2, the Falcons ran the table, beating fellow Ashburn rival Broad Run twice on their way to a Division 4 state title, doing so only five years after opening the doors of the school. In defense of their title in 2011, McSorley and Briar Woods lost the opener to Broad Run 14-0 but once again ran the table, playing all the way into December and winning the state title for the second time in a row. The next year with McSorley, now only a junior, the team would rinse and repeat and this time, not lose a single game on its way to a 15-0 season and its third state title in a row, becoming the first team from Loudoun County to ever do so.

All in all, Ashburn had slowly grown to become one of the dominant places of high school football in Northern Virginia, a statement that in 2000, after Broad Run had come off a 1-win season, would be laughable to the rest of the state. Year after year after the turn of the century, the schools of Ashburn were providing championship-caliber teams and within the community, some of the best football games between the schools imaginable. Ever since their founding, Briar Woods has put on quite a rivalry with Broad Run, meeting the team four times in the playoffs, splitting the postseason series 2-2 and always keeping it way too close for comfort. As always too, The Battle of the 'Burn never fails to excite the community, where after years of being dominated, Broad Run regained momentum in the series, especially after the playoff win against Stone Bridge in 2013.

Heading into the 2010s, Ashburn was a hotbed, with Broad Run, Stone Bridge and Briar Woods leading the way as a measuring stick for all of those in Loudoun County to reach for. Simply put, the football scene in Ashburn had exploded out of nowhere, solidifying Northern Virginia as a "Death Valley" of sorts for visitors. In a blink of an eye, the ever so quiet community of Ashburn had become a testing ground. If you could get through the "Big Three" of the 'Burn, then maybe, just maybe, you were ready to have some respect put on your name.

Civil War (Chapter Six)

Authors Note:
This is the sixth chapter of the book, after a few chapters of lead-up and introduction to our characters. This chapter is meant as a direct follow-up to the Prologue.

In the nights leading up to the Rock Ridge game, Dawson spent a lot of time in his basement mostly by himself, staring aimlessly at the television in front of him. It felt like a broken record, the same thing playing over and over again, bumping back and forth to a worn out tune. Dawson didn't care though. If he wasn't spending time with his girlfriend, if he wasn't out and about for an occasional get together with the group, he was downstairs on the couch either with an Xbox controller in hands or leaned back watching whatever game was on that night. If he had to chose though, it would be the Xbox controller, especially as football season rolled around.

On this night, it was Madden 17, which he had played tirelessly for quite some time. Funny enough, the day of Rock Ridge would be the release of the newest Madden game which Dawson knew he would be getting without a doubt. He made a promise to himself to get through Rock Ridge first though and afterward, he could spend the majority of his weekend mashing in hours on the newest release, even if Tom

Brady was on the cover.

Tom Brady. Tommy Brady. "The Greatest of All-Time", some would argue. Dawson wouldn't. In fact, he wouldn't even put Brady in his list five greatest quarterbacks to ever live. He would from five to one, Dawson firmly believed that it went John Elway, Dan Marino, Joe Montana, Peyton Manning and then Drew Brees as the greatest quarterback ever. Brady didn't deserve to be up there. He was a system quarterback, an above average talent who was blessed with a great coach.

Bias or not (maybe some bias), Brady wasn't someone Dawson entirely agreed with, which when considering Brady's history with the Eagles leading into 2017, would make sense. Ever since Brady came into the league, the Eagles had struggled mightily against the Patriots franchise quarterback. In his first start against the Eagles in 2003 when Dawson was just three years old, Brady torched them in Philly, throwing three touchdowns for 255 yards while completing 68% of his passes. On the other side, Donovan McNabb struggled going 18/46 with two interceptions on the day. The Patriots would win 31-10.

And then, there was the big game, the one Dawson remembers ever so vaguely that took place on February 6th, 2005 in Jacksonville. Super Bowl XXXIX, the defending champion in the New England Patriots against the rising Philadelphia Eagles, with the Patriots only favored by a touchdown.

Led by McNabb and Terrell Owens, the Eagles would strike first in the second quarter, but Brady and the Patriots ran down the field quickly, with Brady feeding receiver Deon Branch all throughout the game. Entering the fourth quarter, things remained tied at 14-14 when all of a sudden, Brady and the New England offense would explode. Kevin Faulk would put together a 39-yard performance on the nine play,

66-yard drive that would eventually end with running back Corey Dillon plunging into the end zone to make it 21-14.

After a bomb from McNabb to Owens, things seemed to swing in the Eagles fortune when all of a sudden, an errant pass from McNabb fell into Tedy Bruschi's hands, giving the Patriots the ball back. With eight minutes to go, the Patriots took a 24-14 lead, stifling the Eagles offense for almost six minutes until McNabb found Greg Lewis for a 30-yard touchdown. The Eagles would get one more shot to tie or win the game with 46 seconds to go, but another costly mistake by McNabb allowed Patriots safety Rodney Harrison to intercept the ball, clinching the Super Bowl for the Patriots and sending heartbreak through the Drake household.

With the stakes less high for the Eagles but the disdain still there, Brady kept his dominance on the Eagles even after the Super Bowl, beating them again in a close 31-28 game in 2007 and smacking them 38-20 in 2011. Ever since Brady arrived in New England, the Eagles failed to solve him, throwing quarterbacks like McNabb, AJ Feeley (against the aforementioned legendary 2007 Patriots) and Vince Young at him. All three up, all three down. All in all heading into 2017, only one quarterback had ever defeated Tom Brady while playing for the Eagles. That man was former #1 pick turned journeyman Sam Bradford in 2015, where the Eagles escaped New England with a 35-28 win.

Not on this night, but sometimes, Dawson would jump on Madden and pit himself against Brady and the Patriots, just to get the satisfaction of beating the man. He would do so and smile, but hen realizing it was just a simulation, wipe the grin off his face and return to his Ultimate Team on the game. Sitting there in his thoughts as his speaker played quietly next to him so he wouldn't disturb anyone above him, Dawson played onward, his thoughts ranging from what player he would unlock next to of course, inevitably, the Rock

Ridge game.

Dawson had played sparingly against the Phoenix in 2015 when he was a sophomore, mostly relegated to long snapping and other special teams duties due to his already impressive speed by the age of 15. He remembers the game vividly, the debut of the Rams as they visited Rock Ridge High School in what was a game of nerves and sheer excitement for the young Dawson Drake. Rock Ridge, who had spent the 2014 season with a junior varsity and freshman team had the advantage over the extremely green Riverside squad who was jumping right into varsity football. It showed early, as junior Briar Woods transfer Eric Vivian dominated the Riverside defense in the first half, scoring two touchdowns on the way to a 14-6 lead at halftime.

Riverside would respond quickly though, as on their first defensive series of the half, Riverside junior Drew Lewis would block a punt that would be recovered for a touchdown, setting things up to be a hotly contested finish. Vivan continued to dominate for Rock Ridge though, scoring once again and forcing the Rams to put together one final big drive in the fourth. Behind quarterback Blake Kinkoph, Riverside would do just that as a 58-yard pass to junior Drake Barlock would help tie the score a 21 and send the game to overtime. Riverside would continue the momentum, with Kinkoph continuing his strong showing after halftime by throwing a quick touchdown to Corey Forst to begin overtime, giving Riverside their first lead.

Vivian wouldn't go away for Rock Ridge, however, and after a 10-yard to put the game at 28-27, Rock Ridge made the decision to go for the win. The decision made the crowd roar, both sides getting on their feet as Dawson stood on the sideline in his #81 jersey, his heart pounding at the situation. Three yards was all Rock Ridge would need to win their first game in program history. Two yards was all Riverside would need to let up for their first win in program history. Rock Ridge lined up with Vivian in the backfield. The Riverside staff knew exactly who it was going to, Dawson Drake knew exactly who it was going to… the entire stadium knew who it was going to.

It didn't matter. Vivian bulldozed his way into the end zone to cap off a 280-yard four touchdown performance but more importantly, to cap off Rock Ridge's first win with it coming against none other then their new rival in Riverside. For 365 days, Dawson didn't let that one go. For 365 days, Dawson worked, eventually earning a spot at strong safety to take on the Rock Ridge Phoenix himself. In 2015, he felt helpless, only a social teams player who watched on the sideline as Vivian massacred the Riverside defense. In 2016, he wanted to be on the field and be the guy to stop Rock Ridge from scoring.

Rock Ridge wouldn't score as much as Dawson made his first real impact on the varsity squad in 2016, but that wouldn't matter, because the Rams offense sputtered completely. As the clock winded down on another loss to Rock Ridge, Dawson stood on the sideline, this time not so helpless. He was on the field, he had a chance to help Riverside win. They didn't. Another 365 days, another year of grueling agony, all for one final shot at a legacy-defining win against Rock Ridge. Turning off his Xbox, Dawson sighed, standing up slowly and moving towards the stairs, turning off the basement lights and heading up, supporting his legs on the railing as he made his way to his bedroom.

* * *

Dawson Drake had not heard the stadium at Riverside High School sound this loud, probably ever. Standing in the team meeting room right outside the stadium, Dawson stood at the front of the bunch, eagerly awaiting the signal to run out towards the fans who had for once made a large presence felt at the sometimes half-empty stadium. Maybe it was the news of the Tuscarora scrimmage, how Riverside had held their own against a much better school, or maybe it was the simple eagerness that came with the start of a new football season. Or maybe, just maybe, it was because it was Rock Ridge.

In the minds of a lot of people, a game between two programs who had existed for only two years and in those two years had put up historically bad numbers, a game like this would be considered a joke. To bigger programs within the state or even the county, they probably didn't even know or care that Riverside and Rock Ridge would be doing battle for the right to claim themselves as the fourth-best team in Ashburn. Down the road in Ashburn, Briar Woods was set to defend their home turf against West Potomac, a respectable 6A school who was coming off a 9-3 season. That's where the excitement was, as the majority of the Stone Bridge students who were on a bye that week went down to Briar Woods to check that out. That game, in theory, was the one that should've mattered. That game, in theory, should have been the one to fill a stadium.

Yet, the aura surrounded Rock Ridge and Riverside, a two-year-old rivalry that seemed to be going on for decades, at least in the minds of the teenagers who played in the game. And to the students who filled the student sections, smelling of cheap beer and vodka brands you probably never heard of, it meant a world of bragging rights. This wasn't Broad Run vs. Stone Bridge, the famed Battle of the 'Burn, but it held the same meaning to the students who had been populating the newly opened schools of the 'Burn. For Rock Ridge and Riverside's student populations, it wasn't just their "rival" school. These were former classmates, former teammates, neighbors who they could hold bragging rights over for 365 days. Sure, Riverside could beat Rock Ridge in basketball or lacrosse, but who the Hell cared? Down in the Commonwealth of Virginia, if your team took the football game in the rivalry, you could have every other sport for the rest of the year. Those didn't matter. Football mattered. And for Dawson Drake as his heart rate continued to rise while the clock ticked down closer and closer to 7pm on the east coast, putting Rock Ridge in their place was the 2017 season, for all he cared.

Standing in the doorway, Dawson heard a chorus of jeers rain down from the Riverside crowd, signifying that the boys of Rock Ridge had made their entrance onto the turf. Donned in all white with maroon accents against their new matte grey helmets, the words "The Rock" written on the front of the jerseys. Dawson remained focused, channeling any anger deep inside him, saving it for when he would need it most. Standing there waiting for what seemed like an eternity, Riverside finally got the signal to head out.

Both student sections continued to grow as the Rams made their way towards the banner held by the cheerleaders in the end zone. The Riverside section was covered in a sea of blue, the Rock Ridge section responding with an all-white look. The chants echoed through the stadium, the crowd growing louder as they caught a glimpse of Riverside making their way to the entrance point. Standing behind the banner that read "Go Rams, Fight the Phoenix!" Dawson stood collected. The rest of the Rams jumped around, the adrenaline rushing through their bodies at alarming rates. All spring, all summer, they had waited for their shot against Rock Ridge. The overtime loss in 2015, the grueling game in 2016… Dawson and his senior teammates had one more shot.

The Rams exploded through the sign, led by Drake and the other seniors as the Riverside faithful became fully alive. Dawson's heart continued to race while he made his way to the sideline, looking up towards the student section and the rest of the crowd that continued to file in. The sun continued to set on the stadium, the lights making it more and more apparent that soon, darkness would overtake the field and it would be time for some Friday night lights.

Cool and collected on the sideline, Coach Ryan Day paced back and forth his his headset in hand, staring down the Rock Ridge sideline. He looked to the 50-yard line where his captains for the game were lining up. Day, never one to believe in true captains for a season, committed to four for the Rock Ridge game. Giving them the "good to go", junior Trevor Jackson, sophomore Jack Selman, senior Brady Lipson and senior Christian DeVault went out for the coin toss as the remainder of the Rams stood eager on the sideline.

Rock Ridge would receive to start the game, putting Dawson and the defense out to begin the 2017 Riverside season. The experience in the secondary put a wave of confidence in the Rams, especially after the performance they put on against Tuscarora only nine days prior. Taking the field for the first time, the blood pumped viciously through Dawson's body as lined up against Rock Ridge's receivers. Taking a deep breath as he looked at Rock Ridge junior quarterback Tristan Berry, Dawson locked in once and for all.

Berry took the snap on the Rock Ridge 35-yard line and Riverside immediately got pressure on him, forcing him to look right towards junior running back Aryan Hedge, who he dumped it off to in the flat. Hedge caught the ball and looked up field, where Riverside junior Nathan Ayoub came rushing down to make the tackle on his assignment. With the slightest hesitation cut to the right, Hedge sent Ayoub flying behind him, opening up the field to the joy of the Rock Ridge sideline. Dawson, who had been deep in coverage against Rock Ridge's receivers, saw the missed tackle and immediately changed directions, avoiding the Rock Ridge receiver and making his way downhill. Hedge, who had made his way all the way to the Riverside 47-yard line, used the same move he used on Ayoub, this time to the left. Dawson broke down though quickly and got his hands on Hedge, twisting him down as Rock Ridge began the game with a 20-yard gain.

Just like that on a simple dump off pass, Rock Ridge had deflated the Riverside enthusiasm in the stands. For Dawson though, he got up quickly and refused to get angry, remaining calm and understanding that one play wasn't going to define the game. He was right to believe it, as Riverside would hold Rock Ridge stiff, not allowing them any points on the drive. Dawson and the defense did their job to start, now it was on Jackson and the unproven Rams offense to make some noise to start off the season.

Rock Ridge returned the favor, however, as dropped passes and missed reads plagued the Rams right off the bat. Quickly, Rock Ridge got the ball back on their own 10-yard line and went right back to work. With 90-yards to go, Berry and the Phoenix lined up in the shotgun where he took the snap and rolled out to his left with plenty of time. In hopes of tricking the Riverside defense, Berry made it look like a run before quickly dumping it off to to Hedge in the flat once again. Engaged with the Rock Ridge receiver, Dawson quickly read the play and moved off the blocker, coming down into the open field and breaking down on Hedge. The two collided at the 12-yard line, where Dawson's head smashed into Hedge's shoulder pad as the running back braced for the hit. Hedge went to the ground and at the sound of the whistle, Dawson stood up and immediately noticed something was not right. He looked briefly to the sideline but quickly pushed those thoughts away. This wasn't just a football game. It was Rock Ridge, and a hit to the head wasn't going to pull him from it.

For the remainder of the quarter, the two teams traded

punts and possessions, ending the first at a 0-0 tie. The first four minutes of the second quarter gave more of the same, as both teams struggled to get moving offensively, especially Rock Ridge after their opening play. Riverside was making some moves, though, mostly due to the running of Lipson as he made his full debut as the feature back of the Rams. As they neared the 50-yard line, Day put the trust in his junior quarterback who had struggled to start the game. Going under center, Jackson took the snap and faked to Lipson before rolling to his left. Rock Ridge tore through the Riverside offensive line as four defenders closed in on Jackson. Setting his feet, Jackson saw Jack Selman streaking down the Riverside sideline. He planted his feet and launched the football while getting smacked by the Rock Ridge defenders, sailing it towards Selman. The ball landed safely in his hands as Selman scampered the rest of the way, giving Riverside the lead on a 53-yard bomb from Jackson. The Riverside fans exploded as the student section volleyed out blue balloons at the sight of the first touchdown of the season as the Rams led 7-0 nearly half way through the second quarter.

Momentum shifted heavily towards the Rams. With a fired up sideline and a hot crowd behind them, Dawson and the Riverside kickoff team lined up as the crowd grew louder and louder. Riverside kicked off, where Rock Ridge fielded int right outside the end zone. The return man elected to take the ball out where he was met by junior Isaiah Bryant at the 20-yard line. Bryant slowed the Rock Ridge returner down, allowing for Dawson to come flying in and lay a massive hit that popped the crowd even more. Getting to his feet, Dawson ran towards the student section and punched his fist through the air, giving off the signal that maybe finally, it was Riverside's turn to own the rivalry.

As the second quarter came closer to an end, Berry and the

Rock Ridge offense moved swiftly down the field all the way to the Riverside 22-yard line. The Riverside defense would anchor down, forcing Rock Ridge head coach Bobby Lalli to make a decision on fourth and 15. He decided to go for it, where Berry dropped back and ripped it to Payton Hunter on a deep out route, causing confusion in the Riverside secondary and allowing Rock Ridge to tie the game going into halftime.

There was no other way for the game to go it seemed, as history told the players that no matter what, the game would have to go down to the wire. Due to that preconceived notion, Riverside remained calm during halftime, fully aware that they were by far the better team and by far the better conditioned team. In Day's mind, as he had instilled in July and early August through his brutal conditioning sessions, all Riverside needed to do was outlast Rock Ridge. Then, an opportunity would open up. All Riverside had to do was do their jobs, stick to their responsibilities and before they knew it, an opening would show itself.

Riverside couldn't get anything going to start the second half and after a few trades of possessions, Rock Ridge found themselves driving against Riverside's defense. As they got into Riverside territory, Berry dropped back to pass and dumped the ball off to receiver Ben Wright, who tore through the Riverside defense all the way to the end zone. On the Rock Ridge sideline though, Coach Lalli was livid as he saw the sight of a yellow flag placed on the field. An illegal blind-side block called the play all the way back, destroying the moral of the Rock Ridge offense. It showed two plays later, as a distracted Phoenix offense fumbled the ball back to Riverside to the absolute joy of the Rams home crowd.

Things remained at a full stalemate between the two teams, as both defensives continued to shine against struggling offenses. As time continued to dwindle in the fourth quarter,

Riverside was given one final chance when they received the ball at their own 45-yard line with just about three minutes to go. With Jackson struggling to connect with his young receivers, the Rams offense turned to its workhouse, feeding Brady Lipson on the first play, resulting in a thunderous 33-yard run that livened the crowd. Moving quickly to the line, Jackson took matters into his own hands, pounding forward on his own runs, moving Riverside to the 1-yard line. As Rock Ridge scrambled, Jackson took the snap under center and pushed forward into the end zone, giving the Rams the lead with little time remaining as the Rams sideline and fans exploded into celebration.

Dawson and his defensive teammates though remained poised, realizing that Berry and the Rock Ridge offense had just enough time to put together a drive and possibly tie the game. Riverside was ready. Berry dropped back and in a desperation move, launched the ball right into the hands of senior linebacker Alex Gonzalez, sealing the game.

14-7 Riverside. For the first time ever, the Riverside Rams had defeated Rock Ridge High School, causing an eruption from the students as they stormed the field. For Dawson and the other seniors, a massive weight came off their shoulders as the teammates hugged each other with smiles growing from ear to ear. It was a monumental moment as Dawson looked up to the stands, finding his mother and giving her the sign of approval that he was okay and that even better, he was happier than he could imagine. The past two years no longer mattered to him, the heartbreak of 2015 and 2016 non-existent. Riverside had their win against Rock Ridge and to most of the players on the Rams' roster, they had the only win that mattered to them for the entire season.

As the celebration continued on the field, Dawson started moving off the field with his teammates, the crowd still cheering as their undefeated Riverside Rams made their way towards the locker room. Their helmets in the air, for once, a sense of identity and pride overcame the Rams, a moment that had evaded them ever since they arrived on campus in 2015. After two years of being the kids from Stone Bridge, Broad Run and Tuscarora mixed together, this was their defining moment. They were now fully entrenched as the boys of Riverside, a team not of misfits, but a team of players proud to wear the name on the front of the jersey.

His eye black wearing off, his pads soaked, Dawson looked up towards the scoreboard, confirming that it had truly happened. 14-7 Riverside, it still read. He continued to smile, ignoring the aches and pains that covered his body. The gauntlet was still ahead, with plenty of teams a lot better than Rock Ridge sitting in front of them. But to Dawson in that moment, none of that mattered. As the lights shone down on the boys of fall, only one thing mattered.

Riverside was 1-0.

Riverside High School's football stadium in Ashburn, Virginia

The Unbelievers

Going into 2017, the Riverside Rams had won two games in program history...

This is their story.

Britton Barthold

Cover to *The Unbelievers*

Endnotes

All statistics and scores were used and found on the website Max Preps. In the introduction, all Darien football history was found on the site listed in the endnotes. All other websites used in this book are listed as well.

Darien, Connecticut

1 https://www.neighborhoodscout.com/ct/darien/real-estate

2 https://www.zillow.com/home-values/

3 https://www.neighborhoodscout.com/ct/darien/demographics

4 DiGiovanni, the Rev. (now Monsignor) Stephen M., *The Catholic Church in Fairfield County: 1666–1961*, 1987, William Mulvey Inc., New Canaan, Chapter II: The New Catholic Immigrants, 1880–1930; subchapter: "The True American: White, Protestant, Non-Alcoholic," pp. 81–82; DiGiovanni, in turn, cites (Footnote 209, page 258) Jackson, Kenneth T., *The Ku Klux Klan in the City, 1915–1930 (New York, 1981), p. 239*

5 https://www.nytimes.com/1947/11/12/archives/-gentlemans-agreement-study-of-antisemitism-is-feature-at-mayfair.html

6 https://datausa.io/profile/geo/darien-ct/

7 https://datausa.io/profile/geo/stamford-ct/#demographics

8 https://www.stamfordadvocate.com/sports/article/Darien-girls-lacrosse-coach-Lisa-Lindley-3604710.php

9 https://leagueathletics.com/Page.asp?n=13377&org=DHSSPORTS

* * *

Chapter Two

1 https://www.greenwichtime.com/sports/article/Greeenwich-Darien-set-to-renew-football-rivalry-4828366.php

2 http://www.therudenreport.com/with-2-0-start-darien-leaving-opponents-feeling-blue/

Chapter Three

1 https://www.nytimes.com/2007/11/24/nyregion/24rapist.html?rref=collection%2Ftimestopic%2FKelly%2C%20Alex&action=click&contentCollection=timestopics&region=stream&module=stream_unit&version=latest&contentPlacement=1&pgtype=collection

2 https://www.stamfordadvocate.com/local/article/5-Darien-football-players-banned-for-prank-831662.php

3 https://www.darientimes.com/13817/sons-of-former-first-selectwoman-arrested-for-new-canaan-urination/

Chapter Five

1 http://articles.chicagotribune.com/1989-01-03/sports/8902220801_1_pete-graham-irish-locker-room-kent-graham

2 https://www.gametimect.com/2014-fciac-football-team-preview-capsules/

Chapter Six

1 http://www.therudenreport.com/darien-33-greenwich-26-the-blue-wave-overcome-the-error-of-their-ways/

Chapter Seven

1 https://docs.google.com/document/d/1_fwDR4EFOch3RB7mnVIKIx16jfR--bDOxs4Ycn6yzMM/edit?ts=5ac503fa

2 http://www.ourdarien.com

3 https://www.stamfordadvocate.com/local/article/5-Darien-football-players-banned-for-prank-831662.php

4 https://www.stamfordadvocate.com/news/article/Fight-sends-

student-to-hospital-Darien-football-2285698.php

Chapter Eight

1 https://www.gametimect.com/football-3-darien-comes-back-17-point-deficit-beat-5-st-joseph/
2 https://www.darientimes.com/36957/fireworks-finale-wave-sounds-alarm-for-full-house-vs-north-haven-on-saturday/
3 https://www.gametimect.com/the-week-12-gametimect-register-top-10-football-poll/

Chapter Nine

1 https://www.stamfordpublicschools.org/stamford-high-school/athletics/pages/boyle-stadium
2 https://newcanaanite.com/darien-shocks-new-canaan-football-to-win-fciac-championship-17752

Chapter Ten

1 https://newcanaanite.com/theres-no-better-ending-new-canaan-football-overcomes-darien-to-win-class-l-large-state-title-18902

Chapter Thirteen

1 https://www.stamfordadvocate.com/sports/article/Darien-girls-lacrosse-coach-Lisa-Lindley-3604710.php
2 https://www.nytimes.com/2010/01/31/sports/31youth.html
3 http://www.therudenreport.com/the-ruden-report-podcast-darien-girls-lacrosse-coach-lisa-lindley/
4 http://www.foxnews.com/us/2011/12/17/connecticut-coaches-spark-uproar-by-burning-eighth-grade-football-teams.html

Chapter Sixteen

1 https://www.gametimect.com/the-preseason-gametimect-new-haven-register-top-10-football-poll-southington-is-no-1/
2 https://www.gametimect.com/2015-football-rose-ready-to-make-college-choice-lead-southington-to-ll-three-peat/

* * *

Chapter Eighteen

[1] https://www.greenwichtime.com/sports/article/Greenwich-junior-Scooter-Harrington-commits-to-6094195.php

Chapter Twenty

[1] https://www.gametimect.com/the-week-7-gametimect-register-top-10-song-remains-the-same-but-for-how-long/

[2] https://www.darientimes.com/57402/t-200-a-winning-program/

Chapter Twenty-Two

[1] https://www.gametimect.com/fairfield-county-thanksgiving-day-preview-capsules-and-pick-the-winners/

[2] https://www.gametimect.com/fairfield-county-thanksgiving-day-preview-capsules-and-pick-the-winners/

[3] https://www.gametimect.com/no-2-darien-edges-no-3-new-canaan-to-win-2nd-consecutive-fciac-championship/

Chapter Twenty-Three

[1] https://www.gametimect.com/football-the-2015-class-ll-quarterfinal-preview-capsules/

[2] https://www.gametimect.com/the-gametimect-register-top-10-playoff-football-poll-southington-loses-support-but-still-no-1/

[3] https://www.gametimect.com/football-dariens-mark-evanchick-named-gatorade-state-player-of-year/

[4] https://twitter.com/JohnHoltTV/status/672569289531068416

[5] https://twitter.com/SPBowley/status/672467874582253568

[6] https://www.gametimect.com/football-southington-offensive-line-up-for-challenge-vs-cts-sack-king/

[7] https://www.gametimect.com/class-ll-football-darien-crushes-no-1-southington-to-reach-3rd-consecutive-state-final/

Chapter Twenty-Four

[1] https://www.gametimect.com/class-ll-football-trifones-lead-darien-to-first-title-since-1996/

* * *

Epilogue

[1] https://www.gametimect.com/the-final-2015-gametimect-register-top-10-football-poll-darien-is-no-1/

[2] https://www.gametimect.com/the-84th-new-haven-register-all-state-football-team-second-third-honorable-mention/

[3] https://www.gametimect.com/football-dariens-evanchick-trifone-awarded-walter-camps-player-coach-of-the-year/

[4] http://usatodayhss.com/rankings/computer/boys/football/US/2015/1

[5] https://www.gametimect.com/football-new-tape-compels-darien-school-district-extend-trifones-suspension/

[6] http://www.courant.com/news/connecticut/hc-news-darien-football-players-snapchat-20171201-story.html

[7] https://www.ctpost.com/sports/jeffjacobs/article/Jeff-Jacobs-Darien-students-emails-abusive-12627923.php

NoVA (Chapter One)

[1] https://www.maxpreps.com/news/2othfwVzOkaRn2-m4CxzEQ/top-50-winningest-high-school-football-programs-of-all-time.htm

[2] https://web.archive.org/web/20130329185318/http://www.ashburnweb.com/history/index.htm

[3] https://www.census.gov/data/academy/data-gems/2018/cdp.html

Made in the USA
Middletown, DE
27 June 2020